Black in Print

SUNY series, Afro-Latinx Futures
———————
Vanessa K. Valdés, editor

Black in Print
Plotting the Coordinates of Blackness in Central America

Jennifer Carolina Gómez Menjívar

Cover photograph of Carl Rigby spray painting in Pearl Laguna, Nicaragua, by María José Álvarez Sacasa, co-director of *Antojología de Carl Rigby* (2017).

Published by State University of New York Press, Albany

© 2023 State University of New York

All rights reserved

Printed in the United States of America

No part of this book may be used or reproduced in any manner whatsoever without written permission. No part of this book may be stored in a retrieval system or transmitted in any form or by any means including electronic, electrostatic, magnetic tape, mechanical, photocopying, recording, or otherwise without the prior permission in writing of the publisher.

For information, contact State University of New York Press, Albany, NY
www.sunypress.edu

Library of Congress Cataloging-in-Publication Data

Name: Gómez Menjívar, Jennifer Carolina, author.
Title: Black in print : plotting the coordinates of Blackness in Central America / Jennifer Carolina Gómez Menjívar.
Description: Albany : State University of New York Press, 2023. | Includes bibliographical references and index.
Identifiers: LCCN 2022035320 | ISBN 9781438492810 (hardcover : alk. paper) | ISBN 9781438492834 (ebook) | ISBN 9781438492827 (pbk : alk. paper)
Subjects: LCSH: Black people—Press coverage—Central America. | Race relations and the press—Central America. | Black people—Race identity—Central America. | Central America—Race relations—History.
Classification: LCC F1440.B55 G66 2023 | DDC 972.800496—dc23/eng/20221013
LC record available at https://lccn.loc.gov/2022035320

10 9 8 7 6 5 4 3 2 1

For Melisa.

Contents

List of Illustrations	ix
Preface: Coastal Stories	xi
Acknowledgments	xvii
Introduction: Fictions of Blackness and Their Narrative Power	1

Part 1. Pacific/Pacífico

Chapter 1	Disappearing Acts	29

Part 2. Interior/Centro

Chapter 2	Strategies of Containment	63
Chapter 3	Mesoamerican Core, Kriol Periphery	93

Part 3. Caribbean/Caribe

Chapter 4	Multicultural Plots	125
Chapter 5	From Caribbean Sea to Digital Shore	149

Conclusion: The Battlegrounds of Central American Identity   179

Appendix: Transcript of the "Cocorí" Episode on *Radio Ambulante*   193

Notes   217

Works Cited   245

Index   263

Illustrations

Maps

P.1	Administrative Map of Nicaragua	xiii
I.1	Central American Caribbean Coastal Towns	12
I.2	Guatemalan Caribbean Coastal Towns	14
I.3	Honduran Caribbean Coastal Towns	15
I.4	Belize and Belize City, Capital of British Honduras from 1638 to 1961	17
3.1a & b	Areas of Belize Affected by Guatemala's Land Claim	110 111

Figures

3.1	Belize-Guatemala Border Dispute	109
5.1	"La beca del guerrillero" (The Scholarship of the Guerrilla Soldier)	168
5.2	"Para los terremotólogos" (For the Seismologists)	170
5.3	Rigby Admiring His Writing	171
5.4	"Constancia" (For the Record)	174
5.5	Rigby's Anthology	176

Preface
Coastal Stories

The Central American isthmus consists of seven distinct countries, but the stories about Afrodescendant citizens in the region are more strongly correlated with their proximity to either the Pacific Ocean or the Caribbean Sea than they are with the nations that they inhabit.

Never was this clearer to me than when I traveled to Nicaragua in 2009 to conduct research on Afrodescendance. I arrived in Managua and I commenced my work in Granada, which is relatively close to the Pacific coast (Region IV, map P.1). I lived with a Nicaraguan family while I studied the Miskito language, a language spoken on the Caribbean coast of the country. I attended class at a local organization, and there, as well as in other key Nicaraguan cities (Managua and León), I met individuals who openly expressed their surprise at my interest in Afro-Nicaraguan history. Among them were several who openly expressed their disdain for the *negros* of the Región Autónoma de la Costa Caribe Sur (RACCS, Region VIII on map P.1) and the Región Autónoma de la Costa Caribe Norte (RACCN, Region II)—the two departments with the greatest number of Afrodescendants, according to recent national censuses. For my part, I was perplexed that many of the folks who expressed negative sentiment could very well "pass" for Black in the United States, yet they clearly distinguished themselves from the compatriots they deemed "truly Black." When we spoke about my course on the Miskito language, many admitted that they had never given much thought to the ethnic and linguistic diversity of their country, much less traveled to RACCS or RACCN. Yet they avidly warned me about the dangers of the two Caribbean coastal departments, recounting stories that they had heard about "violent" Creole drug dealers stealing from and assaulting women on the streets of the town in broad daylight. Those same individuals who professed themselves to be progressive were clearly wary about the *tipos* who lived in that part of the country. Poignantly, those exchanges emphasized a racialized geographic conceptualization of place: Black individuals in the RACCS and RACCN were Creole, Caribbean, Jamaican, Rastafarian, you name it. Anything but Nicaraguan.

Few of my contacts in Granada, Managua, or León had ever interacted with Afrodescendants on the opposite coast, and most knew nothing about the history of Black peoples in the country. By the time I completed my work in Regions III and IV and had established contacts with the Centro de Investigación y Documentación de la Costa Atlántica (CIDCA) in Region VIII, I looked forward to investigating how Regions II, III, and IV were perceived by Region VIII. I boarded a small airplane and in about an hour I arrived in what was a netherworld for many Nicaraguans in the principal cities of the country. In this side of the country, I heard Creole, English, and Nicaraguan Spanish languages and passed Caribbean colonial architectural styles as I headed to my lodgings. They were markedly distinct sounds and sights from those I had observed closer to the Pacific Ocean. Walking the streets of Bluefields, I heard US country music and Jamaican reggae. I searched for the former headquarters of the Universal Negro Improvement Association, and en route I met a Black elder who was raised in Bluefields and who offered to walk with me and show me some of the landmarks, like the Moravian church in town. While we strode through the streets and he greeted friends in both Creole and Nicaraguan Spanish, he told me that Marcus Garvey had rescued slaves and brought them to Bluefields to safety. Though historically unsupported, I was captivated by the heart of the story: the acknowledged fact of West African enslavement and the perception of Bluefields as a coastal haven for enslaved Black peoples and their descendants. He told me about how much the dynamics of the coastal town had changed in the last three decades with the arrival of an increased number of Spanish speakers. The conversation with him was almost a prelude to what would come. In the weeks henceforth, I heard a similar sense of urgency in discussions between scholars, students, and activists working on Creole and Miskito language preservation, bilingual educational policies, and the region's (multi)cultural identity. In content and scope, the perception of Blackness in Regions II, III, and VIII was dramatically distinct from that which I had encountered during my time in Region IV.

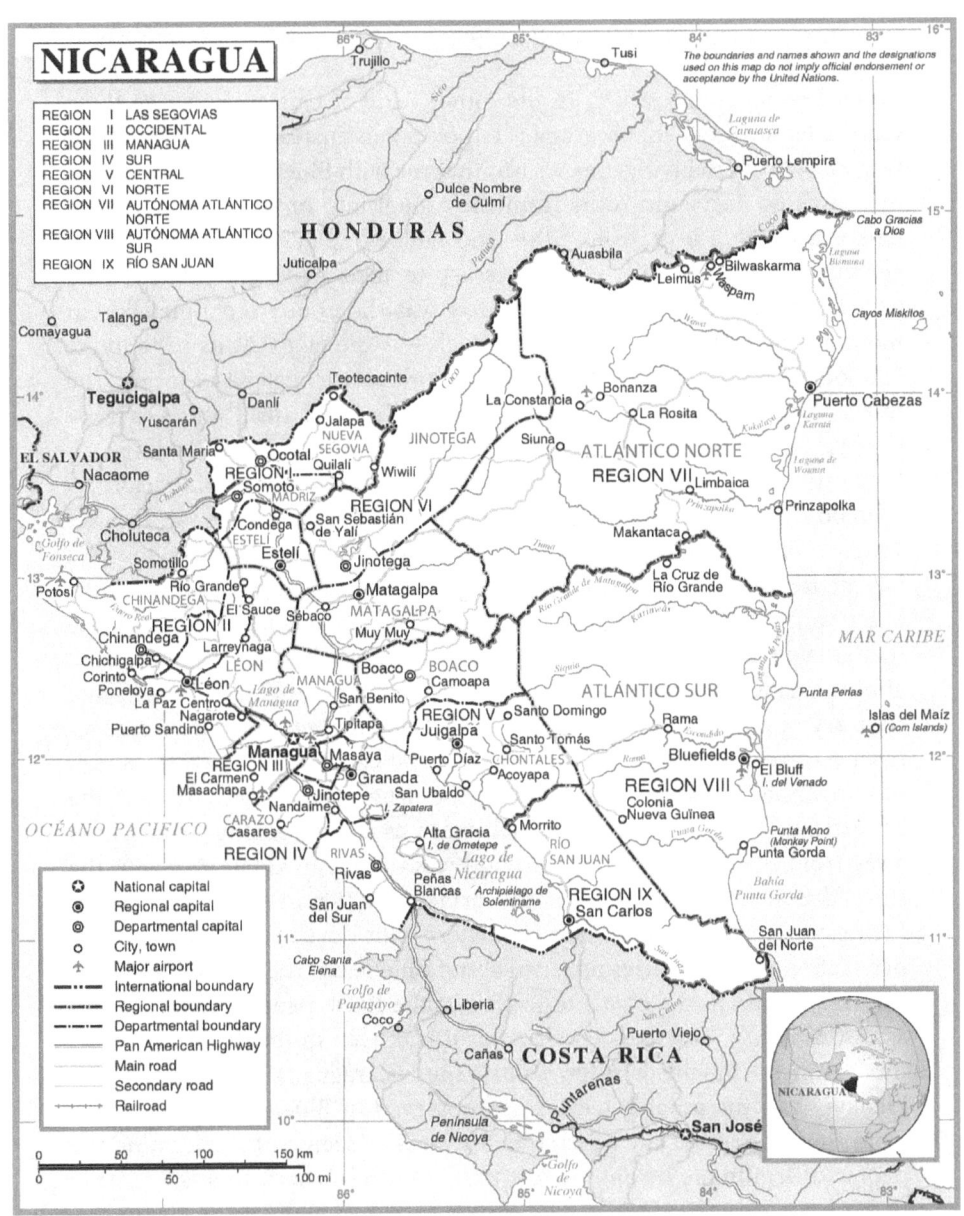

Map P.1. Administrative Map of Nicaragua. *Source*: Cartedumonde.net.

~

When I conducted research in the "other" side of Guatemala some three years after my stay in Nicaragua, I took a bus instead of a plane from Guatemala City to Livingston. As was the case with Bluefields until recently, there was no easy land route from the capital into or out of Livingston.[1] One must take a boat from either Río Dulce or Puerto Barrios, and, to get to either of the two, it is necessary to take a bus from Guatemala City for about seven hours. Livingston was different from Bluefields in monumental ways, not the least of which was the fact that its restaurants and locales clearly marketed themselves for tourists instead of locals. The restaurants displayed images of *tapado*, a Garifuna dish, and Garifuna performers were present at nightly events in local hotels. Blackness in Livingston was clearly on display in a way that it was not in Bluefields. As I would discover some years later when conducting research for *Tropical Tongues* in Punta Gorda, Belize, just across from Livingston, tourism has altered and left its mark on the cultural landscape of Livingston.[2] In other ways, however, Livingston was similar to Bluefields. It was a place that Guatemalan *mestizos* in the principal cities believed to be inhabited almost exclusively by Black peoples, despite the demographic fact to the contrary. It was also a place that many Guatemalan *mestizos*, despite never having traveled to the Caribbean part of the country, believed to be full of dangerous Black men involved in the drug trade. The story that the Ministry of Tourism crafted for Livingston as a Caribbean getaway miles away from the ancient Maya heartland was unique to Guatemala, but the story that had been crafted in the principal cities of Guatemala about Livingston contained the same characters, plot development, and anticipated climax as the stories repeated about Bluefields. The tone of antipathy was manifested in the characterization of the Black peoples of Livingston as distinct from "true Guatemalans" as it had been in the depiction of the inhabitants of Bluefields as far from "true Nicaraguans." In that matched ideology was the notable tenet I had observed in Bluefields: the distance from the geographic site of legitimate citizenry seemed to determine the degree of legitimate belonging, of "true" Central Americanness.

~

Narratives about Blackness have changed over time, crystallizing geography as a central factor for reading the tales of Afro-Central America. On the one hand, Afrodescendants have always resided in Central America's cultural and political centers, a practice of placemaking that afforded them the stamp of *mestizaje* and a position of legitimacy since 1821. On the other hand, Afrodescendants residing closer to the Caribbean Sea—the principal locus of the polyphonic Trans-Atlantic slave trade—have constituted a marginal populace in the isthmus for nearly two hundred years. The coexistence of the two narratives—of time-weathered Blackness folded into the bodies of *mestizo* citizens who unquestionably belong to Central America and reside in close proximity to the Pacific coast vis-à-vis the story of the typecast Blackness attributed to the liminal citizens who live adjacent to the Caribbean coast (and thus much farther away from critical national socioeconomic sites)—is central to the analysis in this book. Its pages track the ways in which the two stories have adopted distinct threads over time, reflecting the aspirations and desires of plot generators as the isthmus's two coasts pass across pivotal moments that redefine the axes of rightful and liminal citizenry.

Acknowledgments

This book has been years in the making and I am indebted above all to my family for walking this journey with me. I am filled with enormous gratitude for my grandparents and my parents who have held more than a century of family history, which is also regional and national history. I am also grateful for my siblings, whose keen observations and genealogical knowledge have contributed so much to this study of the shifting racialized stories in Central America.

My earliest treatment of the Belize-Guatemala border dispute was in a class taught by Beatriz Cortez, and I thank her for allowing me to choose that topic and for being an incredible mentor to me throughout my years as an undergraduate student. Ileana Rodríguez challenged me to think about Central America historically and philosophically, a practice manifested here in the book's consideration of the effects of print across time and ideologies as well as in the labor of love it has been to bring it to fruition. The mentorship of Lúcia Costigan, Abril Trigo, Ana del Sarto, and Laura Podalsky provided this project the wisdom, critiques, and suggestions of critics whose remarkable points of departure allowed me to ask and answer hemispheric questions I would never have otherwise imagined. My adopted mentor, Terrell Morgan, led the seminar in Nicaragua that forever changed the direction of this book by putting me in contact with Danilo Salamanca, who put me in touch with the Cento de Investigación de la Costa Atlántica (CIDCA) in Bluefields, Nicaragua, which then connected me to the incomparable Carl Rigby. Lowell Gudmundson, Catherine Komisaruk, Todd Little-Seibold, and Ben Vinson III all responded to my inquiries about their work with admirable generosity and, without ever having met me, shared copyedits of their work with me before publication. Darío Euraque generously read a very early version of this manuscript and provided fruitful suggestions for working with Paca Navas de Miralda's work. U-Spatial graciously provided many of the maps that appear in this book, Caroline de la Garza assisted with the preparation of the final manuscript, and talented proofreader, k. Hadley, read every word. *Black in Print* would not have been possible without the encouragement I received from the anonymous reviewers who carefully examined every chapter of this book, and I am truly grateful for their insight and suggestions. The version in readers' hands was made richer thanks to them, and any faults herein are solely my own. I thank the entire team at State University of New York Press, especially series editor Vanessa K. Valdés, acquisitions editor Rebecca Colesworthy, former acquisitions editor Beth Bouloukos, and production editor Susan Geraghty for seeing promise in this project and supporting it all along its trajectory from proposal to publication. The appendix to this book is the full transcript of the podcast episode "Cocorí" from *Radio Ambulante*, a leading podcast that reaches listeners worldwide with stories from Latin America. A very special thank you to the team for permitting me to use the transcript of "Cocorí" in its entirety; to Daniel Alarcón, Camila Segura, and Luis Fernando Vargas for bringing this episode to an audience beyond Central American borders; and to Lorein Powell Benard, Quince Duncan, and Tanisha Swaby Campbell for putting themselves on the line to fight racism on behalf of Black and Afrodescendant children in the isthmus.

I accepted a new position across the country in the midst of completing this book, and I am truly grateful to everyone in leadership positions, especially Steve Cobb and Harry Benshoff, for helping me make a smooth transition to Texas. I thank my students in my Seminar in Spanish Language Media for embarking on the exciting journey to review print media in the Viceroyalty of New Spain and for opting (to my delight and surprise!) for an after-class session on textual-visual mediations of caste paintings that much improved the opening to this volume. Finally, I am absolutely indebted to the friends and colleagues who filled my heart with happiness with their generous laughter in the years during which I teased out the nuances of this project. Through unexpected upheavals, their gifts of time, example, insight, joy, and friendship helped me on the path to completing this book. I wish to especially thank Arturo Arias, Osmer Balam, Courtney Brannon Donahue, Gloria Elizabeth Chacón, Cristina Coc, Rebecca De Souza, Jill Doerfler, Jacqueline Foertsch, Elena Foulis, Paula Gudmundson, Sue P. Haglund, Mariaelena Huambachano,

Lindsey Jungman, H. Julie Kae, Tania Khalaf, Karen López Olonzo, Susan Maher, Valerie Martínez-Ebers, Rita Palacios, Héctor Nicolás Ramos Flores, Jacqueline Ryan Vickery, Daniela Salcedo Arnaiz, Noel St. James Salmon, William Alejandro Salmon, G. Juan Sánchez Martínez, Jeanine Schroer, Silvaana Utz, and Ms. Leela Vernon, may she always rest in peace. And, Bill.

Introduction

Fictions of Blackness and Their Narrative Power

"Color-coding" in colonial Central America implied establishing a system of marking bodies, spaces, and written/visual discourses with different colors as a means of identification. Leagues away from the Spanish Crown and kilometers away from the Viceroyalty of New Spain, the social landscape of the Captaincy General of Guatemala was drafted using a palette that arranged colors according to a perspective that differed significantly from that employed to sketch populations with lesser autonomy. Sightlines, imaginary lines from the eye to the object in focus, foreclosed and annulled possibilities to ascertain certain colors and yet were also at stake in throwing other colors into relief. Those sightlines were made manifest in print, and it has also been in print that a reversal of the color-coding systems in Central America has been negotiated, creating apertures at different times in the isthmus' history for Black Central Americans themselves to control the palette and the font used to write narratives—it is not by accident that the cover of this book is a photograph of the Nicaraguan poet Carl Rigby spray-painting the title of his digital poetic volume on a wall in Pearl Lagoon, on his own terms.

Tracking the history of Central American Blackness in post-independence and post-manumission print necessitates, however, the brief excavation of its colonial form and a conceptualization of Black agency from within coloniality before laying out the core arguments of this book. The Curse of Ham, a biblical narrative used to justify African enslavement, was likewise deployed to explain the position of Black subjects in the caste system used throughout New Spain, to which the Captaincy of Guatemala belonged until 1821. According to the story found in the book of Genesis, a man named Noah became drunk from after drinking the wine from his vineyard one night. He lay uncovered and in a state of drunkenness when his son, Ham, entered his father's tent and beheld his bare body. Upon awakening, Noah sentenced Canaan, son of Ham (who had disgraced his father), to perpetual enslavement at the hands of his uncles, Shem and Japheth. Early Biblical interpreters would go on to associate Carthaginians, Egyptians, and Ethiopians with the "Hamite" ancestral line. God enlarge Japheth, and let him dwell in the tents of Shem; and let Canaan be his slave."[1] Juan de Torquemada, a Franciscan friar and historian, repeated the story in his *Monarquía Indiana*. Although his specific concern had been to document the oral histories of the Totonac in present-day Mexico, the Pipil in present-day El Salvador, and the Nicoya in present-day Costa Rica, he layered his accounts with descriptions of many colonial subjects, including Black peoples in the Spanish-instituted caste system. According to the friar, Ham's son begat children who "nacieron negros, y feos, como los Egipcios, y Getulos, Gente barbara, que viven, en una Region en lo interior de Libia . . . que son Negros, como carbon, y tienen la boca podrida"[2] (were born Black and ugly, like the Egyptians and Gaetuli, barbarous people, who live in a region in the interior of Libia . . . as black as coal and with rotten mouths). Such presumptions, based on biblical print, were largely unchallenged until the Age of Enlightenment brought Europeans to seek alternative explanations for the social hierarchies they instituted in their own kingdoms and in the colonies under their dominion.

Theories about the effect of climate on skin color and temperament, as well as hypotheses about blood quality and human character, supplanted the widely held perception of Africans' damnation. Casta paintings by Miguel Cabrera, Juan Rodríguez Juárez, and Juan Patricio Morlete Ruiz illustrated an idea of "blood-mending" and included, in fine print, a formula that progressively diluted Indigeneity—Spaniard and Indian, Mestizo; Spaniard and Mestizo, Castizo; Spaniard and Castizo, Spaniard.[3] These same paintings condemned subjects of African heritage—Spaniard and Black, Mulatto; Spaniard and Mulatto, Morisco; Spaniard and Morisco, Albino; Spaniard and Albino, Torna atras—to endless Blackness.[4] These paintings were the legible medium through which accounts of "positive mestizaje" and "negative mestizaje" were put into circulation. The classification of bodies according to their color and, hence, their caste served to ensure enmity instead of solidarity between those lower in the social hierarchy. After all, the caste system had been a "cognitive and legal system of hierarchically arranged socioracial statuses created by the Spanish law and the colonial elite in response to the miscegenated population in the colonies" since its inception.⁵

Intellectuals like Carlos de Sigüenza y Góngora feared the transgression of the line separating the "right" people from the rest. The frequency of miscegenation led him to express his despair over its disruption of the social order: "Porque siendo plebe tan en extremo plebe ... por componerse de indios, de negros criollos y bozales, de chinos, de mulatos, de moriscos, de mestizos, de zambaigos, de lobos y también de españoles que, en declarándose zaramullos (que es lo mismo que pícaros, chulos y arrebatacapas) y degenerando en sus obligaciones, son los peores entre tan ruin canallada"⁶ (Because being commoners so extremely commonplace ... due to their composition as Indians, Blacks, Criollos and Bozales, Chinos, Mulattos, Moriscos, Mestizos, Zambiagos, Lobos, and Spaniards, who in declaring themselves Zaramullos [which is the same as thieves, bandits, and cape snatchers] and degenerating in their obligations, are the worst of the ruinous rascals). Sigüenza y Góngora easily lists the castes that comprise the plebeians in his city, covering the gamut of the racial mixtures associated with Blackness. The terms negros criollos and bozales, for instance, referred at the time to Black slaves who had been born in New Spain in the case of the former term and on the African continent in the case of the latter. Mulattos were attributed equal parts Spanish and African ancestry, while moriscos, or quadroons as they were known in Anglophone contexts, were believed to possess a quarter of African blood and three-fourths of Spanish blood. Lobos were the progeny of an African and an Indigenous subject, while chinos were the fruit of a union between a lobo and an Indigenous partner. Classification was thus as much based on perception as it was on documented parentage. In fact, such was the indeterminacy of racial compositions after subsequent generations that the term zambaigo was often used interchangeably with lobo or chino when designating a newborn's caste. That they would be included in the list of plebians is not surprising. What is striking and merits further attention, however, is Sigüenza y Góngora's belief that behavior—becoming affected, conceited, finicky, foolish, and all the other synonyms for the term zaramullo—could result, along with color and blood quantum, in a subject's fall into a lower caste.

The initially well-ordered social hierarchy in New Spain had fallen into chaos, according to Sigüenza y Góngora. It had become a landscape that could only be divided into two groups: *gente decente* (respectable people) and *plebe* (plebeians).⁷ It was a society in which the distribution of wealth had permitted descendants of Africans to contribute to and benefit from the colonial economy: "castas with buying power daily flouted Spanish sumptuary regulations."[8] Though some Black women and mulattas, for instance, could face confiscation of their property if they wore gold jewelry, pearls, or full-length embroidered *mantas*, affluence across classes had begun to erode the old distinction between Spaniards and castas. Determined to denounce the bourgeoning intimacy between castes, Sigüenza y Góngora nonetheless captures for his readers a subtle change in the rubrics of color-coded spaces in the Viceroyalty of New Spain. He was witnessing and contributing to a narrative in which the signposts related to Blackness were changing across the important cities of the Viceroyalty of New Spain, which at the time included Mexico City (once known Tenochtitlán) and Santiago de los Caballeros in Guatemala (once known as Iximché). When Mexico and Guatemala became independent nations, these cities and their peoples did not lose their importance. Rather, they became cultural epicenters in which ideas took shape and circulated through print media outward into smaller rural towns. By that time, however, Afrodescendants in urban areas had ceased to be classed according to phenotype, and many had been absorbed into the category of *gente decente* (decent people) of the new nations.

What happened to these descendants of African slaves trafficked into Central America? Why has their destiny in the Central American Caribbean rimlands been markedly distinct from that of Black peoples in the Caribbean islands? Why are the stories about Blackness plotted in the Pacific coastal areas distinct from the stories charted in Caribbean coastal areas? *Black in Print* is a study of these questions. Mainstream print media, I argue, has since the nineteenth century had the powerful effect of making Central American Black experiences first disappear into home-grown *mestizaje* and then malignly reappear to divide and conquer the "decent people" of Central America. I likewise find that the independent print media stream that begins to appear in the region in the early twentieth century brings Blackness back to the center of national discourses, at times in celebratory multicultural tones and at others as part of the isthmian and regional movement that asserts the powerful legacy of Black life and thought in Central America.

Black in Print puts Central American conceptions of race and ethnicity under a microscope, though its observations are applicable to a myriad of discourses about Blackness that have taken shape throughout the Americas. From Mexico to the United States, from Canada to Argentina, from Haiti to Ecuador, from Cuba to Brazil, narratives about Blackness have shape-shifted according to the sociohistorical and political demands for fresh national narratives to better identify the welcomed and excluded inhabitants within national boundaries. For that reason, this book honors the critical contributions of Lélia Gonzalez's theory of "Améfrica" and sheds light on the enduring Indigenous legacy of Blackness in the Americas, despite centuries of loss, dismissal, and disparagement on a hemispheric scale. As Gonzalez writes in her essay, "A Categoria Político-Cultural de Amefricanidade": "Já no caso das sociedades de origem latina, temos o racismo disfarçado ou, como eu o classifico, o *racismo por denegação*. Aqui prevalecem as 'teorias' de miscigenação, da assimilação e da 'democracia racial.' A chamada América Latina que, na verdade, é muito mais ameríndia e amefricana do que outra coisa, apresenta-se como o melhor exemplo de racismo por denegação." (In the case of societies of Latin origin, we have disguised racism or, as I term it, racism by denial. Here, the "theories" of miscegenation, assimilation and "racial democracy" prevail. The so-called Latin America, which, in fact, is much more Amerindian and Amefrican than anything else, manifests itself as the best example of racism by denial.)[9]

Given the prevailing denial of Blackness in Central American contexts (and in many sites in mainland Latin America), Blackness after manumission became what Ben Vinson III has called "a moving target." As Vinson III explains in his observation about Blackness in Latin Americanist research: "Quite simply, for us, the contexts in which Blackness is produced often eschew the very category of study, and among Latin American diasporans themselves, Blackness possesses a proverbial fluidity. As scholars we are well aware that within our region, Blackness is simultaneously segmented, denied, and reluctantly embraced—all while morphing into something that seemingly stretches beyond Blackness. Herein lies a great research opportunity."[10] Gonzalez found it to be an opportunity to engage with a "gigantesco trabalho de dinâmica cultural que não nos leva para o lado do atlântico, mas que nos traz de la e nos transforma no que somos hoje: *amefricanos*" (gigantic labor of cultural dynamics that does not take us to the other side of the Atlantic, but brings us away from there and transforms us into what we are today: *Amefricans*).[11] These are the discursive points of entry into print media with which I now proceed.

Independent Narratives

Narratives about Blackness in Central America have been shaped by both hegemonic and counter-hegemonic forces in situ. They were devised in the isthmus itself, created as the republics were born and, more specifically, put into circulation through the principal influencing print media of every historical period post-independence. To illustrate more clearly, I turn to the events that led to manumission in the isthmus. The *moreno* (Afrodescendant) populations in the province of San Salvador and the province of Guatemala were crucial constituents to take into account in January 1822 when José Matías Delgado of the Liberal party submitted his petition for the abolition of slavery before the Salvadoran junta over which he presided.[12] Afrodescendants, he reasoned, had been active in the independence movement.[13] He determined that as political actors, they merited the same rights as other categories of (non-Indigenous) people who could exercise their rights as citizens. Propelled by this shift in the hegemonic narrative, six enslaved men from Trujillo (Honduras) surnamed Álvarez, Morejón, Berardez, Hota, Cabal, and Navarro presented their petition for freedom in September 1823. In an eloquent statement, they argued that the freedom of man was an "inestimable joya" (priceless jewel) without which he could not partake in the good of the social pact offered to his equals. They founded their observations in religious scriptures arguing that God did not authorize the servitude imposed upon wretched slaves. Furthermore, they appealed to the fiscal tenets of slavery, stating, "No es otro mas que la relajada avaricia de los hombres que, por aumentar sus caudales, han infestado las desgraciadas costas de la Africa, esclavizando a sus habitantes, que en sentido claro, no es otra que robarles la preciosa joya de su Libertad." (It is nothing but the extravagant greed of men who, to fill their coffers, have infested the wretched coasts of Africa, enslaving her inhabitants, which is clearly nothing other than stealing the precious jewel of their Liberty.)[14] The five [Black] men had developed a persuasive argument appealing to the Central American National Congress on the basis of their inalienable right to freedom.

They were not alone. Across Central America, many of the Afrodescendants who remained enslaved gave their reasons in print for seeking freedom. One group of six men, from the Santo Domingo Convent in Palencia (Guatemala) presented the following petition: "Somos los mas infelices, anaden, pero conocemos que el oro es una tierra amarilla y que la plata es tierra blanca. La Asamblea aprecia a los hombres, y no hace caso de la tierra por blanca o por amarilla." (We are the most wretched, but we understand that gold is a yellow earth and that silver is a white earth. The Assembly appreciates men and does not distinguish between land, whether it be white or yellow.)[15] The print material about Blackness written by the aforementioned petitioners in Honduras, Guatemala, and in other Hispanophone Central American nations in those years positioned Afrodescendants as political actors in the central plot of an isthmus undergoing a change in character from a colonial outpost to a collective of independent republics. The print material was likewise based on the theme of God-given, inalienable rights to all men. Despite being Black and enslaved, they had taken pen to paper and argued for themselves that they wished to be recognized as free men, capable of reason, and willing citizens of the new nation.[16] Like the Afrodescendants before them who sought legal avenues to challenge their racial designation as *negros*, *mulatos*, and *morenos* and to bring to an end to the taxation resulting from such identifiers, these enslaved men used petitions as the means to affirm their own humanity and ability to reason. Their documents, called *gracias al sacar*, have become a part of the archive that documents the experiences and thoughts of Black slaves as a matter of national/regional historical fact.[17] The voluminous writing bore fruit when Article 13 of the Constitution of the Federal Republic of Central America went into effect on April 24, 1824, making manumission official in the five republics of Guatemala, El Salvador, Honduras, Nicaragua, and Costa Rica. African enslavement had been declared illegal in Gran Colombia—of which Panama was still a part—many years earlier, though many Black individuals remained enslaved, and it took many more years for full emancipation to be achieved.

At the time, Central America's Conservative party was comprised of whites, their allies, and the bishop of Central America, who supported enslavement and the colonial Spanish administration. The Liberal party, on the other hand, consisted primarily of *gente de color* (people of color). Within this context, many Afrodescendants became famous for their involvement in the fight for the region's independence and entered other sociopolitical spaces to ensure their freedom in the emerging nations no longer as *people of color*, but as *citizens*. Mauricio Meléndez Obando evaluates the context:

> With Independence and the former substitution of socioracial categories with the term *citizen*, afromestizos finally witnessed the elimination of legal and social barriers justifying their centuries-long exclusion from the halls of power. Some did not fail to take advantage of the opportunity: they had access to municipal offices, the legislative, executive, and judicial branches of government, and the high clergy throughout Central America.

> Now we know the answer to the question frequently posed to those of us who study slavery in Central America: But what happened to the slaves of the colonial period?[18]

In their bureaucratic transformation from *negros* to *morenos* to *citizens*, liberals established an ideological landscape that reinforced the stereotypes of a Conservative white *criollo* class, staunchly old guard, that vehemently opposed progress and the philosophy of liberalism. As the demographic majority in the Liberal party, Afrodescendants in the Hispanophone areas of Central America consolidated the *negro-moreno*-turned-*mestizo* hegemonic ideology that nurtured a color-blind narrative in the five first Central American nations in 1824. There, belonging hinged less on one's racially ambiguous phenotype and more on one's ideological, linguistic, and geographic affiliation. In this scheme, Afrodescendants in Pacific cities were members of the citizenry, quickly establishing the stories of the new nation-states, while Afrodescendants residing on the Caribbean coast were invisible in the print of the independence period. Whether Afrodescendants could be conceived of as de jure and/or de facto citizens quickly came to depend on place of origin, language spoken, and the historical period in question. The designation of de jure and de facto citizenship and even de jure and de facto foreignness carried a narrativized element relating to an individual's perceived degree of national contribution. Put succinctly, Afrodescendants in principal cities were folded into narratives that supplemented ideologies about territory, resources, and legacy posited by the Liberal parties in the new nations.

A Moving Target in Time

As sociopolitical and economic factors changed, so too did the stories of Central America's [Black] citizenry.[19] With time, the converging factors of space, time, and the changing semantic meaning in Central America led to denial of Blackness in plain print. Afrodescendant men who obtained their freedom—both before and after manumission—held positions in cities as artisans or craftsmen, contracted by the upper classes to fashion objects that competed with those made in the Old World.[20] Others remained in the countryside, tilling their own land and overseeing their own haciendas. Movement and dispersal were such constants that even travel narratives written by outsiders, such as that by Jacob Haefkens

(1832), provide their readers with sketches of these Black men and women who moved across the terrain and through the echelons of colonial society.[21] The increasing number of Afrodescendants in skilled professions throughout the Captaincy of Guatemala led to a paradigm shift as an increased number of Afrodescendants began to appear in church registries and official documents not as *negros* but as *morenos* and, with time, as *mestizos*. Absorption through *mestizaje* became one of the central fictional elements in the narratives of Blackness constructed in the five first independent nations of the isthmus.[22]

As an intellectual with the express intention of relating his account to the king of the Netherlands in 1832, Haefkens would have been keenly aware of the writings on race promulgated during the Enlightenment, particularly Johann Friedrich Blumenbach's *On the Natural Varieties of Humankind*. The text posited that there were five races belonging to humankind: Caucasian, Mongolian, Ethiopian (Black), American (Indigenous), and Malay. The four latter races were said to have degenerated from the ideal Caucasian stock. In his account, Haefkens declares that the Central American population "comprende personas de todas las razas imaginables, pero se divide en tres clases principales" (includes people of all imaginable races, but is divided in three main classes): the white upper class, which enjoyed such luxuries as comfortable homes, fine clothing, excellent horses, and delicious food; the middle class—racially unclassified—which had stable work, clean clothes, and enough food; and the Indigenous, who were exploited and subjected to forced labor despite their legal condition as free individuals.[23] The category *mestizos* caused trouble for Haefkens, who recognized that in this context, unlike Europe, Afrodescendants were not relegated to the bottom rung of the social ladder. This class of people, he wrote to his king, consisted of descendants of whites and Indians (his term for Indigenous people) who were known as *ladinos* and added that mixed white and Black individuals, and other combinations of ethnoracial mixtures were also considered *ladinos*. Anyone with a *ladino* classification, reported Haefkens, was distinct from the strata of pure "Indians," reported Haefkens.[24] To soften the message, Haefkens adds a note stating that he does not mention Blacks as a racial category because their number is too low to be mentioned. Though his king would be unlikely to imagine the scene, Haefkens understood that in Central America, Afrodescendants constituted the majority of the populace, and they were on par with other *ladinos* afforded the opportunity to climb the social ladder.

Whereas their forefathers and foremothers had been enslaved and consequently defined by Spaniards as *negros bozales* and *negros criollos* in the colonial period, Afrodescendant citizens entered marriages and careers with the dignity ascribed to any other participant in the wars of independence.[25] These [Afrodescendant] citizens created an imaginary that increasingly posited their society not as Africanized, but *ladino*: a term that exists today as the predominant popular and official descriptor for non-Indigenous peoples in Guatemala.[26] Lowell Gudmundson reminds us that census takers in the nineteenth century "followed what they understood to be their superior's intentions in documenting a presumptive process of national integration via mestizo majority."[27] Mulattos and Blacks in the isthmus henceforth "disappeared" in technical writing before disappearing in other print genres. Moreover, "Black was something one did not lightly accuse another of being in Nicaragua or anywhere in Central America, at least in public. More epithet than descriptor, it ranked right up there with other challenges to honor or masculinity as fightin' words."[28] *Mestizo* became the category used with greater frequency as the use of *negro, moreno, zambaigo, tente-en-el-aire, tornatrás, no-te-entiendo* became outdated markers of phenotype and instead an insult. Bureaucratic lightening and narrative passing techniques after independence concomitantly resulted in a great decline in the number of Afrodescendants who would have self-identified or been identified by census takers as such. Rubén Darío (discussed in chapter 1) would be a clear example of an Afrodescendant who understood the power and assumptions about class, character, and national belonging implicit in the term. *Mestizos* who had Afrodescendant ancestry had a place in all the professions and small-scale business endeavors available in Central American cities; *negros* and *mulatos* did not have the same privilege of belonging.

Throughout Central America, *mestizaje* was embraced as a post-independence means of diluting Indigeneity: from recruiting German coffee farmers in Guatemala, to attracting Muslims in El Salvador, to opening borders to Chinese immigrants in Panama, the regional intention was to reduce the impact of Indigeneity (understood as barbarism, following the writings of Latin American thinkers of the epoch) in the gene pool of the citizenry as the new nations moved toward progress. After all, as Peter Wade observes, "Elite and literate expressions of mestizo identity harbor within themselves a tension between sameness and difference, rather than simply being homogenising expressions pitted against a subaltern consciousness of difference."²⁹ In this framework, Black alterity in the first years of Central American independence was perceived as a means of attenuating the force of Indigeneity that remained present through the Spanish colonial period. Seen thus, a *mestizaje* that could incorporate Blackness was the ultimate requisite of a successful republic aiming to showcase itself as liberal and progressive. That said, political elites were acutely aware of how their populations were perceived by the US and European elites. Juliet Hooker explains that the segmentation of area within national boundaries facilitated the ideological making of *mestizo* cores that subtly enfolded Blackness within their parameters. Drawing from print archival material pertaining to Nicaragua, she states:

> The racialization of some regions claimed as part of the national territory as Black or Indigenous and therefore "inferior" or "savage" served to legitimize the political disenfranchisement of their inhabitants by Nicaraguan and political elites during the nineteenth and twentieth centuries. The mapping of race onto space simultaneously fueled and facilitated the spatialization of race. Thus the designation of some regions of the country as the only ones where racial others resided made it possible to imagine the remaining areas of the country as lacking any kind of racial difference. . . . It also served to legitimize the notion, which persisted well into the twentieth century, that citizens of western regions of the country were peculiarly entitled to exercise political power in the [nation] as a whole, and over "uncivilized" regions in particular.³⁰

Beyond Nicaragua, other nations expressed the same insistence on *mestizo* competence and progress germane to the cities powered by *mestizos* closer to the Pacific coast. Central America had firmly closed its chapter on the colonial period; with that epistemic shift, Blackness was no longer an issue in the cities that mattered to the civilized republics. As Hooker finds with Nicaragua, the reminder of that alterity within emerged when the country entered into a dispute with Great Britain for the Mosquito Coast. Elsewhere in Central America, as the chapters in this book highlight, political turning points likewise ushered keen awareness of Blackness (and Indigeneity) and in more cases than not, resulted in the sharp rejection of *lo negro* (and *lo indio*), which operates largely at the level of slur more so than phenotypical identification.

Hooker's observations are key to the regional consideration I give to narratives of Afrodescendance in this book. In Central America, the Caribbean coastal strip is perceived as *the* site of Blackness in the region. Blackness can be literally seen there, while Blackness in the Pacific coastal areas and in the highlands is utterly unseen even by their own Afrodescendants. Unlike the Indigenous populations that were managed by *mestizo* and white Central Americans through a system of debt peonage well into the 1980s, Afrodescendants in the multilingual Caribbean coastal areas lived on the margins of the Hispanicized Central America (map I.1). Given the lack of roads connecting areas closer to the Pacific

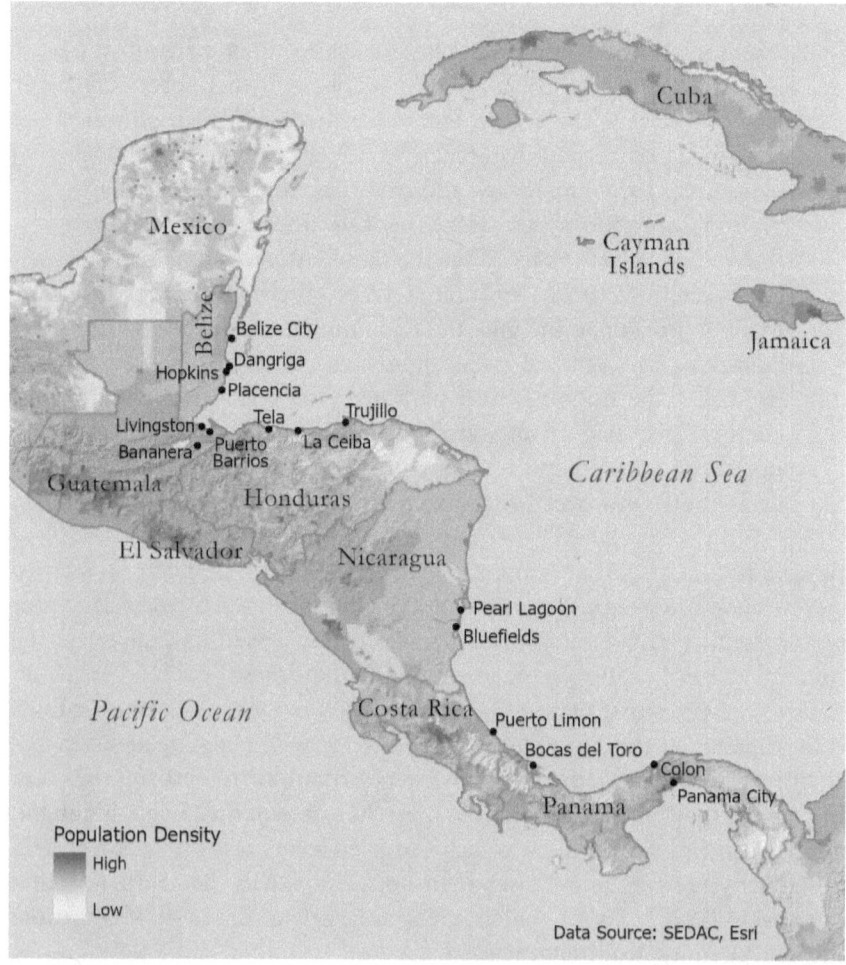

Map I.1. Central American Caribbean Coastal Towns. *Source*: U-Spatial.

to areas closer to the Caribbean, travel to "Black sites" was limited, and Afrodescendants could disappear altogether from their fellow Central American citizens' ken. Furthermore, legislation was used to literally keep Black peoples in place, as many countries of the isthmus established strict immigration laws targeting Afrodescendants.

A Moving Target in Space

Geography was a determining factor in the division of resources within the five United Provinces of Central America. Determining the apportionment of land and resources that would go to each province and how the incipient nations could pose a unified resistance to existing (Mexican and British) and emerging (United States) political threats was central to creating a sense of commonality among leaders and elites from north to south within the isthmus. Terrain was conceptualized as having racial/ethnic/linguistic properties resulting in a homogenizing voice from the capitals of the provinces: the United Provinces of Central America were Hispanicized locales and would continue to foment their unity through the Spanish language and Catholicism. It was a posture that presumed that Afrodescendants had *already* become part of the populace, the body politic, and economic order through linguistic and social "integration." By virtue of the nonexistent infrastructure connecting Pacific and Caribbean coastal areas, it was easy for [*mestizo* and white] Central Americans to imagine Blackness as something outside of their nations and region. National projects involved obtaining the nutrient-rich soils of Indigenous lands, controlling Pacific ports, and harnessing the coffee-picking labor of landless Indigenous peoples, leading to a *convivencia* of the [white and *mestizo*] ethnolinguistic majority that required proximity to Indigenous peoples in order to better dispossess them of their land. In Guatemala, [Black] towns like Livingston, Puerto Barrios, and Bananera register at 0, 33, and at 753 feet above sea level, respectively, in comparison to the towering capital of Guatemala City, which is located at 4,900 feet above sea level (map I.2). The pattern is repeated in Honduras, where the capital of Tegucigalpa is nestled in the hills between mountains at 3,248 feet above sea level in comparison to the [Black] towns of Trujillo, La Ceiba, and Tela, which are located at 114, 10, and 10 feet above sea level, respectively (map I.3). Afrodescendants were systematically restricted to the lowland undesirable "elsewhere" of their Central American nations, keeping them unseen across the other side of mountain ranges well into the twentieth century.

14 | Black in Print

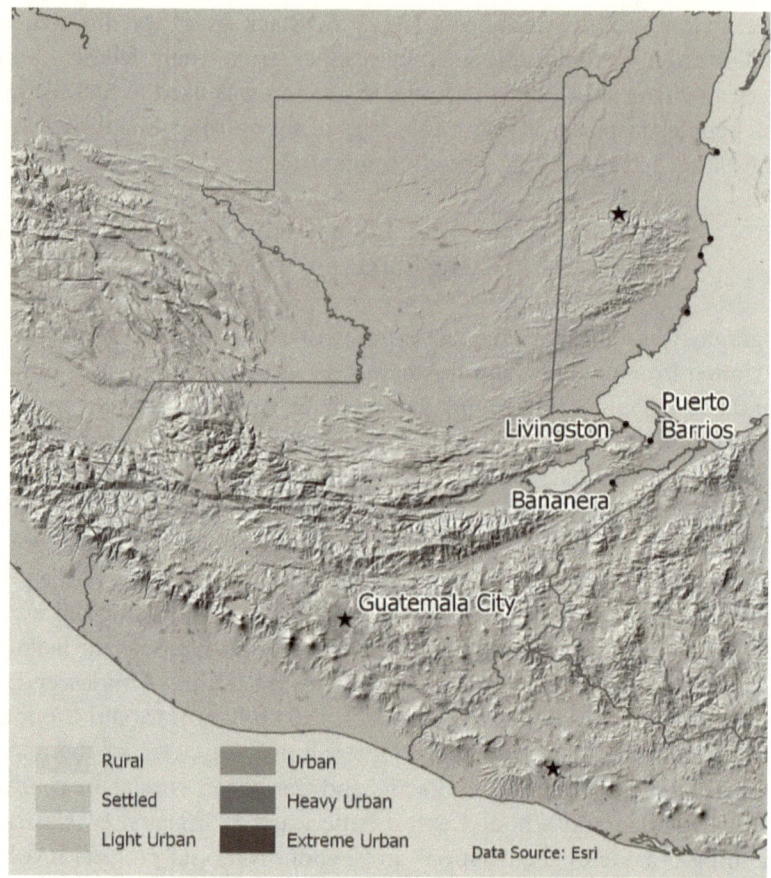

Map I.2. Guatemalan Caribbean Coastal Towns. *Source*: U-Spatial.

Politically and economically, the Pacific coast and mountain ranges were an early strategic area for [*mestizo* and white] coffee producers who exported it through the harbors located on the shores of the Pacific. Controlling the Indigenous (*campesino*) labor force—a group they considered distinct from the more numerous ethnically ambiguous *mestizo* citizenry—created a sense of national identity as national economies and regional financial networks were built.[31] The geographically and linguistically distinct "Black" groups that remained in lowland Caribbean areas existed outside of these larger socioeconomic networks. It was not until 1903 when Panama, with its substantial Afrodescendant population, was brought into the isthmian Hispanic fold that Nicaraguan president José Santos Zelaya and other Central American politicians began to take an

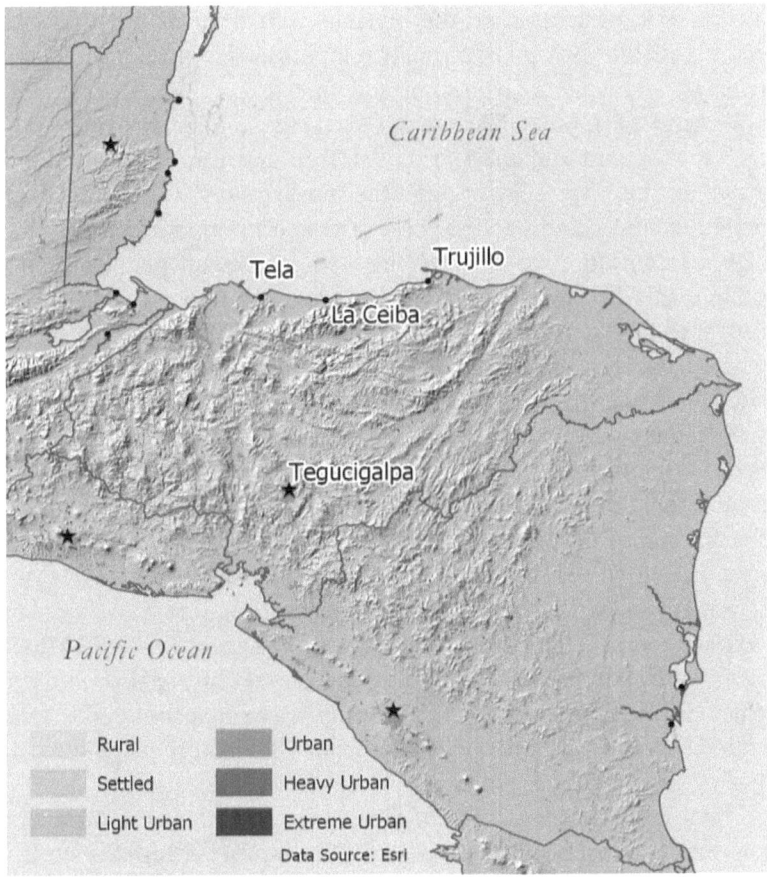

Map I.3. Honduran Caribbean Coastal Towns. *Source*: U-Spatial.

interest in claiming and Hispanicizing the hitherto culturally British and linguistically Anglophone Central American Caribbean coast.[32] As a result, discourses about a distinctly Black presence in Central America only reemerged when Hispanization, intensified nation-building, and territorial expansion all occurred in the [Black] towns that had hitherto been culturally and economically influenced by the British. As this distinct lowland Caribbean coastal topography and climate area was incorporated into the Central American nation, so, too, was the Black populace who was perceived as ethnolinguistically undesirable to the nation.

Thus, the isolated, unincorporated populations that had been essentially ignored by Central American administrations began to be "seen" and recognized as "Black." As United States–based banana companies settled in to make a profit through the banana trade from isthmian Caribbean ports, places like Belize (Belize City, Hopkins, Placencia, and Dangriga), Guatemala (Bananera, Livingston, and Puerto Barrios), Honduras (Tela, Trujillo, and La Ceiba), Nicaragua (Bluefields and Pearl Lagoon), Costa Rica (Limón), and Panama (Bocas del Toro and Canal Zone) were literally put on the map. They became the most important ports in the early twentieth century, and because these critical economic sites were home to a high concentration of Anglophone Afrodescendant peoples (including Garifuna, Miskito, and West Indian peoples with heritages dating back to ancestral enslavement in British Caribbean islands), they were at the center of heated debates when anti-imperialist media increased in circulation. Those [Black] towns on the Central American Caribbean coast were, and remain today, multilingual areas. These locales are polylinguistic areas in which the Spanish language arrived much later than it did in the highlands and the Pacific coast. In these [Black] towns, English, Creole, and Garifuna are just three of the languages in contact with Spanish. As an ethnically diverse nation with Kriol—a language born in conditions of West African enslavement—as its lingua franca, it is unsurprising that Belize would both be excised from Central American regional imaginaries and be the sole country in the isthmus with its first capital, Belize City, resting on the shore of the Caribbean Sea (map I.4). Although Belmopan became the capital after 1961, Belize City was the capital from 1836 and remains the cultural center of Creole culture and the Belizean Kriol language.[33]

I emphasize the existence of plurality even within the isthmian double narrative (described in the preface of this book) because the stories that have circulated about Blackness at different points in Central America's post-independence history has not been uniform. The narratives—organized by three spatiotemporal themes but further isolated into five distinct plotlines from the nineteenth century to the present day—came to determine whether all, some, or none of the descendants of West African slaves, Creoles,[34] Afro-Indigenous peoples,[35] and West Indian immigrants[36] would be subjected to the narratives about Blackness in the Central American countries in the isthmus. Degrees of proximity to capitals and linguistic criteria played a central role in incorporation of Afrodescendants and even in the cultural dis-incorporation of Belize from the Central American regional fabric. Hispanophone Afrodescendants continued to be part of the social, political, and military leadership of post-independence Central American societies. While political enemies in the United States and Great Britain mocked the region for its Afrodescendant politicians, these same

Introduction | 17

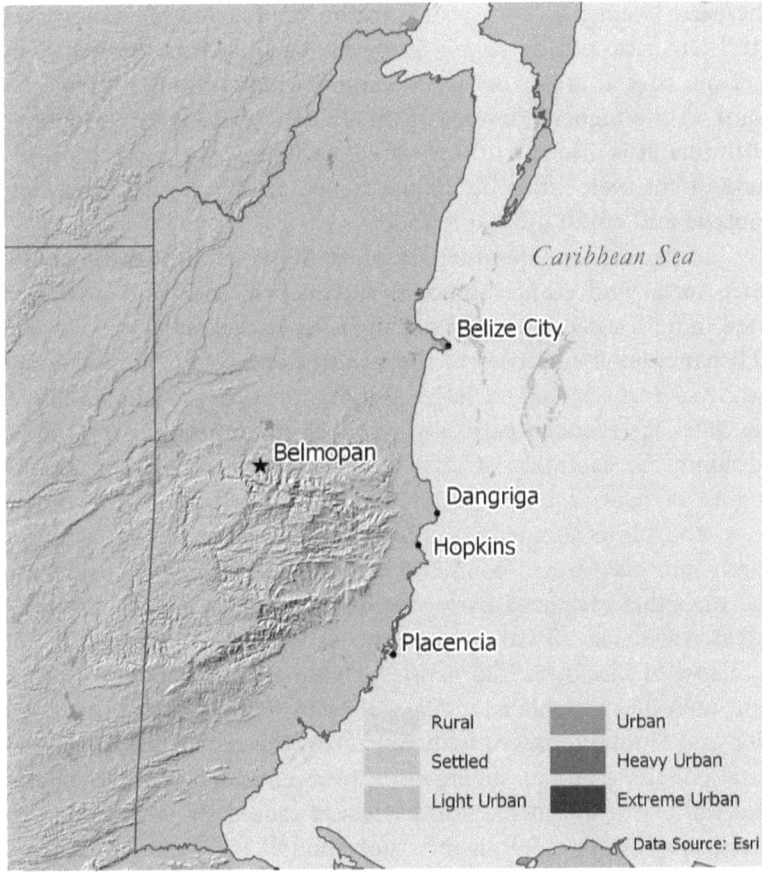

Map I.4. Belize and Belize City, Capital of British Honduras from 1638 to 1961. *Source*: U-Spatial.

leaders were participants in the elite circles that defended liberalism, the constitution of the United Provinces of Central America, and their capital city in Guatemala.[37] Yet, unlike the Afrodescendants on the Pacific coast who passed into all echelons of independent Central American society, multilingual Afro-Indigenous and West Indian groups in Caribbean coastal areas in the twentieth century were quite literally condemned to the fringes of their respective nations.[38] The Miskito, for example, continue to reside in Caribbean coastal communities in Honduras and Nicaragua. The Afro-Indigenous Garifuna have continued to live in coastal towns in Belize, Guatemala, and Honduras. The West Indian community—recruited in the early twentieth century to work on the banana plantations across Central America and the Canal Zone in Panama—has thrived in those very same coastal areas. Belize, the sole nation without a Pacific coast, is home to the highest number of inhabitants who identify as Creole in the isthmus. It is also the sole place where Kriol, a language born in the context of enslavement, is the lingua franca for all citizens, regardless of phenotype and cultural background.[39]

This became the premise of plots in which Blackness could be at once racial and ethnic, fictional and factual, seen and unseen, and defined in both essentialist and socially constructed terms. Consequently, the Hispanophone countries of the isthmus exemplify the phenomenon noted by several scholars, including J. Lorand Matory as quoted in Henry Louis Gates Jr.'s *Black in Latin America*: "North Americans tend to be as blind about the centrality of class in our society and vigilant about the centrality of race as Latin Americans are vigilant about the centrality of class and blind about the reality of race."[40] Despite the centuries of research into class-based conflict, Central America remains impervious to the ways that racialized narratives became institutionalized over time. For that reason, in all isthmian countries with the exception of Belize, the collapse of Blackness into *mestizaje* was held as an indicator of parity among men and republican civility. Therein lies a fallacy. And, as both Rahier and Hooker observe with respect to the region today, the multicultural policies that have emerged in the twenty-first century are merely a legal redress to the ideological exclusion caused by the ongoing myth of mestizaje.[41] Muilticulturalism is not enough to emplace Blackness as an ingredient in ideological biologies of the isthmus.

Axes and Coordinates of Blackness

Forever elusive and thus a challenge to entrap due to early narratives of disappearance, Blackness has continued to change coordinates even as it changed from (1) being incorporated into *mestizaje* after 1824, (2) challenging *mestizaje* in the early twentieth century, and (3) coexisting with Indigeneity as a subaltern subjectivity in these first two decades of the twenty-first century. These are points at the intersection of an x-axis that marks the "when" and a y-axis that marks the "where" of Blackness in Central America. After all, as Michelle M. Wright notes in *The Physics of Blackness*, Blackness is often examined as a "what," though it operates more precisely as a "when" and "where." Blackness cannot be conceived as a common denominator that links Black presence across categories; instead, the question of Blackness requires "focusing on the phenomenology of Blackness—that is, *when* and *where* it is being imagined, defined, and performed and in what locations, both figurative and literal."[42] Not only is the "meaning" of Blackness an epoch-specific attribution, but Blackness itself is experienced as a condition subject to the limits and possibilities afforded by the site and moment in which it is performed and read. In much the same way that the contours of Blackness have changed in the history of US media, so too has Black experience in Central America undergone similar "epistemic" transformations evident in the media of the region.[43] Sociopolitical waves of change have created the historical contexts that foreground narratives about Blackness and Black experience in three distinct regions within Central America: the Pacific coast, the central highlands, and the Caribbean coast. How do time and space converge to release energy in print so powerful as to rearrange the sightlines of citizenry into discreet cartographic zones?

In *México's Nobodies*, B. Christine Arce explains that a nation's "nobodies" make their way through the cracks caused by groundbreaking events, and that when they do, they are displayed in different trappings in order to respond to the needs of the period in question. Like Blackness in Mexico, Blackness in Central America has been thrown into relief at poignant historical moments, and at others, it has been submerged into national and regional oblivion. These matters are, as one critical observer has noted, historical questions, since the meaning and nature of inclusion, exclusion, and recognition are dependent on a variety of social, political, economic, and cultural factors that themselves change.[44] These observations direct us back to Wright's tenet that Blackness and Afrodescendance have a spatiotemporal quality that renders the meanings and *markers* of Blackness as alternately a "race" or "ethnicity"—as well as the philosophical/legal/political grounds for their relevance and applicability—as factors that vary over the course of time. Consider Wright's theory more closely: "Becoming aware of how spacetime operates in our everyday and more formal discourses on identity can help us retrieve those identities that have been consigned to the margins as 'rare' and 'unique' and bring them into their true place as a site for enriching intersections with other bodies, other times, and other histories. This mechanics, or 'physics,' of Blackness ticks in every one of us, because at any given moment we are in the hearts of all sorts of human diasporas."[45] The extent to which

Afrodescendants were included or recognized during the colonial period can be determined by delving into a history that has historically only provided Indigenous, *mestizo*, and white subjects a much more fixed place in national narratives.[46] In this book, I work with the variables of time and space that Wright and Arce discuss in their theories about Blackness as axes on a graph over which to determine the coordinates of Blackness at distinct moments in the history of the isthmus. To their discussion, I add the variable of language.

Print, as shall become clear in the chapters that follow this introduction, has inscribed Black bodies within imagined temporal, linguistic, and geographic boundaries, whether these be regional, national, or continental. Saidiya Hartman suggests in *Lose Your Mother* that this is because the enslaved ancestors of Afrodescendants in the Americas were torn from their families, homes, countries, and continent, perpetuating their condition as plotted strangers in national stories. The case of Juliana Deguis, popularized in the podcast *Radio Ambulante* in 2018, further illustrates this situation by presenting us with a woman whose point of origin and mother tongue is questioned in the Dominican Republic, despite the fact that she has always lived on the Dominican and not the Haitian side of the border. Despite their voices emerging in different languages and nations, Hartman's and Deguis's intellectual and experiential contributions to the literature on Blackness, language, geography, and heritage-home capture the "false rubrics" (per Michelle M. Wright) of Black hypostatic entity imposed on Afrodescendants. Their inventions also highlight the ways that a narrative of rightful belonging is replaced by a narrative of "associative belonging." In the same vein, hypostatic conceptualizations in US media have decreed, for example, that Blackness *is* urban instead of rural. To speak of Black country music in Texas or Black farmers in rural Virginia is as disruptive to mainstream notions of Black associative belonging as it is to read the Black characters crafted in Stephen L. Carter's novels.[47] Like US media's attribution of urban spaces as the locales of Blackness, Central America has designated its Caribbean coast as a strip of land in which Afrodescendance can be ascribed and circumscribed. It is a space where the miscegenation laws imposed by the British distinguished it from, first, the Pacific coastal areas where *mestizaje* became normalized and a foundational platform for creating Central American citizenry and, second, from the remote highland areas where many of the isthmus's Indigenous people were forced to flee to escape genocide.[48] It is this existence of a distinct space within the national context that creates the identity that Emily

Clark describes in *American Quadroon* and Lorgia García Peña captures *The Borders of Dominicanidad*. In these contexts, a nation is ideologically carved into a quintessential racially homogenous space counterposed to its racially ambiguous opposite. Whether or not a physical border divides the two spaces, the imagined hypostasis of Blackness is transposed to one of the geographic fragments of the nation in question.

This book joins others in questioning the historical reluctance to "trouble the water" in order to see Blackness. Richard L. Jackson was among the first to dedicate his extensive scholarly oeuvre—*The Black Image in Latin American Literature* (1976), *Black Writers in Latin America* (1978), *The Afro-Spanish American Author* (1980), *The Afro-Spanish American Author II* (1989), *Black Writers and the Hispanic Canon* (1997), *Black Writers and Latin America: Cross Cultural Affinities* (1998), and *Black Literature and Humanism in Latin America* (2008)—to the "black phobia" across the Americas and the concepts of "positive *mestizaje*" and "negative *mestizaje*" that resulted in problematic representations of Blackness in the print media of Central America and beyond. Santiago Valencia Chalá's *Blacks in Central America* (1986) provided the anthropological perspective on Afrodescendants' culture and discrimination, spanning Garifuna, West Indian, and descendants of enslaved African peoples trafficked into Central America during the colonial period. The demographic data recorded by Valencia Chalá facilitated an understanding of Afrodescendants across the *mestizo* nations of Central America. Ian Smart's groundbreaking *Central American Writers of West Indian Origin* explored the isthmus in detail, observing how immigration patterns from the Caribbean islands to what he calls "the rimlands" resulted in a new type of literature: "Black Central American literature." Focusing on literature produced by members of the third generation of the Caribbean diaspora in Panama and Costa Rica, but also including writings by *mestizo* authors, Smart argued that African heritage constituted one of the defining features of the cultural production not only in the Caribbean basin and but also in the Central American rimlands.[49] Like Ian Smart, Dorothy Mosby focused on writers of West Indian origin. Her landmark contribution to the field, *Place, Language, and Identity in Afro–Costa Rican Literature* (2003), examined the myth of whiteness that contributes to the invisibility of a rich Afro–Costa Rican literary tradition that crystallizes in the reconstitution and reconceptualization of identity from West Indian to Afro–Costa Rican identity. Mosby's central argument, that Afro–Costa Rican writers' ability to affirm "belongingness" in their native land and assert a presence in the country's literary culture is still a "dream deferred," is key in this book as I consider the region from 1821 to the present day and broaden the scope to consider the seven countries of the isthmus as well as today's coexistence of traditional and digital print media platforms.

Central American print continues to be marginal in the Latin American tradition, and print material related to Blackness in the isthmus is even more so. As a result, many of the texts examined in this book have yet to be translated to English; I have noted my translation of the fragments from those texts at the onset of their mention in the chapters.[50] What is clear, regardless of the language or translation of the texts, is formulated according to the variables of place, time, and language, which ultimately result in formulas for Blackness that refuse geographic, temporal, and linguistic essentialism. There are few places outside of the Caribbean islands and Brazil where constructions of Blackness have turned over at a speedy pace since the nineteenth century. As this analysis demonstrates, Central America is one. These are all the very same reasons why Blackness in the isthmus must be understood as a complex cartography over which mapped constellations consisting of plotted coordinates have disappeared, emerged, and reappeared in discrete positions in variations of time.

Print Media, from Independence to the Present

Black in Print is based on a range of print media from the region as a whole instead of a specific country with the aim of identifying constructions of Blackness in Central America, from the nineteenth century to the present. The analysis situates the work of the prolific Costa Rican novelist and essayist Quince Duncan, as well as the fresh voices of Nicaraguan poet Carl Rigby and Guatemalan Garifuna poet Wingston González, who were all born and raised on the Central American Caribbean coast. Since narratives of Blackness in the isthmus have been penned by outsiders, this analysis excavates writings by several influential Central American *mestizo* literary figures, an emerging Belize Maya author, and an Ecuadorian journalist. The mainstream writers included here are the Salvadoran Francisco Gavidia, who is considered an important founder of the Central American literary tradition established after independence. Two literary beacons in the wider Latin American literary tradition, Rubén Darío—himself an Afrodescendant, though fiercely opposed to what he saw as uncouth Blackness—and Nobel Prize winner

Miguel Ángel Asturias, are also included in this analysis. Anacristina Rossi, Tatiana Lobo, and David Ruiz Puga represent newer voices whose work has attained importance in Central American literary circles. The corpus of print media includes poetry, plays, canal literature, and banana novels sent to press, as well as print distributed and read through the vehicles of film and digital platforms. This body of work thus encompasses print material produced, circulated, and consumed in traditional as well as new media arenas.

This analysis begins with part 1, Pacific/Pacifico, which examines how the isthmus's founding fathers and the literary beacons equated Blackness with foreignness. The few literary works that addressed Blackness ascribed a purely ornamental place to it, further reinforcing its otherworldliness. In texts that centered the Pacific coastal areas of Central America, Black bodies and Black experience were located on any other shore but that of the Pacific Ocean. Hence, chapter 1 discusses the early work of Rubén Darío and Francisco Gavidia, two Central American intellectual giants, whose nineteenth-century profiles of Blackness have been largely overlooked despite the plethora of studies devoted to their oeuvre. The high degree of intertextuality in their works results in compositions that are influenced by classical, Orientalist, religious, and positivist perspectives of Blackness. Their texts situate Blackness as an experience outside of the isthmus, fitting for other times and sites, and thoroughly subject to the biblical Curse of Ham.

Part 2, Interior/Centro, examines how borders and boundaries became a central concern in political and literary discourses of the early twentieth century. It also explores the rhetoric of eugenics and xenophobia that were applied in narratives that featured Afro-Indigenous and West Indian immigrants in the region's early twentieth-century novels. With Mesoamerica as the reference point for national and regional discourses, "belonging" to the isthmus was predicated on the degree of imagined proximity to an Indigenous, precolonial past. This has resulted in the artificial, yet historical, dividing line between Black and Indigenous peoples in the isthmus. Chapter 2 treats banana novels and canal fiction as maps that divide nations like Honduras and Panama into two distinct geographic regions: the *mestizo* zone along the Pacific coast and the *negro* zone along the Caribbean coast. The Black zones in Honduran "banana novels" and Panamanian "canal novels" are posited by writers of the period as densely populated tracts of land where the rule of law does not reach. This type of mapping establishes a chasm between what are perceived as the legitimate citizens of these nations and Afrodescendants on the Caribbean coast—the English-speaking Afro-Indigenous Garifuna and West Indian workers on banana plantations and the Canal Zone. Meanwhile, chapter 3 focuses on narratives written as authoritarianism surged in the mid-twentieth century. This period was critical in shaping ideas about ethnicity, race, and belonging in Central American countries. Writing from Guatemala, Miguel Ángel Asturias leverages indigenista rhetoric and religious iconography to augment Black "difference." Belizean Maya David Ruiz Puga examines how the settler colonialist designs of the British empire created divisions between Indigenous and slave-descendant Creole peoples in the sole Anglophone nation of the isthmus. Taken together, narratives cement the Black/Indigenous divide that is at stake in the rightful claim to Central American belongingness.

Finally, part 3, Caribbean/Caribe, analyzes contemporary stories of Blackness as a response to the global discourses of diversity and inclusion. Print media has been tinged and transformed by the rhetoric of international organizations that validates the experiences of marginal groups like Afrodescendants in Central America. I begin with a chapter that examines the discourse of restorative justice that permeates one direction that narratives have taken, before launching into the discourse of autonomy on what I call "digital shores" embraced by contemporary Black writers. Hence, chapter 4 follows Central America out of the region's civil wars through the emergence of human rights discourses in the political and literary spheres. This resulted in multicultural initiatives at the local and national levels that have had a spillover effect on print material, including the novels of Anacristina Rossi and Tatiana Lobo, whose fictions take readers to hitherto unknown Black communities on the Caribbean coast in order rewrite a national history with material from Black experience. Lastly, chapter 5 examines the work of Wingston González and Carl Rigby as Black writing that resists temporal and thematic compartmentalization, both in content and in the manner produced and circulated. It pays particular attention to the use of new media in the diffusion of Black thought, the role of these print-on-digital platforms in extending the networks of Black writers beyond the isthmus and historically restrictive literary circles.

As these sections make clear, narratives about Blackness have at times reified and at other times challenged the geographic, ethnolinguistic divides that have ideologically severed Central America into three distinct ethnolinguistic zones: the Hispanophone [*mestizo*] Pacific coast, the Hispanicized [Indigenous] highlands, and the Anglophone [Black] Caribbean coast. In hegemonic Central American thought and discourse, Pacific coastal areas are the cradle of Central Americanness and its inhabitants are perceived as the unquestionable citizens of the isthmus. While manumission in 1824 discursively resulted in the legalistic absorption of Blackness into the *mestizo* ethnolinguistic category in coastal areas, Afrodescendant populations closer to the Caribbean coast were not similarly folded into the category. Central American Black peoples remained, in all countries except Belize, communities that purportedly neither existed nor had contributed to building Central America. The inexistence of infrastructure connecting the Pacific coastal areas to Caribbean coastal areas resulted in over a century of willful oblivion of Black constituencies in the isthmus. Blackness is a moving target in these narratives—shifting from the Black "foreigners" in chapter 1 of part 1, to the Black "contaminants" and "pests" in chapters 2 and 3 of part 2, to the Black "sovereign, autonomous peoples and creatives" in chapters 4 and 5 of part 3—creating a multidimensional field onto which the coordinates of Blackness have been mapped across time.

Before closing this introduction, it is important to me to emphasize that *Black in Print* rejects the treatment of the descendants of West African slaves, Afro-Indigenous peoples, and West Indian immigrants as a monolithic racial group. It does, however, ultimately posit that the print material that has circulated in the long durée of Central American history has erased the very important ethnic and historical differences between these populations. Despite great differences between Black communities, Afrodescendants in Central America have all been equally erased from national and regional grand narratives while still physically residing in the isthmus. Those who were not accepted as racially ambiguous *mestizos*—the Black populations residing in the Caribbean coast—have borne the same legacy of endemic poverty and anti-Black racism.[51] Meanwhile, scholarly studies like Nancie L. Solien González's *Dollar, Dove, and Eagle*, Lok Siu's *Memories of a Future Home*, and even the documentary *The Civilizers* directed by Uli Stelzner and Thomas Walthe all attest to the perceived contributions of other "minorities" in Central America, despite their much more recent arrival in the isthmus. From Guatemala to Panama, it is the Afrodescendants whose ancestors arrived in the isthmus centuries ago whose "fit" in the region has been repeatedly questioned. The power of print has made Central American Black legacies disappear and reappear at different times in the isthmus's history. As such, I seek to honor the Black lives in Central America (including those in my own family in El Salvador) that have been lost, dismissed, and disparaged. The narratives of Blackness that have upheld hegemonic systems of biopolitical and socioeconomic power throughout the isthmus have been plentiful, but today, in this twenty-first century, there is a new take on Blackness that resets the controls on the print produced, circulated, and consumed in the isthmus and beyond.

Part 1
Pacific/Pacífico

Chapter 1

Disappearing Acts

Goods and Black bodies were trafficked across the great expanse of the Atlantic Ocean. The colonial period transformed this body of water into a grid over which positions of subjectivity and alterity were carefully plotted. The deterritorialization of enslaved Black peoples as well as the transatlantic commerce effectuated by their masters have been amply documented, allowing us to gauge the critical transactions that resulted from these journeys. The Atlantic Ocean has historically shown itself to be an anachronic system of cultural exchange with linguistic, political, and intellectual repercussions.[1] However, the hermeneutic practices that flew over the Atlantic Ocean and across the Caribbean Sea only to be refashioned on the shores of Central America have not been sufficiently explored. Neither has the isthmus been sufficiently examined as a landscape narrated by the same complex mechanisms. Taking Stuart Hall's concepts of dominant-hegemonic encoding and decoding through the lens of the Black Atlantic theorized by Paul Gilroy, I examine the waterworld between two continents as a field onto which Orientalist and romantic influences were transformed into a narrative about Blackness for an independent Central America.[2] This first chapter is focused on the intertextual relationships in a selection of Rubén Darío's earliest poetry and in Francisco Gavidia's *Júpiter*—all of which appeared first in periodicals before they were published in volumes.[3] The overlapping narratives, I observe, respond to the political circumstances of nineteenth-century Central America and interweave a range of temporally discontinuous influences from across the Atlantic Ocean. These texts subject the reader to an aesthetic education by supplying copious allusions to influential works, demonstrating the Central American intellectuals' literary prowess through their conversion of Blackness into a literary element that, once fictionalized, could be understood as having faded away from Central American history itself.

A Cosmopolitan Isthmus

The liberal reform period of the nineteenth century had the greatest transformative power of any other critical juncture in the history of Central America. No other phase—including the colonial, the depression of the 1930s, or the sociopolitical reform period of the 1940s and 1950s—resulted in infrastructural changes of critical importance to the future development of the region to the degree seen during this period.[4] The increased demand for Central American agricultural products in the mid-nineteenth century led conservatives to gradually surrender their commitment to colonial land systems and to concur with liberals on such matters as land privatization and the transition to an agro-export economy. The Central American landscape was forever altered as a result of the influx of global capital in a region that had been peripheral, at best, during the colonial period. Contests were held for architects who wished to build the grandest of national theaters throughout Central America, and, when the first national theater was built in El Salvador, it was only fitting that it should reflect the Versailles, rococo, and romantic architectural styles that had become popular among the elite.[5] The expansion of commerce had allowed Central America to take great progressive leaps toward becoming "modern."

Cosmopolitanism was highly valued in nineteenth-century Central American society. As the elite classes defined themselves against the poorest sectors of their societies, they made a distinction between those who were worldly and well read and the lamentable "provincial" subjects in their countries.[6] The rise of print culture led to an unprecedented volume of writing that was devoured by the elites in early nineteenth-century Central American intellectual circles. The vast majority of books, newspapers, and other printed materials that were read in Central America came from Spain, but also from the Low Countries, Italy, Switzerland, and France.[7] These publications included dictionaries, grammars, histories, geographies, novels, theological treatises, and the latest in philosophy—all of which enabled the illustrious elites to keep abreast of cultural and scientific developments as well as the debates in French and British societies.[8] Despite the hundreds of books published in the five original Central American countries, however, the first presses and libraries of the region supported translations of European books; less than 5 percent were written by writers in the isthmus.[9] Though this might have been perceived as challenge, it also presented an opportunity for emerging intellectuals from the region who had the opportunity to single-handedly create a national/regional style and print following. Iván Molina Jiménez observes that in order to do so, they had to construct their own collective identity distinguishing them from Europeans that would nonetheless allow them to be accepted in their countries of origin, legitimize their stylistic aesthetics and specific ideologies via *modernismo*, and diversify and widen cultural markets to guarantee the printing, circulation, and readership of their works, all of which entailed collaboration between presses and libraries in promoting "national" and "Central American" selections and series.[10]

Rubén Darío, who was not only part of this world but came to define it, had strong opinions about the role of print in extending the grandeur of the isthmus. Darío fiercely advocated for the union of the five nation-states that together formed the federation, and within that political vision, he saw the production, circulation, and consumption of print materials a critical avenue for intellectual freedom and progress. Leaving behind the commissioned work by local politicians, Darío abandoned the topic of Nicaraguan politics and immersed himself in ornate lyricism for a wider readership. Meanwhile, Francisco Gavidia, the father of Salvadoran national letters, shaped new elite sensibilities and aesthetics within his own repertoire of characters in theatrical works, prose, and poetry. So great was his influence in the national literary canon that the incorporation of his work in public school curricula has resulted in readers across generations since the nineteenth century. Blackness appears in a selection of their works as an aesthetic motif of an Old World/old colonial remnant on the verge of disappearing into the rapidly restructured Central American reality. Integrating a wide range of sources arising from intellectual circles across the Atlantic allows both Darío and Gavidia to make beauty and passion recenter that which the divisive political rhetoric of the day risked suffocating: the zeitgeist of progress that was fueling Central America's transition into an important player on the world stage. Blackness died—either through suicide or fate—in the works of Darío and Gavidia, while the copious cosmopolitanism of their pieces jealously guarded the nascent and future narratives of the isthmus.

Pacific Privileges

On the eve of Latin American independence, Simón Bolívar proclaimed in his "Carta de Jamaica" that the glorious destiny of the Federal Republic of Central America was ensured by its very location and the degree to which this could be used strategically to increase the wealth of the continent: "Esta magnífica posición entre los dos mares podrá ser con el tiempo el emporio del universo; sus canales acortarán las distancias del mundo; estrecharán los lazos comerciales de Europa, América y Asia; traerán a tan feliz región los tributos de las cuatro partes del globo. ¡Acaso sólo allí podrá fijarse algún día la capital de la tierra como pretendió Constantino que fuese Bizancio la del antiguo hemisferio!" (Its magnificent strategic position between two oceans may in time result in a universal emporium, its canals shortening the distances between worlds and reinforcing commercial ties between Europe, America, and Asia, bringing tribute to this happy region from the four quarters of the globe. Here alone, perhaps, it will be possible to establish a world capital, as Constantine aspired for Byzantium to become for the ancient world!)[11] According to this vision, the Federal Republic of Central America would serve as a broker for trade with Europe and Asia and soon the promised wealth of Nuestra América would make its way through the isthmus before being redistributed to the north and south.

This was the promising future imagined for Central America and, by 1875, its ruling elites incorporated into their societies the symbols that they considered relevant to their assumed cosmopolitanism: Napoleonic codes, new editions of Sir Walter Scott's novels, flushing toilets, French interior home decorating, and Victorian roofs were purchased with capital garnered through the exportation of coffee.[12] Aesthetic conceptions were intimately tied to the cultural patterns permitted by the economic boom resulting from Central America's position in the world markets. Accordingly, critics hold that Rubén Darío freed Spain from its "neoclassical dungeon" and released Latin America from a "hazy romanticism" borrowed from abroad by producing a type of poetry that was full of life and anguish.[13] Two poems about Blackness, "El porvenir" and "Alí," that I examine in this chapter are from Darío's first poetry volume, *Epístolas y poemas*.[14] The volume represents the poet's first attempt at transgressing his regional borders and concerns, allowing him to venture into the terrain of artifice as it was crafted across the Atlantic. This collection of poems precedes the publication of his classic *Azul . . .* (1888) and marks

Darío's transition from the political poems commissioned by the Liberal party in Nicaragua to his venture into the modernist compositions he is known for today. *Epístolas y poemas* is a bridge to his most renowned oeuvre and as such it explicitly manifests the poet's debt to the Spanish classics, Victor Hugo's romantic models, and the neoclassical influences in the epistles directed to key literary figures. It allows the poet to fashion an artistic identity independent of a strictly Central American geopolitical position and assume the position of a poet-inheritor of transcontinental aesthetic concerns.

The poems composed prior to *Epístolas y poemas* allowed Darío to make his mark on intellectual circles and, as his commissions from dictators and politicians increased, so did his diplomatic privileges and access to travel. These early commissions exemplify three qualities not found in his canonical *modernista* poetry: provincialism, regionalism, and patriotism. However, it would be extreme oversight to label Rubén Darío a political ideologue of any persuasion due to the commissioned nature of the compositions.[15] The commissioned political rhetoric comes to an end abruptly, suspended when he ceases to believe in the dream of convening the Federal Republic of Central America.[16] *Epístolas y poemas* thus marks the onset of Darío's poetry for poetics' sake. It is also the first indication of Darío's mastery of poetics and of imparting the sensation of the referent as it is perceived instead of how it is manifested physically. This is what the Russian formalist Viktor Shklovskij called *ostranenie*: "The technique of art is to make objects 'unfamiliar,' to make forms difficult, to increase the difficulty of length and perception, because the process of perception is an aesthetic end in and of itself and must be prolonged."[17]

Blackness and Orientalism are thrown into sharp relief in "El porvenir" and "Alí," which allow the reader to experience the artfulness of Darío's carefully sculpted verse, his range of literary influences, and his encoded ideologies of Blackness. This content reflects a Central American poet's cosmopolitan yearnings through new rhythms, love for elegance, and the rejection of the prosaic. It is also written at a time when physically and metaphorically exploring the Orient was a means devised by cosmopolitan Europeans (and Latin American aspirants) to find answers to transcendental questions that could not be found in their own context due to what they perceived as the lack of the sensibility in their surroundings.[18] Darío grappled with transcendental questions that involved an inquiry into the possibility of using poetics as a vehicle to achieve an ideal spiritual state, surpassing the physical and the empirical. This was accomplished through what is commonly known as defamiliarization, or, in literary formalism, as *ostranenie*: a strategy that subtracts substance from the referent and "remove[s] the automatism of perception; the author's purpose is to create the vision which results from that deautomatized perception."[19] Narratives about Blackness and the Orient were commonplace among the intellectual elites of Central America, but what brought about *ostranenie*, the unfamiliarity of the themes and symbols, was their encasing in the Spanish language and a Central American voice. As the reader experiences defamiliarization with the sketches of Blackness and the Orient drawn by Darío, "El porvenir" and "Alí" situate her at the crossroads of four continents.

This is exemplified in "El porvenir" where the poetic voice takes the reader across continents to arrive at what the future holds for Darío's homeland. Without referencing trade routes, it includes a repertoire of mystical symbols associated with literary motifs associated with Asia. This continent *is* the Ganges, Brahmans, armed nomads, forests, elephants, hippopotamuses, and rhinoceroses. Asia had been imprinted in the Latin American intellectual imaginary since the sixteenth century, when ships laden with goods departed Acapulco en route to Manila, Philippines.[20] The passages through time and space allow Darío to stress worldliness and refinement in their art without undergoing the inconveniences of crude voyages or opening the pages of vulgar travel narratives for inspiration. Importantly, it cements both the Hispanophone poetic voice and reader at the precipice of discovery of *self*. Correspondingly, Tzvetan Todorov demonstrates that the discovery the *self* makes of the *other* is rife with paradoxes and hermeneutic twists.[21] In "El porvenir," these lyrical maneuvers relate to the consonances and dissonances uncovered as the poet voice transits from specific continental histories and futures.

The *América*-Europe connection in the poem seemingly replicates the ideological relationship manifested by imperialist center-periphery relationships. The poetic voice praises Europe for being the site from whence Voltaire laughed, Cervantes spoke, and Dante was born. It appeases the reader from *América* who expects to read that this continent's arm is London and that its soul is Paris and masterful frescoes decorate the walls of Rome and Madrid. The muses have blessed Europe, but the gods have elevated the Americas by granting them unparalleled riches and beauty. In a swift and unexpected twist, the poem heralds the trumpet of fame that will carry its song from the Chimborazo volcano in Ecuador to the

Argentinean pampas and over the Tequendama Falls in Colombia. The grandeur of *América* isn't located in a particular Central American site, but rather in a poetic conception of the continent's landscape.

Darío maps continents according to myths, legends, and legendary figures, a strategy that he likewise employs in his depiction of Africa. Just as his profiles of Asia and Europe have been derived from narratives circulating between the continents, "El porvenir" likewise relies on an Old World narrative to frame Africa. As stated in the introduction, the Curse of Ham was among the first narratives of Blackness with the power to justify the enslavement of Black peoples in the Americas. According to this story from the Old Testament, Noah became a husbandman, planted a vineyard, and drank from that wine. He lay uncovered in a state of drunkenness when his son, Ham, entered the tent, saw the nakedness of his father, and told his brothers. They, in turn, entered the tent with their backs turned toward their father and covered him without stealing a glance. Upon awakening from his drunkenness, Noah learned of their different responses. The King James version quotes Noah's curse on the son who disrespected him: "And Noah awoke from his wine, and knew what his younger son [Ham] had done unto him. And he said, 'Cursed *be* Canaan; a slave of slaves shall he be unto his brethren.' And he said, 'Blessed *be* the Lord God of Shem; and Canaan shall be his servant. God shall enlarge Japheth, and he shall dwell in the tents of Shem; and Canaan shall be his servant.'"[22] Though none of the phrases state that Ham was Black and translations of the Bible alternate between the use of "servant" or "slave," it became very common to use these verses as a justification for the perpetual enslavement of African peoples in the early modern era.[23] In "El porvenir," the presumed biblical reference generates *ostranenie* while establishing the supremacy of *América* and its peoples over Africa and its peoples:

> El África tostada,
> ya de antiguo sombría, aletargada,
> donde el fiero león sangriento ruge,
> bate el ala el simoun y vuela y muge la tierra en donde
>   moran/ los hombres de piel negra,
> hijos de Cam,
> que su desgracia ignoran
> y a quienes claro día nunca alegra;
> porque es raza de esclavos y precita,
> raza sin libertad, raza maldita.[24]

(Toasted Africa,/ already drowsy from an ancient gloominess,/ where the fierce bloody lion roars,/ the simoom beats its wing and dances and bellows/ the land/ where there dwells/ the men of black skin,/ children of Ham, unaware of their disgrace/ and whom a sunny day never cheers;/ because it is a race of slaves and condemned to hell,/ a race without freedom, a damned race.)

Invoked post-manumission, Darío's poem substantiates a hegemonic belief in Blackness as inferiority and the righteousness of Godly punishment. In this scheme, Africa remains unchanged in its misery while *América*, as Darío has already established, marches forward in its path toward progress. The inclusion of a "periphery of the periphery" relationship in the route across continents is of interest here precisely because the poetic voice fully cognizant of the narratives used to frame his and other "inferior" cultures was constructed through European discourses. The passage replicates a series of narrative elements crafted by Europeans about Africa and, by integrating them into "El porvenir," the poet designates himself master narrator. He is at once creator and designator of the signs used to tell the story and the future of the continents. The Hispanophone reader is subtly invited to assume this same position. The process allows poetic voice and reader to continue along the path toward a racialized cognitive mapping, so to speak, that is critical for disassociating both from the colonial past. Like other early nineteenth-century works, this poem posits Latin American identity as a receptacle to be filled with ideological components that reinforce a continental march toward progress.[25]

More specifically, "El porvenir" invites intended readers to establish themselves as subjects crafted within a lush landscape in contrast to the Black subjects of the Sahara, a desert that is quickly disassociated from the northern and southern extremities of the continent by the use of poetic references. This is a barren, lethargic, scorched terrain void of culture and promise wherein ferocious lions are said to roar and terrorize inhabitants and travelers alike. Colonial accounts of the simooms, a dust-laden wind that blows in the Sahara and parts of the Middle East, serve the poet well as he constructs an account of the oppressiveness of the climate. Through the damning pronouncement that associates Blackness with the Curse of Ham, the poetic voice severs the location-nationality connection that remains in place for *América* and Europe and settles for an interpretation of Blackness based on phenotype and bleak destiny. In the same breath, it provides a religious justification for its manifestation. Positions are mapped through a metonymical transfusion from nature to people: Black subjects are condemned to be slaves, to be ignorant of the curse that has befallen them—here, the implication being that they have not been Christianized and thus do not have the power of understanding the origins of the curse as dictated in Genesis. As neither Christians nor free men, they face the consequences of their ungodliness. This narrative espoused is anchored in the sociopolitical history of Central American society of the time: it dignifies the whiteness of the elite and, perhaps more subtly, aligns Latin American intellectual history with the ideology of biological determinism in vogue in Anglo-Saxon and European contexts.[26] This, while subjecting Asia and Africa to Orientalist and divinely damning depictions. In Darío's early poetry, then, an ideological allegiance with European "greatness" hinges on presenting Blackness as an Old World curse.

Orientalism, like the presumed curse of Blackness, is a discourse that originates across the Atlantic and is refashioned by Darío as he writes from his position of Pacific privilege on the elegant side of the isthmus. Aside from establishing the polarities between rational and irrational subjects, Orientalism stressed that "the Oriental lived in a different but thoroughly organized world of his own, a world with its own national, cultural and epistemological boundaries and principles of internal coherence."[27] A parallel maneuver is deployed in Darío's poem "Alí," which is included along with "El porvenir" in the volume *Epístolas y poemas*. In line with Orientalism, the poem stresses that the Black subject's world has its very own intelligibility and identity, though the reader can discern that the very logic of this microcosm will lead to its own demise. The written and historical commentary of Victor Hugo regarding the Orient is present in Darío's deployment of noteworthy tropes. In Hugo's *Les orientales*, the dazzling colors of the East are present, but it is purely illusory because these bright and cheerful colors are actually set against a background of destruction and death.[28] So, too, with Darío's "Alí," which foreshadows the devastating fate of the title character.

Darío explicitly states at the beginning of the poem that it is dedicated to a friend who enjoys the pleasures of the "mysterious Orient," understood as "luxurious and imaginative."[29] As Darío makes clear in this dedication, the poem is written at the request of someone who delights in Zorrilla's legends and is for that reason composed in a style that the poem describes as "half pearls, half honey and flowers," though the poet self-critically admits that it might lack some of Théophile Gautier's hashish. Written as an epic in verse in a style that overtly draws its inspiration from Zorrilla, the poem achieves a seamless transfer of the ideological content of North African settings as they were represented in the French and Spanish literary traditions. The style manifests itself in the introductory verses that present the reader with two star-crossed lovers against the forbidding sands of the Orient.

Zela is the prototypical female found in Darío's later *modernista* poems—beautiful, graceful, and celestial—but in this early poem, the damsel is a Moor, and her lover is an Ethiopian. The poetic voice describes her as an Oriental nymph whose abundant curls fall over her shoulders and whose hands are like a bouquet of lilies; Zephyrus, god of the west wind, irons her silk vestments.[30] Alí is a slave to none other but Zela's love. As beautiful as he is strong-willed, his soul blends the traits of a panther and a dove. The verses that present him to the reader demonstrate that he is not the broken Black slave under the whip; rather, he is the Black warrior feared by the Bedouin who dare not humiliate him or threaten him with their weapons:

> Alí es el etíope bello;
> negro, hermoso, alto y fornido;
> de ojo brillante, encendido,
> y de encrespado cabello;
> sobre la faz lleva el sello
> de un vigor que no se doma:
> según el rumbo que toma,
> él es en su alma altanera/ feroz como una pantera,
> tierno como una paloma.[31]

> (Alí is the beautiful Ethiopian;/ Black, beautiful, tall, and strong;/ of a brilliant eye, passionate,/ and of curly hair;/ over his face he bears the seal/ of a vigor that will not be tamed:/ according to the path he takes,/ he is in his proud soul/ as fierce as a panther,/ gentle as a dove.)

Like Herodotus, who was one of the first writers in the Western literary canon to express an opinion about the physical appearance of Ethiopians, Darío does not hesitate to highlight the Black subject's beauty. In the texts of antiquity, color does not preclude the requisites for beauty. From

Philodemus, Asclepiades, Theocritus, Suetonius, Vergil, Ovid, Luxorius, and others, there is a plethora of implied and explicit references to the beauty of Blackness.[32] Greek and Roman texts stipulate individual preferences and relative standards of beauty, emphasizing as Propertius did in one text that "tender beauty, white or dark, attracts."[33] Like Zela the Moor, Alí the Ethiopian is an aesthetic figure that destabilizes the expectations of the average nineteenth-century learned reader. To these readers, the description of Alí would rouse *ostranenie* as the reader meditated over the conception of damned Blackness in the verses of "El porvenir" only to turn the pages to find beauty and grace in the verses of "Alí." While both compositions conclude on the same bitter note, satisfying the briefly destabilized reader, these opening rhymes cater to a different intellectual, one quite familiar with the depth of the classical influence on Darío's work who might very well see in the pairing of the two poems the same masterplot that the average reader discovers only upon Alí's demise in the final verses of the poem.

The poem opens with descriptions of the lovers. Alí is docile in Zela's presence, complying with her wishes and sobbing on his hands and knees whenever he disappoints her. Zela, who cries when Alí is away and sighs when her gaze meets his, also demonstrates this absolute devotion. Fearing the wrath of Zela's cruel father, the two lovers meet secretly under the full moon. The Ethiopian promises the Moor wealth and happiness, imploring her to defy her father and part with him. She assents and they race through the desert. The image is captivating, for Alí's beauty and determination even extend to his black steed:

> "Ven conmigo bella flor;
> vente conmigo a gozar;
> mil prendas te voy a dar
> como te he dado mi amor."
> Y cargando con vigor
> la niña, salió en secreto
> del jardín, y a un vericueto
> se dirigió, do tenía
> el corcel, que ya quería
> correr afanoso, inquieto.
> Potro de negro color,
> nariz ancha, fino cabo,
> crespa crin, tendido rabo,

cuello fino, ojo avizor,
enjaezado con primor,
de Alí corcel de combate,
nunca el cansancio lo abate
y casi no imprime el callo,
cuando se siente el caballo
herido del acicate.
En ese va el africano
por el desierto con Zela:
va el corcel como que vuela
para un país muy lejano;
y siguen al negro ufano,
con paso tardo, distantes,
los camellos y elefantes
do puso riquezas mil
de perlas, oro y marfil,
y rubíes y diamantes.[34]

("Come with me, beautiful flower/ Come with me to enjoy/ a thousand garments I will give you/ as I have given you my love."/ And carrying with vigor/ the girl, he left in secret/ from the garden, and through twists and turns/ he headed/ where he had/ the steed, who already wanted/ to run unflaggingly, restlessly.// A Black buck/ wide nose, fine backside/ curly mane, long tail/ fine neck, sharp eye/ saddled up with care/ Combat steed of Alí/ fatigue never abates him/ and he almost doesn't recoil/ when the horse feels/ the wound of the spur.// It is that one the African rides/ through the desert with Zela:/ the steed rides on as if in flight/ to a faraway land;/ and following the proud Black man,/ with a distant stride, in the distance,/ the camels and elephants/ where he has placed a thousand riches,/ of pearls, gold, and ivory,/ and rubies and diamonds.)

The verses in the first stanza characterize Zela as a girl misled to leave her home with Alí's promise of wealth, while the second half of the verses concentrate on the Black man. This same gaze continues in the second stanza's first five verses, which ambiguously describe both Alí and his horse in suggestive sexual language until the final verses of the poem draw focus on the black steed. Encoded in the poem, then, is the same blurred line between Black subjects and "brutes" (horses, cows) as well as their implicit breeding for a slavery economy that was pervasive in the Americas during the transatlantic slave trade.[35]

The foreshadowing notwithstanding, in the last stanza, Darío emulates French poet Théophile Gautier's passion for situating luxury and beauty against an exotic backdrop. In his preface to *Émaux et Camées*, Gautier established a similar pattern of inspiration upon acknowledging the extent to which his own collection of poems had been influenced by German poet Johann Wolfgang von Goethe's *Divan occidental*, whose verses had been in turn inspired by the work of Hafez, the Persian poet. The genealogy traces the Western subject's desire to bridge Christian-Muslim traditions through the artifice of poetry, parables, and epic lyricism. Firmly in place is a schema for reading not only the cultural but also the imagined gendered dynamics in such a context. Creating "art for art's sake," as Gautier and the Parnassians who were influenced by him declared, was nonetheless a reaction to the political and literary circumstances these literary masters faced.

Gautier writes of his predecessor: "When empires lay riven apart,/ Fared Goethe at battle time's thunder/ To fragrant oases of art,/ To weave his *Divan* into wonder."[36] He compares Goethe's struggle to produce art against a tumultuous context to the challenges he also faces: "I, closed from the tempest that shook/ My window with fury impassioned/ Sat dreaming, and, safe in my nook/ *Enamels and Cameos* fashioned."[37] Published in 1852 after Gautier left France to travel through the Middle East, this collection highlights the formalist aspects of Orientalist poetry rather than the emotive qualities of the romanticist compositions he opted to challenge. A world away, Rubén Darío responded in a similar manner to the upheaval caused by the dissolution of the Federal Republic of Central America by favoring Orientalist formalism over divisive political rhetoric. This was a period in which the qualities of a cosmopolitan man prevailed over the concept of a political poet, making Darío evermore devoted to fashioning lyrical poetry and elegant prose instead of partisan ideas.[38] Just when the destiny of Central America was being narrated, Darío outshone the political rhetoric of his commissioned poetry and displayed his passion for artifice and Orientalism germinating across the Atlantic.

In "Alí," the critic can find traces of seemingly opposing literary discourses. Having renounced the "lettered city," Ángel Rama writes, there arose a general opposition to the political material among intellectuals of Darío's generation: romantics, conservatives, liberals, rationalists, the old guard, and the old followers of the Enlightenment.[39] Imitation of form was certainly a vehicle to achieve an aesthetic mélange of influences and, like alchemists, Darío and other poets sought to make gold from the elements with which they experimented. That which was beautiful, that which was strange, exquisite, and luxurious was at the root of their search for a refined, transcendental experience. A rejection of that which they perceived to be vulgar and revolting was implicit. Therefore, Blackness, once it was divested of the silk garments afforded by Orientalism and classical influences, was subject to the power of positivism that had taken root in the Central American isthmus and in broader Latin American intellectual circles.

The two lovers take flight across the sand on exotic verses: beautiful Alí and romantic Zela with their caravan of camels and elephants carrying pearls, gold, ivory, rubies, and diamonds. He is *el africano* (the African) running over the desert sand with Zela, the poetic voice declares.[40] The term works with Darío's rhyme scheme, but the designation strips Zela of her own Africanity. We know that the match between a Muslim North African and an Ethiopian sub-Saharan African would be plausible, per the many archaeological and literary references provided by Frank M. Snowden in his *Before Color Prejudice*, given that conversion from one religion did sometimes occur. Yet "Alí" locates the Black male subject squarely as an African and, in the very identification and omission of the bride's own Africanity, interjects nineteenth-century understanding of "damned" interfaith and/or interracial unions. As the denouement of the poem indicates, this new position subtracts power from the Black male subject in a subtle gesture that highlights Alí's subjection and emasculation. The sub-Saharan African male turned slave is thus cleverly juxtaposed to the North African Muslim male figures, from Zela's father to the sultan who ultimately captures the lovers.

In latter stanzas, the poem turns from exotic considerations to the curse on the two star-crossed lovers. The poem bears the mark of French and Spanish romantic incursions into the Orient in the first stanzas and the mark of Anglo-Saxon positivism and Protestantism by the last verses. Zela's father discovers that they have left and expires before reaching the runaway couple, but not before laying a curse on the lovers. The damsel's realization, "que la maldición de un padre/ desata la ira de Dios" (that the curse of a father/ unleashes the fury of God), clearly foreshadows their doom, though Alí attempts to assuage her by invoking Allah's fairness and wisdom.[41] No longer designated as a Christian Ethiopian, Alí's appeal to Allah marks him as an sub-Saharan African Muslim. An infidel, as it were. The curse over the Black subject that is developed in this poem follows the Judeo-Christian biblical text, the Curse of Ham: a child has defied/defiled a paternal figure and has committed adultery, following the definition of "sexual indiscretion outside of marriage." The wrath of God befalls the lovers seconds before they consummate their love for the first time. In a devastating twist, a band of Bedouin fighters captures the couple and takes them to an opulent sultan. The poetic voice erupts in the narrative to remind the reader of the old man's curse. Just as the Judeo-Christian text posits the Curse of Ham as one that results after a child defies/defiles a paternal figure by committing a sexual indiscretion, so too does "Alí" adopt the parameters of the curse that befalls the Black subject in this poem.[42] Alí, who has always been able to defeat and terrify the Bedouin, is now suddenly powerless. He is committed to slavery and castrated while Zela becomes the sultan's concubine.

The poem reaches its climax when Alí rushes into the bedroom and confronts the sultan just as he is about to copulate with her. Alí has changed dramatically from the beautiful man he once was and is now like any other Black slave owned by the sultan: "Flaco, la frente arrugada/ la mano huesosa y dura/ la crespa melena oscura/ crecida y alborotada/ con la vista extraviada." (Thin, his forehead wrinkled/ his hand hard and bony/ his curly mane darkened/ overgrown and tousled/ his gaze lost.)[43] He threatens the sultan with a weapon, declaring that it is he—the ruined subject who has lost everything, the wretched creature, mud, and rotten seed—who seeks vengeance.

> Zela era mi amor; yo el de ella.
> ahora, ella altiva; yo vil,
> imagínate un reptil
> que habla de amor a una estrella . . .
> Hay un monstruo y una bella . . . ,
> y ese monstruo tiene ardor . . .
> y es un eunuco, ¡oh dolor! . . .
> Mi amada en regazo ajeno;/ yo me revuelco en el cieno,
> y tú . . . ¡tú eres el señor![44]

(Zela was my love; and I hers./ Now, she is proud; I, vile,/ imagine a reptile/ that speaks of love to a star . . ./ There is a monster and a beauty. . ./ and that monster has a burning . . ./

and he is a eunuch, oh how painful!/ My beloved in another's lap;/ I wallow in mud/ And you . . . you are the master!)

Alí cannot bear to look at his beloved Zela, who now only inspires hate and repulsion in him. Having already become a wretched creature upon losing his freedom, Alí descends further into wretchedness and misery by letting his emotions consume his power to reason. Alí thus murders her and the sultan with a passion only equaled by the devotion he once had for her. He kisses her one last time and stabs himself in the chest before falling by her side, thereby frozen in the image of: "La boda terrible/ de un eunuco y una muerta." (The terrible wedding/ between a eunuch and a dead woman.)[45] Darío thus completes a poem that privileges a positivist disposition toward Blackness, which relies on the depiction of Black subjects as ruled by passion over reason. The pen strokes in these understudied poetic compositions amply allude to the intersections of transcontinental and anachronistic influences in the representations of Blackness.

Staging Blackness

Darío captured the explicit message in Giovanni (Cinthio) Battista Giraldi's short story "Un Capitano Moro"—the sixteenth-century inspiration for Shakespeare's *Othello*—in the last verses of "Alí." This was the same sentiment that Salvadoran Francisco Gavidia would echo four years after Darío: that despite their apparent tameness, the nature of Black men is violently irrational. In Cinthio's story, the thought is articulated by Desdemona when her husband accuses her of infidelity: "You Moors are of so warm a composition that every trifle transports you with anger and revenge," to which her husband retorts that he will seek vengeance to his satisfaction for any injustices committed against him.[46] As his jealousy reaches perilous heights, Desdemona expresses a growing concern: "I begin to fear that my example will teach young women never to marry against their parents' consent, and the Italians in particular, not to connect themselves with men from whom they are separated by nature, climate, education, and complexion."[47] The message is clear: a lady who marries a Black man is subject to his capricious passions, which are correlated to his nature and origins. This tragic story also served as the blueprint for Francisco Gavidia's *Júpiter* (1889).

Júpiter, a Salvadoran national drama/tragedy, is the earliest Central American text in prose form to feature a Black slave as the main character and the only isthmian play to delve into the complex question of the Black subject's political and cultural rights in the context of Independence. Carmen Molina Tamaca reports that *Júpiter* first appeared in print in the *Repertorio salvadoreño*, the monthly magazine of the San Salvador School of Sciences and Literature. It was published a second time in 1895 for the San Salvador National Press in a volume under the direction of the editors of *El Figaro* newspaper. The Salvadoran Dirección de Publicaciones e Impresos oversaw its third publication as part of its "Colección Teatro" in 2002. The play has been staged three times—in 1951, 1971, and 1991 as part of Salvadoran Independence Day celebrations—and was adapted for a thirty-minute radio drama in 2006 on Radio YSUCA 91.7, yet it has never featured a Black performer.[48]

Júpiter details the events leading to the 1811 uprising commonly heralded as "the first cry for independence" in which a heavily armed contingent of *morenos* played a key role. The play features three Central American founding fathers: Santiago Celis, José Matías Delgado, and Manuel José Arce. These three *criollos* come to determine the fate of Júpiter, a literate and God-fearing Black man who is granted manumission upon agreeing to enlist San Salvador's slaves and mulattos in his former master's plot against the Crown. In a stunning politicized display of synecdoche, within the framework of the national romance, Júpiter comes to stand for the Black masses in the new Central American republics.

The core events are drawn from a plethora of literary sources, not the least of which is Cinthio's short story and Shakespeare's adaptation for the stage. Meanwhile, the satellite events of the play are drawn from the historical circumstances of the Central American independence movement. The play appeared in print at an important juncture in the production of national literatures within the isthmus and beyond. The entire Latin American region underwent the institutionalization of literature and the proliferation of fiction through newspaper serials and magazines in the nineteenth century. This gave rise to the publication of *folletines*, serial novels and romances that featured "star-crossed lovers who represent particular regions, races, parties and economic interests" whose passion for conjugal and sexual union, argues Doris Sommer, "spills over to a sentimental readership in a move that hopes to win partisan minds along with hearts."[49] Since intellectuals in the nineteenth century were fueled by a desire to establish a literary history that would legitimize their new nations, their foundational fictions equated the ideal of domestic happiness with dreams of national prosperity, consolidation, and growth.[50] These foundational fictions included an abundance of national romances, national poems, and national dramas situated not across the Atlantic but against the backdrop of Latin American landscapes.

As Sommer suggests, the national romances provided "gender models that were teaching future republicans to be passionate in a rational and seductively horizontal way."[51] Like nationality, gender and sexuality standards were assumed to shape modern individuals, and examples of proper femininity and masculinity abound in the nineteenth-century literature of these young republics. Correspondingly, in *Júpiter*, the reader encounters the angel of Santiago Celis's home: Blanca, whose name intentionally means "white." She is a young, illiterate, wealthy young woman who has grown up without a mother and fears the prospect of matrimony because it would imply leaving her father alone. The opening scene introduces her sewing, silently wiping away tears as she ponders the reason for her father's late arrival, utterly oblivious to her father's involvement in the regional independence movement. Blanca exemplifies what Patricia Arroyo Calderón has identified as a new female subject in the new Central American republics whose realm was the internal governance of a home through the correct undertaking of a series of critical economic virtues, such as the control of her own desires—with regard to her moderation of expenditures and of those in her surroundings, the productive management of her time, the efficient administration of objects and people—children, servants, and other dependents—and, finally, the transformation of material austerity into the fountain of aesthetic pleasure.[52] As the ladies' home economics textbooks required at the secondary school levels for all young ladies advised, "Para el progreso de las repúblicas centroamericanas no sólo eran necesarios hombres económicos capaces de acumular capital y acabar con el viejo orden colonial . . . a base de reorganizar el tejido material y social de la patria por medio de desamortizaciones de tierras y liberación de mano de obra, sino también mujeres igualmente económicas encargadas de preservar los recursos de ese modo generados." (The progress of Central American nations required economic-minded men capable of accumulating capital and ending with the old colonial order . . . in order to reorganize the social and material fabric of the fatherland through land grants and the release of a workforce, but also women who were just as economically savvy in charge of preserving the resources generated in said manner.) These women judged themselves and were judged by the men in their lives according to four principal virtues: piety, purity, submissiveness, and thrifty domesticity. Women who complied were guaranteed happiness while those that dared challenge the status quo were "damned immediately as an enemy of God, of civilization, of the Republic," for it was woman's duty to uphold the moral pillars of her society.[53] This gendered ideal was especially applied to privileged women who were tasked with providing their male breadwinners comfort from an aggressive world by providing them a tranquil household and the grace of their feminine companionship.

Blanca is written in such accord with ladylike domesticity that upon hearing Engracia's scornful laughter in the opening scene, she subtly chides Engracia by contrasting the gossipy servant's comment with virtuous generosity toward the Black man standing below her window: "Dicen que es muy listo. El padre Delgado le ha enseñado a leer, a escribir y contar." (They say that he is very clever. Father Delgado has taught him to read, write, and count.)[54] The phrase is less about Júpiter than it is about the white liberal friar, who has indeed taught his slave reading, writing, arithmetic, and religion. The characterization of the founding father is in accord with the post-independence climate of Central America, in which the nation's heroes believed that their new nations were vulnerable if their inhabitants did not feel a sense of debt to the republic and to those who represented enlightened thought. Júpiter, tragic hero of this national drama, is thus constructed in the hearsay of others before his body and countenance appear in a scene. He has, after all, absorbed the teachings of his master that deference is well rewarded. These lessons echo the political romanticism of the period that Leopoldo Zea examines in his important study, *Dos etapas en el pensamiento latinoamericano*: "La Colonia había formado la mente que ahora entorpecía el progreso. Allí estaba todo el mal. Para desarraigarlo sería menester rehacer desde sus raíces dicha mente. Urgía realizar una nueva tarea: la emancipación mental de Hispanoamérica." (The Colonial regime had created the mindset that now impeded progress. Therein lay an all-encompassing evil. It would be necessary to refashion this mindset from its very roots in order to uproot it. It was urgent to undertake a new task: the mental emancipation of Hispanic America.)[55] To the liberal intelligentsia—both those living in the isthmus and those living in the pages of *Júpiter*—discarding the Spanish Crown required loyalty to a new flag: "la autonomía del intelecto fue la nueva bandera" (the autonomy of intellect had become the new flag).[56] The wealth of timeless classic European texts, Spanish and otherwise, were revisited by brilliant individuals who propagated the cherished values of the independence movement.

Both Júpiter's destiny and his position vis-à-vis *criollos* in this text are in accord with liberal maxims, which held that post-independence society could not legally or ethically accept the enslavement of human beings. Firmly locked in the political claims of the leaders of the independence movement, the national drama model allows Gavidia to examine the divergent interests of Central American [white] forefathers and the Afrodescendant masses united for a moment in the isthmus's history on a common quest for independence. The values expressed in the play echo those of Honduran José Cecilio del Valle—appointed editor of *El amigo de la patria* newspaper in 1821—whose readership included elected officials at the provincial and municipal levels. According to this intellectual, the fatherland, both great and small, gave the individual a sense of belonging and had the potential to give rise within the citizen a desire to expand it and possess it so long as he experienced the bond of patriotic loyalty to it.[57] In *Júpiter*, the Liberal party is seeking to overthrow King Ferdinand VII of Spain and form the Federal Republic of Central America. The challenge they face is compelling all the main regions of El Salvador (San Miguel, San Vicente, Sonsonate, and Santa Ana) to take part in the insurrection, making it necessary to reach out to the masses. These include the numerous Black slaves and *morenos* who—according to *criollo* intellectuals in this play and in regional history—were at the ready to fight to ensure their freedom from the figurative and literal forms of enslavement institutionalized by the old colonial regime.

Despite the importance of freedom in the ideology of liberalism, however, the founding fathers did not find liberty and servitude incompatible.[58] Júpiter's character is fashioned accordingly: he is not an upwardly mobile mulatto but simply a literate slave whose Black skin and enslaved condition locate him at the lowest rung of the social structure. The tragic end of Júpiter's life is foreshadowed in the very first lines of the play, as a *mestiza* servant looks out the window contemplating whether to throw water over his head—a thought she relishes with laughter. Far from the judicious figure of Blanca, the servant's mockery matches that of the greater slice of the Central American populace toward Blacks and Blackness.[59] Júpiter is outside of the scene, while Blanca gently deflects the crassness of her servant in perfect keeping with her role as lady of the house. This dialogue, however, serves to encode the ridiculousness of the Black man's romantic daydreams and love for a damsel who sits high above his class and social standing. His delusions, however, position him as malleable bait for the forefathers who conspire to use him to raise interest in the liberal cause among the Afrodescendants of the city.

As the fictional José Matías Delgado explains to the fictional Santiago Celis when the two conspire to involve Júpiter in the independence movement, the slave has served as his master's secretary and has read the works of Elio Antonio de Nebrija, Pedro de Calderón de la Barca, and María de Zayas y Sotomayor. The report of literary influences on Júpiter is critical, for it represents another body of knowledge encoded in the play that is expected to be readily decoded by readers/listeners of the dialogue. Elio Antonio de Nebrija's most celebrated work, *Gramática de la lengua castellana*, was dedicated and presented to Isabella I of Castille with the assertion that language was the instrument of the empire. Such was the case both in Spain and in her colonies, where even subjects who aspired to unleash themselves from imperial rule found that the Spanish humanist tradition continued to be relevant in the intellectual circles of the new nations. "El guineo, blanco los dientes, se enfría los pies" (Guinean, white teeth, cools feet), wrote Nebrija as an example of a synecdoche in his celebrated 1492 text.[60] The author defines the figure of speech and advances his explanation by stating that a synecdoche works on the basis of a mutual understanding between speaker and interlocutor who share the common ground needed to decipher meaning behind the phrase. As nebulous as "Africa" might have been in the imagination of Nebrija's readers, two things were understood in the example given: the "peculiar" contrast between the black skin and white teeth of a sub-Saharan African and the desert heat that that leads the Black subject to the oasis to cool their feet.

The literary references in the play serve as a clear indication that Júpiter is not an "incomprehensible," "ignorant bozal" but rather an "eloquent" and "trained" individual. However, the assertion that language is the most powerful vehicle for the dissemination of the cultural values of the empire highlights the implicit attitudes regarding Black subjects in the example of "synecdoche" chosen by Nebrija.[61] Through the mention of Calderón de la Barca, a writer whose extensive oeuvre includes instances of allegorical figures of Blackness—the most notable being the African continent itself—Gavidia introduces early critiques of the institution of slavery. Three of Calderón de la Barca's plays stand out from others in their critique of the institution of enslavement in the seventeenth century: *La sibila de Oriente y la gran reina de Sabá*, *Los hijos de la fortuna*, and *Teágenes y Caricela*.[62] Finally, the reference to María de Zayas y Sotomayor brings to mind the author's study of violence against women in seventeenth-century Spain in her *Novelas amorosas y ejemplares*. In the Iberian literary tradition, she remains one of the most widely circulated authors in favor of women's independence and educational access. The fact that these readings are among Júpiter's literary repertoire implies that the narratives he has previously read have left a mark on him as a [Black] man desirous of freedom, exactly whom the forefathers of Central American independence needed to convene the Afrodescendant masses. After all, he will be more likely to claim his rights as an individual than a slave who has never read any print materials besides the Bible by his bedside.

Júpiter has read canonical lay literature, but Delgado is quick to point out that his Catholic devotion might make him reluctant to accept liberal principles. A devotion to the Catholic religion is expected from new citizens, but so is their renouncement of loyalty to the Spanish Crown. Júpiter is unaware of the dividing lines between liberals and conservatives, and even more so the dividing issues between men of the Liberal party. Encoded in the play are a series of finer political points, such as the position of Delgado and Celis—in the text and in history—against José Francisco Barrundia. In this detail and others that bind true forefathers to true citizens, characters and the audience would have shared knowledge that Barrundia was a liberal who was opposed to the incorporation of Central America into Mexico and favored its incorporation into the United States following independence.[63] However classic his readings have been, however, Júpiter is constructed as a subject who knows nothing but fictions and lacks an understanding of political theory and strategy. Working with this imposed limitation, Delgado asserts in his conversation with Celis that the best way to cajole Júpiter into taking a recruiting role in the movement is to appeal to the values of honor and freedom within the classics:

> DELGADO: Las historias de príncipes y duquesas le embeben casi tanto, Dios me perdone, como las vidas de los santos. Porque eso sí, es un buen cristiano mi pobre negro: tiene tal vez sus puntos de visionario y fanático; para él no hay sino un malhechor en Centro-América . . . nuestro amigo Barrundia. Pero gracias a eso no cifra toda su devoción en el Rey Fernando. La aristocracia es su sueño. Contrastes de la vida: ya ves que no es más que un esclavo.

CELIS: Con todo, ese esclavo es un hombre.

DELGADO: . . . "El tostado africano/ Es un hombre, es tu imagen, es mi hermano." ¡Admirable poeta es Meléndez!

CELIS: Oye, padre. Precisamente hoy que me dices eso de tu esclavo, siento más vivo deseo de hablar con él.[64]

(DELGADO: The stories of princes and duchesses interest him as much as, God forgive me, the lives of the saints. Because frankly, he is a good Christian, my poor Black: he might have his visionary and fanatic flaws; for him there is no other evildoer in Central America . . . our friend Barrundia. But thanks to that, he does not place all of his devotion on King Fernando. He dreams of the Aristocracy. Contrasts of life: you see he is nothing but a slave./ CELIS: All in all, that slave is a man./ DELGADO: " . . . The toasted African/ Is a man, is your image, is my brother." What an admirable poet, that Meléndez!/ CELIS: Listen, Father. Precisely today when you tell me such things about your slave, I feel an even more burning desire to speak with him.)

These statements reduce Júpiter's aspirations of privilege to the vanity of someone whose readings have deceived him into thinking he is a man when he is nothing but a slave. By quoting Juan Meléndez Valdes's poem "La presencia de Dios," Delgado points to the humanistic values, religious principles, and political objectives that constitute the ideological basis of the poem.[65] If men have been made in the image of God, as the often-quoted biblical verse in Genesis 1:26 reads, then this is the grand equalizer between ethnic groups as diverse as the Tartars, Sami, Indians, and Africans mentioned in Meléndez's poem. The premise that one man is his brother's keeper remains present in this pronouncement, a proclamation rooted in the perception of fraternity (a liberal value) as a horizontal alliance. Yet despite its insistence that men of all colors are men, made in God's image and therefore the poetic voice's brothers, this position does not eliminate the notion of a standing hierarchy. While Delgado's tone is ironic in delivering the poet's verses, the poem is understood by Celis as a call to serve as the worldlier subject in ethical and experiential matters who is ethically obliged to guide his less apt brethren. The parallel task of intellectuals—in fact and fiction—was to instruct the masses in patriotism. In forefather José Cecilio del Valle's words: to love the nation or people is a love that is cultured and moral: to work toward light and virtues, to become interested in an education that keeps giving.[66] Imagining Júpiter's instrumentality, Celis requests that Delgado sell the Black man to him.

In their first encounter, Celis informs Júpiter that he is his new master. He proceeds to shame the Black man into taking part in the liberal insurrection, arguing that his fate is a waste if he declines to fight for his freedom: "Mando que te sientes delante de mí porque somos iguales. Sin embargo, por un puñado de dinero cualquiera puede adquirirte, azotarte. No eres nadie: te llaman Júpiter, llevas un nombre de perro, a menos que sea el de un dios . . . y para ser un dios es preciso poseer en absoluto la libertad . . . Todo en ti, pues, viene a ser irrisión y miseria." (I demand that you sit before me because we are equals. However, anyone could acquire you or beat you for a small amount of money. You are no one: You are called Júpiter, you bear the name of a dog, unless it refers to a god . . . and for one to be a god one must have full possession of one's liberty . . . Everything about you, then, is nothing but derision and misery.)[67] Celis shifts to a condescending tone as he proclaims that Júpiter should do as Celis has done: humiliate other Black men with the same words and in the same manner. Celis commands him to speak with the Black slaves, artists, and laborers in San Salvador and instill guilt in them for their enslavement and provide them with weapons to fight against the colonial government that has taken away their liberty.[68] Celis hopes that using Júpiter to this end will fortify liberal troops, as the number of Afrodescendants in San Salvador is higher than the number of whites. During his impassioned speech, Blanca enters the scene and he sees in her a second opportunity to shame Júpiter:

> CELIS: ¡Y tú, vil esclavo, escoria, nada!; ¿tú no ardes en cólera como yo?, ¿no te ahogas de indignación? ¡No gritas libertad! ¡¡Tú!! ¿Oye? Santiago Celis tiene su libertad en su pensamiento. Llegará hasta ella rompiendo por la muerte, si la encuentra a su paso . . . Puedo matar a mi hija antes que ella fructifique en el pantano como flor aciaga . . . Tú, si amases a una mujer que el destino ha puesto en la cúspide de la babel espantosa, si sólo llegases a pensarlo, serías colgado en la picota y muerto al furor vil del látigo."[69]

(CELIS: And you, vile slave, scum, nothing! Don't you feel the rage I feel? Don't you drown with indignation? Don't you cry for liberty! You!! Listen, Santiago Celis has his freedom on mind. He will have it even if it means fighting to the death, should it come to that . . . I shall kill my daughter before she bears fruit in the marsh like a tragic flower . . . You, should you love a woman that destiny has placed on the cusp of a fearful tower, should you only think of it, you would be thrown into the stocks and killed by the fury of the whip.)

Most of his speech falls on deaf ears, since Júpiter only hears words that matter to his heart. Blanca's arrival and Celis's words give rise to his passionate belief that equality would make it possible for him to marry Blanca. While Júpiter's love for the Church made him initially waver, this romantic thought makes him cry at last: "¡Libertad! ¡Rebelión! ¡Abajo el Rey! ¡Muera el arzobizpo! Decidme que lo maldiga todo: maldito sea todo." (Liberty! Rebellion! Down with the King! Death to the Archbishop! Tell me to damn everything; everything be damned.)[70] This sequencing highlights the emotive, antirational objective that drives Júpiter. This passionate turn to a covenant with patriotic liberalism is a mistake that will result in tragic consequences for Júpiter as the play enters its final scenes.

While Gavidia's "humanistic" motive was to personify the Afrodescendant masses through the character of the Black slave, the play is subject to the same underlying assumptions about interracial marriage in Cinthio's short story, Shakespeare's *Othello*, and even in Darío's poem "Alí," examined in the earlier pages of this chapter.[71] Júpiter understands Celis's words as a guarantee that a new social order would permit a union between him and Blanca, a possibility beyond his wildest dreams and beyond the literary tropes he has found in the classic literature he has read. Júpiter is successful in accomplishing the mission with which he was tasked, but he falls victim to the impulsiveness attributed to a man who has never been more than a slave. Not long after becoming involved, his doomed fate is sealed as he gives way to his impulsiveness. In one scene Júpiter declares he must acquire more weapons and that he will buy all of the liquor in San Salvador. The aside that follows ensures that readers/spectators will not miss the signs of his madness: "Las ideas se me suceden en el cerebro: cada una me deja un nuevo ardid." (The ideas that arise in my mind: each one leaves me with a new burning.)[72] These fervent words offer a striking contrast to the "rational" motives of the *criollo* founding fathers of soon-to-be-born Central American republics. While Júpiter appears in chaotic exchanges with his men, they appear in the company of ideologues and strategists. Whereas Júpiter cedes to feverish desires and is ultimately captured and accused of treason against the king, in both the chronotope of the narrative and in history books, Celis and Delgado become the dignified forefathers of the Republic of El Salvador.

When the conservatives torture him, Júpiter remains steadfast in his refusal to cooperate with them, not because of patriotic loyalty but because he continues to have faith in the prospect of marrying Blanca after being released from prison shackles. Believing wholeheartedly in the possibility of a socially condoned romance with Blanca, Júpiter withstands imprisonment and torture for treason against the Spanish king while keeping his eyes on the prize: the freedom to wed Blanca, the object of his desires and affection. Upon his release, he boldly meets with Celis to ask for her hand. Celis resolutely declines to hand his daughter over to the Black man. In the same condescending manner evidenced in their first conversation, Celis tells him that he has already fulfilled his part of the agreement by proclaiming Júpiter's heroism to the townspeople and kissing the former slave's wounds in public, adding that asking for a blessing over an interracial marriage is going too far. Pouring salt in the wound, Celis adopts a paternal tone and pronounces the words behind the masterplot in fiction and in fact about the destiny of Afrodescendants in the new republics. It's over, Celis says. "Soldado de la libertad, lucha, muere por ella . . . El porvenir verá tu raza igualar los latidos del corazón con los de todas las razas. Así fueron todos los sacrificios; sólo no fructificarán para los mártires . . . Te hablo compadeciéndote, como amigo." (Soldier of liberty, fight, die for her . . . The future shall see the men of your race match their heartbeats to that of men of all races. All sacrifices were thus: they just don't bear fruit for martyrs . . . I speak out of pity, as a friend.)[73] The national drama thus arrives at its narrative closure with a clear message about the destiny of Black peoples within Central American borders. The national imaginary—the legacy of future generations—in fact and fiction will omit the memory of Blackness from its collective Central American experience as it moves from a colonial past to an independent future.

George Lamming's observation in his assessment of *The Tempest*—the second Shakespearean play that clearly informs *Júpiter*—is relevant as the masterplot arrives at narrative closure. In Lamming's words: "Prospero has given Caliban language and with it an unstated history of consequences, an unknown history of future intentions."⁷⁴ Caliban understands speech and concept as the conditions of future possibilities, making this "gift" of language that he has received "the very prison in which Caliban's achievements will be realized and restricted."⁷⁵ The possibility of an Afrodescendant intellectual achieving the same status as his master, even under utopian conditions, is nullified in *Júpiter*. The prospect of an alternative is likewise halted at the precise moment when the trope of Black wretchedness could have been overturned and a future for Afrodescendants in a new nation could have been manifest: irrevocably distraught and betrayed, Júpiter murders Celis. He commits suicide shortly after assassinating a distraught Blanca who offers herself to Júpiter in a futile attempt to save her father's life, crying: "Vedme. Quiero sanar todas las heridas de vuestro amor y orgullo . . . Miradme: Blanca de rodillas os ofrece su mano." (Look at me. I want to heal all of the wounds of your love and pride . . . Look at me. Blanca is on her knees offering her hand.)⁷⁶ The narrative core of *Júpiter* thus develops through satellite events that lead to the closure in the same masterplot of cursed Blackness, the theory of causation that depends on the tragic origin and destiny of the Black body and its passions. After all, as Fernando Unzueta reminds scholars of the period, ethical aesthetics were a criterion of nineteenth-century fictions, as authors of the period fully embraced a didactic purpose when presenting their readers with historical national romances. The tragic plot behind *Júpiter* accomplishes several ethical-aesthetic goals, particularly its disavowal of interracial unions and in the advice to Júpiter to disappear, literally and figuratively, into the history of the republic. To cement the lesson, it precedes the tragic denouement with an unmistakable framing of a Black subject whose passions lead to ineptitude and the murder of a [white] man and his [white] daughter, an angel of domesticity. Celis's recommended martyrdom and Júpiter's double homicide and subsequent suicide fit neatly with the ideologies espoused by the leading [white] Central American classes, since the final scene encodes Júpiter's presence as a threat to the bourgeois liberal order and assuages any sense of complicity or guilt that the intended reader might feel as a result of Celis's contradictory rhetoric. As Johannes Fabian argues in *Time and the Other*, the use of time almost invariably is made for the purpose of distancing those who are observed from the time of the observer.⁷⁷ In this national drama there is a clear distinction between the colonial past in which Black men were enslaved by white men and an independent future in which Black men must self-destruct and disappear themselves at the dawn of a new liberal order. The denial of coevalness between with Blackness or Black experience and a Central American future is achieved through this ideological process of detemporalization.

Facing a New Century with a Cosmopolitan Pen

The Central American independence movement sought to establish a definitive break with the Spanish Crown, though this did not result in a decisive break with European literary traditions. The emerging literary establishment thus created and put into circulation works that negotiated Old World literary inheritance while charting its own legacy. Writing about the entire region's predicament at this critical intellectual juncture, Leopoldo Zea observes in *Dos etapas del pensamiento en hispanoamérica* that the intelligentsia "accumulated" experiences instead of resolving the problems brought upon by the Conquest, Colonial Administration, and the Wars of Independence. As a result, the intellectual undertakings of the period exhibit a conflictive relationship to Europe that is far from being resolved: the past has yet to become an authentic past, Zea writes, for it remains a present that cannot decide to become history.[78] When past experiences are not thoroughly assimilated, Zea observes, they remain latent and repressed by the subject who cannot face them. Their lingering presence results in the manifestation of symptoms that allude to the unassimilated event. These symptoms appear in the very gestures, actions, and discourse-making practices of subjects who interface with a present marked by the past, an uncanny *cauchemar* that does not recede into the background or fade with the passing of time.

The works by Rubén Darío and Francisco Gavidia—two beacons in the modernization of Central American societies and the *modernista* print tradition—that I have examined in this chapter insist on a promising future for the young republics. They reflect a sense of "progress" manifested in their drive to create autochthonous culture, literature, and philosophy for Central America. Both authors concurred in their disdain for Blackness and elided what they perceived to be base sociocultural vectors in their literary art forms. Yet Black subjects and Black experience erupt in these little-known texts as a result of the negotiation of the enslavement of fellow Central American citizens and the continued reality of Afrodescendants among the populace. This unassimilated colonial history of enslavement leaves cracks on the surface of an otherwise unblemished body of texts exploring Central America's destiny.[79] Francisco Gavidia claimed that his oeuvre was born of reason and humanism, a philosophy at the behest of men well versed in the classics. He declared that intelligence, civilization, and art belonged to men who were more likely to have descended from Jehovah than from apes.[80] Rubén Darío, whose grandparents were listed in the civil registry as mulattos, denied his Blackness in his preface to *Prosas profanes* in order to be better seen as a rational man, raceless and capable of creating beautiful things with his hands: "¿Hay en mi sangre alguna gota de sangre de África, o de indios chorotega o nagrandano? Pudiera ser, a despecho de mis manos de marqués; mas he aquí que veréis en mis versos princesas, reyes, cosas imperials." (Is there in my blood a drop of Africa, or Chorotega Indians, or Chief Nagrandano? It is possible, despite my marquise hands; but herein you shall see in my verses princesses, kings, and imperial things.)[81] Blackness did not factor in as a centerpiece of their prolific literary production, but it did in their print material when they attempted to fashion themselves as cosmopolitan, modern subjects.

The stylization and aestheticization of Black experience presented these Central American intellectuals with the challenge—indeed, the game—of turning Black elements into objects of wonder, only to encase them in the positivist masterplots cementing their wretchedness. To weave references of Blackness into romantic and Orientalist motifs was to work with the most disparaged of subjectivities of the European and American continents at their service. Darío and Gavidia prized classical renditions of Black beauty and deliberately omitted the images of Africa populated by savages and legends of the African continent as a land teeming with monsters.[82] Their texts formulated exotic Black characters based on classical constructions that located them in fictive exotic spaces outside the boundaries of the isthmus. Their ideas of race and of its non-place in Central America were nonetheless mediated by ideas of reason and moral worth that had been promoted in Europe since the Enlightenment.

In 1748, David Hume, for instance, had written: "In Jamaica, indeed, they talk of one negroe as a man of parts and learning; but it is likely he is admired for slender accomplishment, like a parrot who speaks a few words plainly."[83] Immanuel Kant, Georg Wilhelm Friedrich Hegel, and others who echoed these words later in the period likewise bequeathed their "objective" observations to the intelligentsia that emerged across the Atlantic on the eve of their independence.[84] Central American intellectuals adopted these philosophical precepts along with the implicit understanding that any slight misstep with European notions of reason and human worth might result in the writers themselves being classified as "talking parrots." At the hour of Central America's grand immanence, they too, could be collapsed into the same category with Black subjects.[85] It was necessary to maintain good taste. The polar opposites of civilization/barbarism—lest we forget that Sarmiento's *Facundo* had already been published and well distributed by the time Darío and Gavidia made their mark on Central American letters—added the criterion of science, ushering the relevance of Darwin and Spencer. Abolition was widely held to be a precondition for a modern society, but so was the intellectual's attachment to an ideology of superior and inferior races following the birth of republics. Despite their intentions to begin anew, print material catalogued social hierarchies that still bore the imprint of coloniality. Central American intellectuals reissued the discourses once used for their own subjection to design the disappearance of Black subjects in the brand new print tradition of the isthmus. They thereby marked their difference from absolute alterity and crafted a safe distance away from Blackness by establishing outside of the boundaries of their nations. In order to avoid collusion with Blackness, they upheld a firm stance in line with the ideas about race as expressed by European thinkers whose empiricist discourses had been adapted to the Americas.[86]

The passion for artifice and pristine aesthetics is at the root of nineteenth-century Central American representations of Blackness, but so are the chronotopes by which to read the Blackness, Black bodies, and Black legacies. The objective is aesthetic as much as it is a perceived manifestation of reason, science, and even religious doctrine. In doing so, these intellectuals achieved what their much-admired literary masters had accomplished: the triumph of upstaging their multilateral, transatlantic sources. This is what Harold Bloom terms *apophrades*, when "particular passages in *his* own work seem to be not presages of one's own advent, but rather to be indebted to one's own achievement, and even (necessarily) to be lessened by one's great splendor. The mighty dead return, but they return in our colors, speaking in our voices."[87] Correspondingly, Darío and Gavidia write about Blackness with the certainty that their words will endure and that their writings will stand as a testament to the literary craft of the new nations in the isthmus. They respond to the defining historical moment by positioning themselves at the behest of a muse with a penchant for form and a graceful look to an awaited future in which Blackness did not have a place. Established in the principal cities of Central America near the Pacific coast, it was not until political rhetoric entered national letters that an ethnolinguistic basis for power over Blackness became necessary and there was another ideological shift in plotting the coordinates of Blackness in Central American print. Anti-imperialist Central American thinkers assumed that portentous task in the early twentieth century, as we shall see in the next two chapters.

Part 2
Interior/Centro

Chapter 2

Strategies of Containment

The banana trade and the Panama Canal became emblematic facets of Central American politics and economics in the early twentieth century, promoting militarization and the concentration of power in foreign hands. Guatemala became the first republic to seal its fate to the United Fruit Company (UFCO) when it hired the corporation in 1901 to manage its postal system. Nicaragua, Costa Rica, and Honduras followed suit, restructuring their countries' armies, economies, and labor force to meet the demands of their new North American business partner. This increased militarization protected the interests of the UFCO, whose investments in railways, docks, and port facilities, the Tropical Radio and Telegraph Company, and the "Great White Fleet" of steamships transformed the Central American landscape and its people. Long "off the map" for most Central Americans, the rapid industrialization of the Central American Caribbean coast suddenly drew *mestizos* and Black West Indians alike to these hubs of modernity and modernization. Meanwhile, the United States was establishing a relationship to Panama with similar dramatic consequences for the landscape and its peoples. Under the 1903 Hay–Bunau-Varilla Treaty, the United States obtained "the use, occupation and control of a zone under water, the lands and waters outside of it and within the limits of the zone" and assumed "all the rights, power and authority over the zone," including absolute monopoly over the construction of the Panama Canal.[1] Construction began in 1904, and by the time the Panama Canal opened in 1914, the Zone had become a de facto United States colony. The mythic privilege and country club prosperity of North Americans lured an immigrant labor force from all corners of

Central America and the Caribbean, though it was the workers from the Anglophone Caribbean, particularly those from Jamaica, who faced the fiercest racism with Jim Crow–styled policies. With Panama, the (now) six Central American "independent" republics had become nations characterized by a dependence on agricultural exports, a reliance on the US market, and unequal distribution of wealth concentrated in a tightly knit landed oligarchy.

They were a far cry from the isthmian dream Simón Bolívar had depicted in his "Carta de Jamaica," noted in chapter 1. Colombia had lost Panama, the US had obtained the most valuable piece of the former province now turned quasi-independent, and all five other Central American countries had sold their Caribbean coasts and fates to the highest bidder. The most rapidly circulating print materials of the period were nonfiction books on Western history and political science—after all, Central America remained proud of her industry and progress, despite the Titan of the North's depiction of her as provincial and retrograde—but even fiction and poetry began to display a response to the imperialism threating Central America. In the year that construction on the Canal Zone began, Rubén Darío himself published "To Roosevelt" in *Helios*, a literary journal of the region. The poetic voice declared in its first stanza:

> The voice that would reach you, Hunter, must speak
> in Biblical tones, or in the poetry of Walt Whitman.
> You are primitive and modern, simple and complex;
> you are part George Washington and one part Nimrod.
> You are the United States,
> future invader of our native America
> with its Indian blood, an America
> that still prays to Christ and still speaks Spanish.[2]

If cosmopolitanism had been the flavor of patriotic print media in the nineteenth century as Central America invested in its future, print media in the early twentieth century displayed its patriotic fervor in its passionate anti-imperialism. While books in serious circulation in the United States included texts like Benjamin Kidd's *The Control of the Tropics* (1898) and an *Introduction to American Expansion Policy* (1908), Central America contributed its own corpus of texts to respond to the North's designs on its republics. Marixa Lasso explains that here "we see a local elite trying to retain its modernity and economic control over modern resources in the face of an imperial elite trying to erase the history of that control and transform the elites into 'natives' in need of stewardship and help."[3] As this conversation gained momentum, the ethnoracial complexity of Panama and the rest of the Central American Caribbean coastal strip was negotiated by *mestizos* who sought to keep themselves firmly anchored in modernity. As a result, as I argue in this chapter, anti-imperialist print media offered a space to make manifest the positivism and eugenic perspectives that were widely held by believers in Western civilization, the same legacy that Central American intellectuals continued to believe was theirs.

The present chapter begins by examining Demetrio Aguilera Malta's *Canal Zone* (1935), a novel that focuses on a second-generation West Indian in Panama and moves into a discussion of Afro-Indigenous Garifuna peoples in Paca Nava de Miralda's *Barro* (1951). It then concludes with a discussion of masterplots in banana novels and canal literature that considers the role of the narrator in facilitating readers' travel to regions hitherto undepicted in print media. As I demonstrate, the literary cartography devised in the anti-imperialist literature written in the first half of the twentieth century established a palpable division between the legitimately Central American "interior" and the spaces of Blackness along its Caribbean coast. The attendant ethnocartographic strategies employed by novelists throw into relief a masterplot wherein the "legitimate" citizens of Central American nations are positioned in contrast to the anti-heroes and illegitimate Black inhabitants of the same republics. Writers like Aguilera Malta (himself just a traveler in Central America) and Nava de Miralda (born and raised in the Caribbean coast) use the same brush to depict two distinct communities: West Indian immigrants and Afro-Indigenous Garifuna.[4] Despite their distinct authorial positionings, however, both writers depict the two different groups as worthless to cause and nation, a Black force standing in the way of national (and regional) sovereignty.

Entering the *Canal Zone*

A faulty enthusiasm for North American empire-building fills the opening pages of Aguilera Malta's *Canal Zone*, where the canal has become a lucrative site drawing millions of people to its miles of rapidly industrialized space. The narrator describes the changes that easy money brings about in the inhabitants: "Hirvió también la ambición de los hombres sobre todas las aceras. La vida fue encareciendo. Los precios de las habitaciones volaron a las nubes. Por los alimentos se pagaron valores increíbles. Nadie hizo el menor esfuerzo sino se le retribuyó maximamente. Por entonces, el panameño se acostumbró a derrochar. Sus manos se conviertiron en una catarata de oro." (The ambition of men boiled over all of the paved streets as well. Life became more expensive. Prices for rooms rose to the clouds. The price of food rose to incredible values. No one made the slightest effort, but they were rewarded to the max. It was a time when Panamanians became accustomed to wasting. Their hands had become gold waterfalls.)[5] This arresting image captures the social transformation that results from modernity and modernization. It is a poignant rhetorical maneuver, for it captures both domestic and foreign sentiment about economic prospects in Panama. The general population seems to concur with Theodore Roosevelt, who justified the United States' control of the Zone with the statement: "There had been fifty years of continuous bloodshed and civil strife in Panama; because of my action, Panama has now known ten years of such peace and prosperity as she never before saw in the four centuries of her existence."[6] Like the *mestizos* who readily betray wholesome Honduran values in *Barro*, the novel we shall discuss in the next section of this chapter, the complacent Panamanians in *Canal Zone* seem to be blind to the sequences of welcoming imperialism in Panama.

Canal Zone paints a landscape of a beautiful, industrial Panama. Thus, the first part of the novel envelops the reader in the rhetoric of progress promoted by the United States that served as the "opium of the people," so to speak, to conceal the dissolution of Panama's sovereignty as an independent republic. The narrator informs readers that streets were repaired, new roads were built, and the population came to include those whom he called newly arrived Jews, Indian "coolies," and North American "Yankees." Prosperity was in the air. The canal promised them all—foreign investors, tourists, the military, and "even Black laborers"—endless riches. "Los persiguió el dolar, en un abordaje inaudito. Aunque no quisieran, tuvieron que verlo llegar, en oleadas. Lo sintieron metérseles en el bolsillo" (Dollars chased them, in a silent approach. They couldn't resist, they had to see it arrive, in waves. They felt it make its way to their pockets), reports one observer.[7] As more Panamanians are lured by promises of wealth to the Canal Zone, "progress" becomes a detriment to national agriculture because their fields lay unsown. Like the incisive passages in *Barro*, the observer's pronouncement foreshadows the grave consequences that await a populace that has abandoned their nation's values in search of imperial riches. As occurs in *Barro*, the robust economy provides prosperity to everyone until the thirst for wealth results in the loss of human lives and national values. They are, in effect, narratives with encoded warnings for readers. The gift of hindsight—print appears well after imperialism has become engrained—allows them to decode the message that the cradle of national culture was robbed in plain sight, right before the very eyes of a citizenry dazzled by riches.

Nationalism, Racism, and [Black] West Indians

Former US president Theodore Roosevelt "took" the canal in 1904, but it was former US president William Howard Taft's 1912 executive order that led to the expulsion of approximately forty thousand Panamanians from the forty-one towns on what were suddenly deemed zone limits.[8] In the process, Marixa Lasso explains: "US policy and rhetoric recharacterized both Panamanian—mostly Black—citizens into 'natives' and the Zone's intricate commercial landscape into a wilderness in need of intervention. The fact that canal officials portrayed and imagined the Zone as a tropical wilderness and its inhabitants as 'natives' made it politically and ideologically easier for the Zone to be depopulated once its Panamanian municipalities had been turned into 'native towns,' its citizens into 'natives,' and its landscape into the jungle."[9] It became a zone without Panamanians, most of whom were phenotypically identifiable as Afrodescendants. After all, as Sonja Stephenson Watson observes, the number of free and enslaved Black peoples in Panama was as high as 65 percent in the colonial period.[10] The removal of Hispanophone Afrodescendant Panamanians notwithstanding, the United States kept the twenty thousand [Black] West Indian men who had held clerical positions for the French canal company that preceded it within the Zone.[11] These West Indians had spoken English in their Caribbean homelands, were largely Protestant, and had already been trained in their respective fields.[12] These salient sociocultural differences marked them as outsiders among the general Panamanian population, even among Panamanian Afrodescendants, and yet made them the most desirable workforce for the North American enterprise. The operators of the Canal Zone project were white North Americans who implemented Jim Crow segregation measures just as they were in place in the US South.[13] The white North American labor force was paid on the "gold roll" while West Indians received the "silver roll" rate, distinctions that were later institutionalized in the euphemistically designated "gold" and "silver" towns, schools, toilets, drinking fountains, and even segregated windows at the Canal Zone post office.[14] Panamanian indifference to the apartheid in this space resulted from the assumption that the Black immigrants would be assigned the most difficult work and Panamanians of any phenotype would reap the riches of the canal.[15] West Indians believed that they would be repatriated, as stated in their contracts, and thus set out to make their fortunes despite the unequal pay and working conditions.

At the time that Aguilera Malta was writing, West Indians had already become scapegoats and a "metaphor" of "the race problem" purportedly caused by US occupation in newspapers, pamphlets, books, and other print materials that sought someone to blame for intervention and neocolonialism.[16] Like other writings in the same print tradition, *Canal Zone* situates the reader in a sociopolitical context rife with conflicts and contradictions, at the center of which is the debate over the [Black] West Indian labor force that was recruited to work on the Panama Canal. It takes place at the height of the backlash against [Black] West Indians in Panama and addresses the news that made headlines in that period. The hostile response to this immigrant labor force was triggered in the early twenties' soaring unemployment rates. Panamanian policymakers wrote editorials and delivered speeches declaring that West Indians had taken jobs that rightfully belonged to Panamanians and initiated immigration restrictions that dubbed the Black masses "undesirable immigrants."[17] Since it became increasingly difficult for Panamanians to find employment in the Canal Zone unless they spoke English, the government soon passed legal measures to require all organizations to have Spanish names and conduct business in Spanish. Store signs had to display their Spanish name first and in larger letters than their English appellation; elementary schools had to conduct all their classes in Spanish, and where English was taught, it was to be done so as a foreign language.[18] A nationalist movement arose under the banner of "Panama for Panamanians," demanding the West Indian community's repatriation, fastening itself on the Spanish language as one of the sacred symbols of the homeland. The movement culminated in the new constitution of 1941, which stipulated that all children of "prohibited immigrants" who had come since 1903 would have their citizenship revoked. Though the constitution of 1946 restored their citizenship, English-speaking West Indians could not immigrate to Panama until 1949.

Chombo became the pejorative term of choice to refer to the Black men who worked in the Canal Zone and who were increasingly perceived as a threat to the Spanish-speaking Panamanian community. With an anti-imperialist masterplot in place, Aguilera Malta presents these Black men and women as the "lumpenproletariat," a layer of the working class who cannot be expected to ever achieve class consciousness and therefore do not have a place in the class struggle.[19] The Black masses described in the text are vulnerable to discrimination and unjust practices because they are paralyzed by "un miedo animal a lo desconocido" (an animalistic fear of the unknown).[20] Meanwhile, their oppressors—the US Panama Canal Company as well as racist Panamanians—capitalize on the immigrants' inability to organize themselves collectively. The novel dialogues with historical data from the period to incorporate newsworthy instances of Panamanian racial discrimination. One character, Panga, for instance, is one of the many landlords in the city who responds to the rising unemployment, inflation, and the call to protect *mestizo* interests by expelling the Black tenants from his buildings. The narrative voice provides psychological insight into the character: "Ahora cuando lanzaba un *chombo* sobre todo a un *chombo* que tuviera extensa familia, sentía una dulce alegría interior." (Nowadays when he threw out a *chombo*, especially a *chombo* with an extensive family, he felt a sweet happiness deep within.)[21] His frequent use of the word *chombo* for West Indians working in the Zone and the pleasure he garners from evicting his Black tenants provides readers with a window into the Panamanians in fiction and history who saw Black workers as encroaching upon their land, property, and nation.

The West Indian immigrants' inability to assume agency and respond collectively to the injustices they suffer in Panama is a pivotal aspect of this text. Their misery is, in fact, palpable. Forced to leave well-populated areas close to the Canal Zone, they seek refuge in the savannah. The dispossession of the Black masses is poetically described, as the artist-narrator sketches "vetazos de ébano a la piel de la tierra uniforme. Manchas humanas incontables. A lo lejos, parpadeaba el incendio de los colores chillones de sus trajes" (the strokes of human stains on the smooth land. Innumerable human stains. From afar, there flickered the fire of the bright colors of their clothing.)[22] The narrator continues, describing a savannah that trembles with every new Black brushstroke indicating the arrival of a new *chombo*. The human stench in the savannah refocuses the reader's attention to the rank smell of unwashed human bodies and stench of their breath, "que, como una red invisible, aprisionaban el ambiente" (which, like an invisible net, caged the atmosphere around them).[23] These masses, initially recruited to work in the Canal Zone, are represented by the narrative voice as lumpenproletarians who, without a voice, without a worker's movement, and without the possibility of being repatriated, are destined to destitution and humiliation on Panamanian territory. They lack the cultural capital at the disposal of Panamanian *mestizos* and, unable to return to the Caribbean islands from whence they came, Black workers are doomed to languish in their plight.

In contrast to [the predominantly Afrodescendant] Panamanians, the [Black] immigrants in *Canal Zone* are not given a place in the anti-imperialist struggle waged by Panamanians in the Zone. They live on the margins of society after being shut out of industrial work, and they remain uninterested and unengaged in the [*mestizo*] Panamanian-led revolutionary movement. In order to drive this message across to the reader, Aguilera Malta shifts from a macro-level description of Black immigrants to the daily life of one [Black] immigrant mother and her mixed-race adult son struggling to survive. The narrative voice blurs the line between fiction and fact by describing the mother to the reader as a first-generation Jamaican immigrant whose passivity resembles that of her generation: "Para ella todo tenía el mismo color uniforme, el mismo horario cotidiano. Aún cuando el griego llegaba borracho y la insultaba, aún cuando le pegaba, ella conservaba su pasividad extremada, su tranquilidad de esfinge de ébano." (To her, everything had the same flat color, the same daily schedule. Even when [her Greek husband] hit her, she maintained her extreme passivity, the peacefulness of an ebony Sphinx.)[24] Her stoic dignity is an asset to her role in the informal economy since, as a laundress, she toils on a daily basis under the harsh sun in the company of other Black women who bear the weight of their color and gender: "En el patio húmedo y gris, repiqueteaba el jadeo de las lavanderas *chombas*, encuclilladas, mostrando sus piernas gruesas y vigorosas. El Sol les arañaba las espaldas, les encendía el rostro y les lamía cruelmente los senos." (In the wet and gray patio, one could hear the panting of the *chomba* laundresses, squatting, their thick and vigorous legs uncovered. The sun scratched their backs, lit their faces, and cruelly licked their breasts.)[25] Like the poetic image of the masses setting up camp in the savannah after being expelled from the city, this image reinforces the narrative voice's displeasure with the Black lumpen. To advance this position, the narrative voice uses Coorsi's character to pose a rhetorical question: Will the Panamanian-born children of West Indian immigrants awake and take a position in the consciousness-raising movement in time to save themselves from the North Americans who profit from them and redeem themselves in the eyes of the Panamanians who resent them?

Like Rubén Darío and Francisco Gavidia, whose texts were examined in chapter 1 of this book, Aguilera Malta seems to have a ready answer. From the opening pages, Coorsi's destiny seems predetermined. When the economic crisis strikes Colón City, he is laid off from the newspaper agency where he works. He roams the streets lamenting his inability to support his mother while also regretting his "inferior" color.[26] The narrative voice frames Coorsi's circumstances as a destiny ensured by the very blood that pulses through his veins, using the Black man's mother as the voice box for the thoughts sourced in *mestizo* ideology. As she washes a symbolically white suit, Coorsi's mother thinks about the obstacles that lie in wait to crush his spirit: "Algo contra lo que no podía levantarse. Ni siquiera protestar. Ella lo había visto frecuentemente en los hombres de su raza. Pedro llevaba inútilmente ese poquito de sangre blanca. La sangre negra imperaba, era más fuerte. Y tenía que arrastrarlo al precipicio." (Something against which he could not rise up. Not even protest. She had seen it frequently in the men of her race. [Coorsi] had some white blood but his black blood was stronger. And it would drag him to the cliff.)[27] The Black men among the lumpen, Aguilera Malta suggests, are cursed with a color that brings them to the precipice, the metaphor of suicide. This foreshadowing leads the reader to correctly identify the eventual demise of this central, tragic Black male subject. Coorsi walks through Colón unable to assert agency in an economic situation exacerbated by the racism of the broader Panamanian society; he is unable to see himself out of his predetermined "checkmate" situation.[28]

Following his two-week engagement with the failed grassroots movement that sought justice for the Black immigrants who were expelled to the savannah, Coorsi is hired as one of the many chauffeurs serving the forty thousand newly arrived United States Marines on a mission to "pacify" the streets of Colón. While the white Panamanian aristocracy prepares to attend balls in honor of the Marines, Coorsi drives along thinking about the futility of his existence: "Pedro Coorsi—marginal, como la mayoría de los *chombos*—había conseguido, por fin, trabajo. Era chofer de un carro destartalado, que se especializaba en llevar marinos de uno a otro lado. . . siempre el volante. Su mundo, hoy, mañana, siempre el volante. Volante, cadena. Auto, cárcel. Yanquis que pasean en auto, centinelas." (Pedro Coorsi—marginal, like the majority of the *chombos*—had gotten, finally, a job. He was the driver of a beat-up car that specialized in taking Marines from one side to another . . . always at the wheel. His world, today, tomorrow, always at the wheel. Wheel, chain. Car, prison. Yankees who wander in cars, sentinels.)[29] Unlike his mother, Coorsi feels the sting of alienation. Born in the Zone, he is a Panamanian citizen who faces the racism of his countrymen as well as that of the Marines. His passengers are oblivious to his resentment, since they have never considered the possibility of a Black subject being utterly conscious of his position among them. From this scene forward, the narrative voice that Aguilera Malta deploys establishes a high level of intimacy with the [mestizo] reader as it takes a psychological turn to explore what it posits as "the Black mind." In these last moments, Aguilera Malta escapes the confines of nationalist leftist politics and turns to psychoanalysis as he circles back to the masterplot of the tragically doomed Black man.

That night, a Puerto Rican Marine named D'Acosta decides to amuse his white friends by inviting Coorsi, their Black driver, to their table. The white men are disappointed and bored with the stern Black man before them: "Hubieran querido verlo hacer movimientos acrobáticos de simio. Que riera a mandíbula batiente, enseñando los dientes blanquísimos. Que rompiera algo, en un desbordamiento animal. Se sentían defraudados." (They would have liked to see him do the acrobatic tricks of an ape. To see him cackle, showing them his white teeth. To see him break something, like a wild animal. They felt cheated.)[30] D'Acosta calls a Black prostitute over to the table to dance with Coorsi, hoping that the two will put on a show and that he will be able to save face in front of the white Marines. The dance becomes increasingly sensual, the Black man proves to his spectators—and the reader—that they were right all along, that this Black man is exactly the marionette they knew him to be. The very fact of his Blackness obliterates any possibility of their consideration of Coorsi as a rational human being. As Frantz Fanon recalls of his own experience: "I was expected to behave like a black man—or at least like a nigger."[31] Coorsi is utterly humiliated. As he drives the Marines back across the Canal Zone, he thinks about the West Indian immigrants like his mother who came to Panama to build the Panama Canal:

> Los negros trabajando para que los barcos de los blancos no pasaran por el estrecho de Magallanes; los negros, como verdaderos puentes para unir dos océanos; la estridencia de sus carnes alborotadas, como polvo, con el jadear estruendoso de

la dinamita; las enfermedades traidoras que desaparecieron a los pocos sobrevivientes de la épica hazaña. Después acá, en la ciudad, los mismos negros haciendo calles para que las transitaran otros. Casas para que las habiten otros . . . Siendo odiados. Formando un mundo aparte: un mundo de Chorrillo y de Calidonia, o el de los barrios marginados de la Zona.[32]

(The Blacks who toiled so that the ships owned by white men wouldn't have to pass through the Magellan Strait, Black people who were like true bridges bringing together two oceans; the shrillness of their agitated bodies, like unsettled dust in the wake of exploded dynamite; the treacherous illnesses that led to the deaths of the few who survived the epic feat of building the Canal. Then, here, in the city, the same Black men building roads so that others could travel over them. Living in homes that would be overtaken by others . . . Being hated. A world apart: the Chorrillo and Calidonia world, the marginalized neighborhoods in the Zone.)

Coorsi crashes his car, committing suicide and killing the Marines in the process, following the preceding words of the narrator. The last words of the novel are as striking as the suicide-murder: "Within a short time, the whole world forgot about Coorsi. No one spoke of him again."[33] Coorsi—a Black man who always existed outside the wage-labor system—faced the same destiny as the other Black lumpenproletarians in the country when the car crash was forgotten. The self-destruction of the Black lumpenproletariat broken by humiliation fits neatly into the larger narrative of listless, unrooted Black masses with no place in Panama's future.

Leon Trotsky referred to the lumpenproletariat as the "countless bands of declassed and demoralized human beings whom finance capital has brought to desperation and frenzy."[34] In this vein of political philosophy, the lumpenproletariat was a potential threat to the revolution because they were especially vulnerable to reactionary ideology. *Canal Zone*, geared to the anti-imperialist reader, called attention to foreign domination over Panama and highlighted the costs of engaging in business with the enemy. Nonetheless, the framework of the narrative does not identify even the smallest glimmer of defiance in the West Indian immigrant masses and their children. As Sonja Stephenson Watson observes, this would not appear in print until 1977 upon the publication of Carlos

"Cubena" Wilson's historically revisionist work.³⁵ In Aguilera Malta's 1930s narrative, Coorsi and the others are the lumpenproletariat who succumb to serving the imperialist enemy and become perpetual outsiders. Never fully integrated in the national and political economy, they are presented to readers as the dispossessed Black masses now marooned on the shores of the Panamanian national imaginary.

A Banana Republic among Many

Paca Navas de Miralda's *Barro* opens with songs of praise to the fertile Honduran lands along the Caribbean coast, a lush region where oranges, grapefruit, pineapple, mangoes, avocados, soursops, coconuts, and bananas grow in abundance. Moments later, however, a train charges through the landscape: "El ruidoso correr de la locomotora empaña la opalina transparencia de las montañas y las tardes costeras, y la jungla cargada de pólenes y savia nueva, pareciera estremecerse al vaivén apresurado de las máquinas que se detienen aquí y allá, recogiendo los pesados racimos de 'oro verde' al borde de los extensos bananales." (The loud engine of the train fogs the opalescent transparency of the mountains and the coastal afternoons, and the jungle laden with pollen and fresh dews seems to shudder against the hurried passing of the machines that stop here and there, loading the bunches of "green gold" at the edge of the extensive banana plantations.)³⁶ These pages highlight the omnipresent traces of industrialization and modernization in a tropical context where the relations of production are feudal rather than fair. The steel locomotives make the lush landscape flinch, for it is nature's wealth that is being exploited with the power of their engines. The rich setting enables the narrator to establish the powerful sway of modernization over the peoples that inhabit this landscape. Hearkening to Marshall Berman's assessment of the experience, "to be modern is to find ourselves in an environment that promises adventure, power, joy, growth, transformation of ourselves and our world—and at the same time that threatens to destroy everything we have, everything we know, everything we are."³⁷ The owners of the means of production and their underlings can find the experience thrilling, but the critical reader can decode the message to anticipate devastating effects of this new mode of production.

North American imperialism has transformed the hearts and minds of the inhabitants of the coast, who have become outlandish consumers overnight and thrive in a context where machinery devours nature in order to produce the "green gold" they so ardently seek. Their debauchery, states the narrator, runs parallel to the inexhaustible flow of dollars:

> El derroche de que hacían alarde los campeños de aquella zona, corría parejas con el inagotable riego de dólares. Individuos había que al ensuciárseles la camisa de crepé de china, con valor de diez dólares, preferían al engorro de darla a lavar, tirar ésta a la basura reemplazándola en las tiendas por una nueva. Cualquier caitudo recién llegado del interior, usaba en tal época, calzado de la mejor calidad de marca norteamericana o europea. Los sombreros de Ilama y Macholoa, tejidos de fibra, industria nacional de los pueblos de tierra adentro, de los cuales llevan el nombre, eran reemplazados de la noche a la mañana, por los elegantes sombreros de vicuña importados o de fieltro y paja, conforme a la estación.[38]

> (The debauchery that the country people from that area engaged in ran parallel to the inexhaustible spill of dollars. There were people who, upon soiling a shirt made of crêpe de chine, valued at ten dollars, favored, at the thought of washing it, to throw it in the garbage, replacing it with a new one purchased in a store. Any country bumpkin newly arrived from the interior used, in that period, North American or European footwear of the finest quality. The Ilama and Macholoa hats, woven with natural fibers, national handicraft of the peoples of the interior, which lend them their name, were replaced overnight with elegant, imported vicuña, felt, or straw headpieces, according to the season.)

There are those who prefer to throw away ten-dollar crêpe de chine shirts instead of washing them when they become soiled, those who trade their country sandals for European and North American footwear upon stepping foot in the coast, and those who trade their traditional Honduran hats for imported hats made of vicuña wool, felt, or straw according to the season.[39] The *costeños*' free spending is an affront to the Honduran narrator of the "interior," to whom the purchase of these imports is nothing but gluttonous excess. The behavior observed in the Caribbean coast, according to the narrator, is foreign to any self-respecting Honduran who continues to value locally produced items over transcontinental luxuries.[40] The individuals who avail themselves of such luxuries do so, suggests the narrator, because they have quite literally bought into imperialist design.

Nationalism, Racism, and Garifuna Peoples

This lavish lifestyle, *Barro*'s narrator explains, lures rural *mestizos* from the "interior" to seek employment in the Caribbean coast. Historical documents indicate that this migratory flow created an early and intense competition between Spanish-speaking *mestizos* and Black workers that had been recruited from the Anglophone Caribbean. Froylán Turcios, an ally of Augusto Sandino and close friend of Navas de Miralda, denounced Honduras's flexible immigration standards in 1906.[41] Turcios argued that the generous labor clauses of the immigration law prevented the Honduran government from expelling West Indian subjects of the British Empire, "a race made arrogant by their nationality," from the country, and he added that Hondurans would do well to guard against "the possibility that this inferior race might mix with the Indian element."[42] In tandem, labor leaders associated with the Federación Obrera Hondureña (FOH; Honduran Workers Federation) introduced legislation that sought to prohibit "the importation into the territory of the Republic of negroes of the African race and coolies."[43] Honduran intellectuals who viewed the US-owned banana companies as a threat to national sovereignty promoted a united *mestizo* front against the Garifuna and West Indian workers employed by the banana companies. In 1926, Ramón E. Cruz, a future Honduran Supreme Court justice and presidential hopeful, denounced the Black "race" on the Caribbean coast and openly declared that "the compensation received from Black labor could not be compared to the incalculable damage done to our species."[44]

In line with these assertions, Nava de Miralda's *Barro* fans the flames of anti-Black sentiment with racist depictions of the Afro-Indigenous Garifuna communities in Honduras.[45] *Barro* promotes the idea that the Garifuna are outsiders, a strategy that acts as a smoke screen to the reality that the Garifuna were deported to Honduras by the British in 1797, well before the nation was established. It also glosses over the undeniable fact that mestizo settlement in the area did not occur until well after Garifuna tenure of their ancestral lands on the coast.[46] As Charles David Kepner observed in 1936, *mestizo* Honduran citizens were loath to move to the "fever-infested" Caribbean coast, and so Garifuna farmers sold bananas to Italian steamship companies sailing to New Orleans and Mobile even before the United Fruit Company began to invest in the region.[47] Consequently, a majority of the early United Fruit Company banana plantation's labor was Garifuna.[48] The Garifuna were the first Afrodescendant group affected by banana company expansion, since it was they who were first employed by the United Fruit Company and theirs the land coveted by the rapidly expanding enterprise. Nancie González reports that the Garifuna left the United Fruit Company work to *mestizo* Hondurans and West Indian laborers when labor competition ensued between the diverse ethnic groups.[49] They remained engaged in local and national Honduran economies, however, refusing to leave their ancestral lands of San Juan, Tornabe, Triunfo de la Cruz, and La Ensenada where they continued to practice *ejidal* (communal) landownership for subsistence farming and artisanal fishing practices. It would not be until the twenty-first century that they would obtain recognition of their status as Indigenous peoples with ancestral ties to the Caribbean coast and rights stipulated in the United Nations Declaration on the Rights of Indigenous Peoples. In the pages of *Barro*, they are nothing more than appalling *morenos*.

The opening pages depict benevolent *mestizos* who arrive in the Caribbean coast with dreams and riches and are soon contaminated by the greed for "green gold" that circulates in the region. Yet, the most alarming experience for these "good" *mestizos* is to live in the same region as *morenos*. Adopting the posture of an anthropological guide, the narrative voice blurs the line between fiction and ethnography for a reader who has presumably never encountered a Garifuna. The author thus follows the *principle of minimal departure* that, as Marie-Laure Ryan explains, is a theory of narrative cognition: "When readers construct fictional worlds, they fill in the gaps in the text by assuming the similarity of the fictional world to their own experiential reality. This model can only be overruled by the text itself."[50] Thus, when the narrator of *Barro* shifts attention from *mestizos* to the Garifuna of the Atlantic, she does more than just include another group into the narrative. There is a register shift that promotes a scheme in terms of which Honduran cultures are placed in a temporal slope, a stream of Time, that perpetuates the denial of coevalness between the *mestizo* self and the Garifuna other. As Johannes Fabian reminds us, "there is no knowledge of the Other which is not also a temporal, historical, and political act."[51]

In what reads as an aside to her readers, Navas de Miralda informs them that the Garifuna live on the edge of the sea in a town called Nueva Armenia in homes that are built from laced palms and are found through the entire length of the coast, forming small clusters under the shade of the coconut tree. They are said to benefit from subsistence farming, but also depend heavily on the trafficking and contraband of a wide variety of items, including weapons and liquors.[52] The narrative voice adopts an "objective" ethnographic tone from whence moral and cultural observations about the Garifuna are made. This allows her to claim, for instance, that it is Garifuna women who "siembra[n] y cosecha[n] la yuca, en el terreno preparado por su hombre; la que corta leña y cría los hijos sin taza. Una de las características de la raza negra, es la de reproducirse como ratas" (sow and harvest yucca, on the land prepared by their husband; who chop wood and raise their children without a cup. One of the characteristics of the Black race is to reproduce like rats).[53] The accurate observation about Garifuna women's labor for their family is paired in the same breath with commentary that elicits revulsion in the reader, while comparing them to rodents subtracts their humanity and dignity. The comment also bears undeniable eugenicist underpinnings based on the Manichean dichotomy of civilization/barbarism in which Garifuna peoples are clearly the backward object to be studied by the civilized reader. As Ernest Gellner observes, the "systematic study of 'primitive' tribes began first in the hope of using them as a kind of time machine, as a peep into our own historic past, as providing closer evidence about the early links in the great Series."[54]

In that vein, the narrative voice informs the reader that there are relatively "civilized" tribes in Port Trujillo and La Ceiba, but that they nonetheless hold rambunctious weddings and dances. It dismisses their knowledge with statements such as: "El atraso de esta raza, aunque muchos saben leer y escribir en forma elemental, merced a la difusión de escuelas en algunos sectores, ha contribuido mediante influencias ancestrales, a la divulgación de un sinnúmero de prácticas de hechicería, como la magia negra, en las cuales se inspiran—como las tribus salvajes de África u Oceanía—sus danzas rituales de Pascuas y Carnestolendas." (The backwardness of this race, though many can read and write at a basic level, thanks to the availability of schools in some sectors, is contributed to by ancestral influences, the widespread practice of countless witchcraft practices, like Black Magic, in which they are inspired—like the savage tribes of Africa and Oceana—to produce their Easter and Shrovetide ritual dances.)[55] By deploying the binary opposites of civilization and barbarism that would be easily decoded by progressive readers, the narrative voice clearly establishes the Garifuna as wild elements, impeding a steady march to national progress. These details prepare the reader for a transition from the discussion of the daily lives of the Garifuna to a lengthy exposé of Pocomania and Carnival celebrations that renders the readers' disassociation of Garifuna experience from Honduran culture even clearer.[56] This focus is important, as writers across the Central American print tradition, especially those of the anti-imperialist stripe, had well established Hispanism and Catholicism as the mainstay foundations of their identity and belonging.

Narrative authority in *Barro* depends on the reader's lack of direct knowledge about Garifuna peoples, which facilitates the reader's reliance on the narrative voice for a fictionally factual account of the peoples of the coastal strip. The covert influence of the narrator is kept hidden through the pedagogical tone of descriptions that range from gendered division of labor, as cited earlier, to the masks and headdresses worn for Holy Week and Pentecost. The generous descriptions of extravagant apparatuses in the shape of buildings, towers, boats, and globes that Garifuna women wear on their heads are offered to the reader as evidence of reliability. The seamless transfer of authorial-authoritative content encompasses the descriptions of the rattles and tiny mirrors that adorn these headpieces along with the transmission of judgment over Garifuna peoples in brief phrases, like the purported "scandalous and deafening" sound these adornments make when Garifuna women dance and bounce along a street.[57] The narrative voice's selection of diction is evident when she refers to these celebrations as "rituals" and to celebratory dress as vestments in bright, loud colors and bracelets made of rope and shells that together constitute "extravagant and demoniacal" outfits.[58] The narrator affirms that the Garifuna all gather in groups, dancing to rhythms that "deben tener un sentido especial, desconocido para los ladinos" (must have a special meaning, unknown to *ladinos*) in street corners, outside the homes of the wealthy and in the port of Trujillo. Taking a retrospective glance to the economic boom, the narrator describes magnates throwing down packets of *soles* from their balconies to the dancers as they move their bodies to the rhythm of "canciones guturales o jerigonzas en su propio dialecto, al compás del pito y la timbala" (guttural songs or chants in their own dialect, to the beat of the whistle and percussion).[59] These details—like the aforementioned comments about Garifuna mothers—reinforce the image of the dislocated quality of the Honduran Caribbean coast as an uncivilized site that is home to Black peoples who have been severed from the cultural, social, and political attributes of the Honduran national imaginary.

Despite the novel's central focus on a *mestizo* family's tribulations on a banana plantation, the material about Garifuna peoples in *Barro* constitutes its most important nationalist element. As Pierre Bourdieu observes in his classic *Outline of a Theory of Practice*, "Objectivism constitutes a social world as a spectacle presented to an observer who takes up a 'point of view' on the action, who stands back so as to observe it."[60] By transferring into the Garifuna community the principles of her high position in the social structure, the narrative voice strengthens the authoritative authorial position that there is no coevalness between morally reprehensible [Black] coastal peoples and good [*mestizo*] Hondurans.[61] For example, to exacerbate the rendition of the Garifuna community's incivility, the narrative voice comments: "Finalizan las fiestas pascuales con orgías desenfrenadas, acompañadas de diversas ceremonias de magia negra, de contenido escalofriante y satánico, las cuales hubieron de ser prohibidas un poco más atrás del tiempo que situamos estos relatos, o sea a principios de siglo." (They conclude the Easter festivities with wild orgies, accompanied by diverse frightening and satanic black magic ceremonies, which should have been prohibited much before the time our narrative takes place, at the beginning of the century.)[62] The Indigenous community's actions are morally judged while being presented in discourse that simulates truth. The narrator's direct signaling of the Garifuna people's ceremonies as Satanic is a clear arrow to the reader:

> Además del ritual de oraciones e imploraciones a falsas deidades, al espíritu de Satán o el Diablo, se valen estos traficantes de raros amuletos, siendo los más usados los muñecos de cera acribillados con alfileres por medio de los cuales, el entendido en la materia o brujo, provoca en la persona enemiga que pretende dañar, fuertes Dolores o retortijones, según el órgano o parte del cuerpo que dicho muñeco tuviese agujereado. . . . También hacen uso tales individuos de ciertas plantas afrodisíacas, algunas de las cuales—según versiones—idiotizan al que las toma, cuando no suscitan en él mismo, graves estados patológicos sexuales o accesos de vesania o locura furiosa.[63]

(Aside from the ritual of prayers and imploring false deities, to the spirit of Satan of the Devil, these charlatans use rare amulets. Among the commonly used is a wax doll stuck with needles, through which the master of the black arts or witch causes the enemy to experience pain and suffering, according to the organ that has been punctured by the needle. . . . These individuals also use aphrodisiacs, which—according to some accounts—either renders the individual lethargic or cause grave states of sexual pathology or excess of insanity or fury.)

The novel's "anthropological" observations, which begin with descriptions of Garifuna seaside villages early in the novel and culminate in the descriptions of orgiastic rituals, frame the text as it is meant to be digested by the nationalist-oriented reader. It assumes an individual who is invested in understanding how imperialism has impacted the *mestizo* population and how the existence of this Black community might impact the nation's future and its reputation among its fellow Hispanophone Catholic neighbors. After all, both the constituent events and the satellite events of the plot add to the trials and tribulations faced by the *mestizo* family in focus.

National identity is solidified in this text by demarcating the lines of the "rational" and the "irrational" and by correcting the gray areas by attributing responsibility to Black peoples and absolving *mestizos* by explaining their accidental fall to immorality. As alterity is associated with primitivism, so too are the geographical boundaries put in place by nature and aggravated by the unwillingness to connect the two worlds and join them as one in the national imaginary. The branding of Black bodies ensures that the implicit reader closes the text with a firm resolve that, although the spatial distance between *mestizos* and Garifuna has been reduced by the new mode of production that draws *mestizos* from the interior to the coast, the fact remains that the distances in evolutionary time cannot be breached. The anthropological gaze permits the narrator of *Barro* to revisit Honduran labor history and to relegate the Black bodies of the Garifuna to the margins of the formal economy. The politics of the anthropological gaze weigh heavily in this text where, by invisibilizing the contributions of [Black] West Indians and highlighting the otherness of the Garifuna, the narrative voice makes a clear distinction between the "productive" *mestizo* bodies and "inefficient" Black bodies in the Honduran Caribbean coastal landscape.

Anti-Imperialist Masterplots

Aguilera Malta and Navas Miralda's print legacies posit that Central America is "locked in a life-and-death struggle with first-world cultural imperialism—a cultural struggle that is itself a reflection of the economic situation of [the third world] in their penetration by various stages of capital, or as it is sometimes euphemistically termed, of modernization."[64] These stories are allegories of the embattled situation of the national culture and society in question with the North American colossus. With labor relations a central issue in their masterplots, the positionality of Black subjects becomes a key element in the historical materialist analyses devised by Nava de Miralda and Aguilera Malta.[65] In a manner without precedent—because previous treatment of Blackness had relegated it to contexts back across the Atlantic, in the Old World—these authors directly address Black labor and Black presence within their nations. The historical moment itself is an aperture that allows writers to pique their readers' curiosity about labor relations on the Central American Caribbean coast. The novels serve a didactic purpose by mapping the rapidly industrialized coastal strip and its workers, while identifying the racial groups that merit the anti-imperialist reader's compassion and mistrust.

Aguilera Malta and Navas de Miralda were hardly alone in their use of print material to challenge the United States' influence in the isthmus while discussing what they perceived to be the racialized future of Central America. They were members of anti-imperialist intellectual circles in the isthmus that circulated readings and knowledge with like-minded thinkers in the hemisphere. Together, they promoted the political unity of Latin America and the nationalization of land and industry over the globalizing force of the United States, a country that in 1848 through the Treaty of Guadalupe Hidalgo had usurped half of Mexico's land, turned Puerto Rico into a protectorate under the 1898 Treaty of Paris, and taken over the Canal Zone with the Hay–Bunau-Varilla Treaty in 1903 all while controlling the military and ports in the Central American Caribbean coast. Most importantly, these groups represented a collective voice in favor of [*mestizo*] workers' rights and against US capital's control of national governments.[66] The political periodicals, ephemera, and books that emerged from within these circles shared common features. They highlighted the governing classes' allegiance to the United States and the manner in which, Haya de la Torre notes, "the natural resources which form the riches of our countries are mortgaged and sold, and the working and agricultural classes are subjected to the most brutal of servitude" in exchange for loans and other favors from the United States.[67] While their political leaders clamored for more US involvement in their countries' affairs, these intellectuals objected to the loss of national culture and the dissipation of their republics' natural riches.[68] They believed the land had been handed over too easily and that the United States had assembled a [Black] immigrant workforce to replace the [white and *mestizo*] nationals.

Ana Patricia Rodríguez observes in *Dividing the Isthmus* that the wealth of social realist print media focusing on the production of bananas and the construction of the Panama Canal was published between 1930 and 1960: "Produced by some of the most outspoken, progressive, and militant writers of Central America, the social protest literature challenged not only the corporate order but also national rule and foreign economic intervention in the isthmus."[69] Anti-imperialist writing constituted a unifying discourse that scrutinized the impact of United States intervention on Central American nations and their local populations. These novels were written from within a Pan–Latin American intellectual movement and railed against a new mode of production that by the mid-twentieth century had not only transformed the isthmus but also earned Central American nations the pejorative nickname of "banana republics."[70] The classics as well as the understudied texts in this genre evidence the fact that authors had shed the cosmopolitan air that had been central to earlier isthmian plots in favor of a sociopolitical and ethnoracial review of the new republics. However, they did so by making the Spanish language—and its speakers—the ultimate signifier of protagonism. In doing so, these narratives establish ethnolinguistic boundaries between Spanish and English that mark Hispanophone peoples as undeniably Central American and Anglophone peoples as foreign trespassers. Authors take politically sympathetic readers from the Pacific capitals to the Central American Caribbean coast, draw the landscape under the tyrannical power of American imperialism, and sketch the [Black] bodies colluding with the enemy in the hostile takeover of the isthmus.

One notable text in the banana novel genre, Carlos Luis Fallas's *Mamita Yunai* (1941), focuses on Costa Rica. The novel follows José Francisco Sibaja, as he makes his way to the Talamanca Province, a place he describes as overridden by Black and Indigenous faces surrounding him and where Spanish is seldom spoken. He describes the boxes, suitcases, bags on floor, and the Black men who, "instead of men, looked like Black muscular demons shining under the sun" while their women laughed and sang.⁷¹ From afar, Sibaja attests, the scene looked like "an extravagant Carnival parade that gave off the feeling of a barbarous and wild party."⁷² Sibaja is self-described as the only [white] man among "eleven thousand devils" and, consumed by boredom, he begins a conversation with the sole Black man who converses with him in Spanish. The Black interlocutor explains their migration to Panama as the last resort open to a people who can no longer live on bananas and crab on the Caribbean coast. Since they are not allowed on the Pacific coast or the interior of Costa Rica, they will seek opportunities where they can work legally: "White people have a chance in the Pacific, but us? Can't you see that they make it difficult for us to become citizens! There aren't any jobs, we can't sow the land and they don't let us make a living in the Pacific Coast. Are we to starve, then?"⁷³ The plethora of references to Black men and women in this novel, however, is of the Black population that has stayed in the country, and its depiction is of servants and filthy, disease-ridden workers in competition with "real" Costa Ricans. Fallas's novel thus establishes the debates about eugenics and biotypology that widely appeared in print in Costa Rica as the referent for the plot developed in these pages.

Similarly canonical, Miguel Ángel Asturias's banana trilogy *Viento fuerte* (1950), *El papa verde* (1954), and *Los ojos de los enterrados* (1962) focuses on an "unfamiliar" Guatemala.⁷⁴ David Caballero Mariscal explains that the trilogy depicts Mayan migration to the coastal zones as a betrayal of the land, an act that is punished with a curse on all who have left the heartland of the country for the "other" Guatemala.⁷⁵ Thus the author disengages from narratives focused on *criollo* characters in Guatemala City or Mayan characters in the highlands. The first novel in the series describes the new landscape where Mayan and *ladino* migrant workers, drawn to jobs on banana plantations, suddenly find themselves. In this unfamiliar strip of Guatemalan landscape, man rules over almost every aspect of nature: "Todo dominado, menos el húmedo, el inmovil, el cegante calor de la costa. Se impuso la voluntad del hombre. Manos y equipos mecánicos modificaron el terreno. Cambios en el desplazarse natural de los ríos, elevación de esctructuras para el paso de caminos de hierro, entre cerros cortados o puentes o rellenos, por donde máquinas voraces, consumidoras de árboles reducidos a troncos verdiones, transportaban hombres y cosechas, hambre y alimentos." (Everything had been dominated, except the humid, the immobile, the blinding heat of the coast. Man's will had been imposed. Hands and machinery modified the land. Changes in the natural course of the rivers, raised structures for steel railways, between halved mountains or bridges, from whence voracious machines, consumers of trees reduced to green trunks, transported men and harvests, hunger and food.)[76] Not only is Asturias's banana trilogy set in an "other" landscape, it brings into focus the familiar steel machinery that signals the rapid industrialization of the tropical Central American landscape. The lush and mangled vegetation, the furious coast, the wild birds of the jungle, and the sweltering heat work together to situate the reader in a context utterly unlike the Indigenous highlands we are used to encountering in Asturias's earlier novels. "Traveling" to the Caribbean coast thus becomes, for Guatemalan readers in Asturias's time, an unsettling venture to a perilous unfamiliar strip of Guatemalan land.

Asturias's banana novels focus on a complex framework of social relations that involves Indigenous, Black, *mestizo*, Chinese, and [white] North American cultural groups. The reader is left in the unrelenting heat of the jungle on the other side of Guatemala and is suddenly surrounded by a host of characters that constitute a social pyramid unlike that which would be readily understood by readers in the highlands or Pacific Coast of the country. This is the "other" Honduras that Ramón Amaya Amador describes to his readers in his novel *Prisión verde* (1950):

> En Culuco, como en todos los campos bananeros, se reunían hombres de distintas categorías y lugares, de diversos grados de cultura, de heterogéneas cualidades, pero que al convivir, en los campamentos de banana, se conocían bajo el común denominador de *campeños*. Blancos, indios, mestizos, negros, hasta algunos amarillos; salitreros del Golfo de Fonseca, tabaqueros de Copan, chalanes de los llanos de Olancho, morenos y zambos de Colón y la Mosquitia, isleños de Guanaja o de Roatán; de todos los rumbos del país y no pocos también de los demás países de Centro América y Belize y más allá. Valleros, montañeses, costeños, citadinos; exmilitares, excomerciantes, obreros, campesinos, vagabundos; desde analfabetos, hasta con títulos profesionales; solos o acompañados de familia.

> (In Culuco, as in all other banana camps, there were men of different categories and places, of different degrees of culture, of heterogeneous qualities, but whom, after living in the banana camps were all known under the common denominator of *campeños*. Whites, Indians, *mestizos*, Blacks, and even some

yellows; *saltpeters* from the Gulf of Fonseca, tobacco dealers from Copán, horse dealers from Olancho plains, *morenos* and *zambos* from Colón and the Mosquito Coast, islanders from Guanaja or Roatán; from all parts of the country and not only a few from other Central American countries, Belize and far beyond. Valley people, mountain people, coastal people, city people; former military men, former businessmen, laborers, *campesinos*, vagabonds; from illiterates to those who held professional degrees; alone or in the company of their families.)[77]

Far from being a melting pot, the jungle becomes a site in which these differences are salient reminders of the turbulent landscape in which the reader finds herself immersed. Like others in the tradition, Asturias's and Amaya Amador's novels allow their readership to embark on a voyage to a part of the Central American country that many will never actually travel to, but which has a dramatic impact on the political, economic, and social conditions of the country at large. They map the Caribbean coast and provide rich descriptions of that strip of land as a treacherous space, dividing Central American populations into those whose principles are more closely aligned with leftist Central American nationalists and those whose values are molded by North American imperialism.

This sharp distinction between a familiar [Central American] country and its "other" counterpart is also a key feature of an inexhaustible list of texts, including those that are rarely examined by scholars, Hernán Robleto's *Sangre en el trópico* (1930) and Emilio Quintana's *Bananos: La vida de los peones en la Yunai* (1942). Carmen Lyra's narrator in *Bananos y hombres* (1931) presents her sketches of the "other" Costa Rica for a reader who discovers that the inhabitants of the Caribbean coast of her country operate under a code of ethics and the sin of greed, a locale distinct from the values presumably held by the people of the Costa Rican Central Valley. Finally, Afrodescendant Joaquín Beleño's banana novel, *Flor de banana* (1962), and his canal trilogy, *Luna verde* (1951), *Gamboa Road Gang* (1960), and *Curundurú* (1963), all unveil an "other" Panama wrought with strife unbeknownst to those outside of these zones.[78] While this brief account of the anti-imperialist texts is by no means exhaustive, it does highlight the masterplot repeatedly put into circulation by Central American intellectuals over the course of approximately thirty years that opened the door to a discussion about the "unknown worlds" within national borders to their readers.

Whether included in the Central American literary canon or on its margins, anti-imperialist writers challenge assumptions that ideological novels are beset by a certain "simplicity—or, to put it in more brutal terms, the simplistic character of [their] rhetoric."[79] Neither Navas de Miralda, Aguilera Malta, or their regional peers sacrifice aesthetics in order to showcase their leftist principles: Marxist ideology, an association with the working class and popular masses, socialist humanism, internationalism, historical materialism, and nationalism. As Valeria Grinberg Pla and Werner Mackenbach demonstrate, authors in the anti-imperialist tradition went beyond the concerns of the social protest novel. The voices of the characters in their novels come to have a profound influence on national imaginaries and, in turn, narratives about these landscapes have had a profound effect on national identities.[80] The eloquence with which their narratives are stylized positions them as intellectuals clearing the capitalist rhetoric that serves as the opium of the people across Central America. These authors are far from "dead."[81] Their voices do indeed echo the concerns of the [mestizo] masses, but they do so while evidencing their authorial posture in their portrayal of contexts and characters. Their banana and canal narratives map North American–controlled territory for a readership to whom the area is a great mystery. Cartography gives way to human geography as the anti-imperialist text proceeds to catalogue the communities and cultures of the landscape.

Eugenics, Biotypology, and Literary Mapping

Writing just four years after Ecuadorian Aguilera Malta's shocking *Canal Zone* began circulating across intellectual circles, shaming Central American elites, Dr. Clodomiro Picado of Costa Rica exclaimed in his 1939 editorial: "OUR BLOOD IS BLACKENING! And if we continue like this, it will not be a nugget of gold that comes out of the crucible, but rather a piece of charcoal."[82] His was an urgent call to rescue the "European sanguineous patrimony" that had saved the country from "falling into systems of African type,[83] whether in the political or in pastimes that imitate art in distinction in sad and ridiculous styles."[84] As an alumnus of the Pasteur Institute and director of the national laboratories in San Juan de Dios during the first half of the twentieth century, Picado's observations supported Central American intellectuals' fervent belief in this powerful biopolitical movement. Eugenics and biotypology became an integral aspect of the political discourses of Central America's progress, permeating literary representations of the flow of Black subjects across and within national boundaries.

Literary and political print was not produced outside of the parameters of nationalist self-making that creates the identities of citizens by establishing boundaries between the self and the "other." As Nancy Leys Stepan observes in her landmark study, *The Hour of Eugenics*, scientific and medical discourses provided the framework for inquiries into Latin American national identities in the early twentieth century. Eugenics was, first, "a science of heredity that was shaped by political, institutional, and cultural factors particular to the historical moment and place in which it appeared" and, second, "a social movement with an explicit set of policy proposals that appeared to their proponents to be suggested by, or be logically derived from, hereditarian science itself."[85] Argentina, Brazil, and Mexico were foremost among those countries with an established interest in eugenics, but the presence of Haitian, Costa Rican, Salvadoran, Honduran, Nicaraguan, and Panamanian delegates at Pan American Sanitary Conferences and Pan American Conferences of Eugenics and Homoculture in the early 1930s reveals the broad scope of the appeal of the movement.[86] The political and scientific institutions in these countries adapted the theory to suit their contexts, conceiving of it as a means of improving the nation by cleansing from the milieu those factors considered be damaging to its citizens' hereditary health. In those Central American nations where the United Fruit Company recruited a largely West Indian labor force to work on the plantation, the discourse of eugenics became the rhetoric of choice among intellectuals who warned the populace as to the impending doom faced by nations otherwise destined to have a "purer" and more "pristine" genealogical composition.

During the thirty years that banana and canal masterplots were produced—both by Central American thinkers and equally appalled Latin American onlookers—isthmian intellectuals faced the challenge of legitimizing their countries. They faced scathing critiques from comrades such as the Argentinean socialist Alfredo Palacios, who considered Panama nothing but a "Yankee colony" undeserving of respect due to its imminent absorption by the "North American colossus."[87] Thus a central concern in these Central American foundational banana and canal fictions was to present Central Americans as a unified *mestizo* people in the fashion of the ruralist movement espoused by proponents of the movement who deliberately depicted the peasant subject as the basis of their nationalism.

The harmony and homogeneity that arose from these folkloric representations meant that Black subjects couldn't play a role in the conception of *mestizaje* promoted in foundational fictions, despite their demographic dominance in these regions since the colonial period.[88] The discourses that addressed ethnic and racial plurality did so by asserting the authenticity of their citizens' *mestizo* identity in contrast to the foreignness of the Black populations living in their nations.

The novels suggested the Central American Caribbean coast was not the site of the supposed "Hispanic heritage" that was emblematic of Central American nations, but that challenging Anglophone domination would return it to its purer state. While affirming an anti-imperialist stance, these discourses also reified eugenicist and biotypological discourses. Doubly anthropological and social realist in their choices for narrative voice, these fictions gave authorial authority to writers who uncovered the Central Caribbean coast as a Black coastal strip, alien to the citizens of Central American nations. Furthermore, language and nationalism were intimately tied in Central American anti-imperialist texts of the period. Where there were linguistic policies to bolster the position of the Spanish language, there was institutionalized racism against Afrodescendants. Where print media were concerned, they served as a space to denounce the usurpation of *mestizo* rights by those who unjustly reaped the profits of Central American nations. They also fueled legislation, especially immigration laws, and the release of census data.

Eugenics and biotypology were at the root of historical conflicts between Hispanophone Central Americans and Anglophone West Indian/Garifuna communities on the Caribbean coast. Print, meanwhile, was used to designate the geographic position of Black subjects in this key historical juncture in the history of Central America. Factually speaking, there were few roads that connected the Central American "interior" to the Caribbean coast until the postwar period (1992–present). *Barro*, for instance, was written ten years before the first paved road in Honduras, and to return to the interior after having failed to amass the fabled green gold of the coast, a family would have had to walk fourteen days through the Atlántida and Olancho jungles.[89] *Canal Zone* was written fifteen years after thousands of Panamanians were cleared out to make way for the many swimming pools, tennis courts, movie theaters, and restaurants that were closed to Panamanians unless invited by a Zone resident.[90] It belonged to the United States, and as the 1964 *Time* magazine article proclaimed, it was "more American than America," and a few Zonians even boasted that they rarely crossed the border to what they considered "the other side."[91] But more than simply revolutionary declarations, these banana novels and canal literature served to map the origins and transit points of migratory flows of Black peoples who could no longer be ignored but would be vehemently rejected from national space. They allowed like-minded readers to track Black bodies—and their position in the formal and informal economies—in the farthest reaches of national imaginaries. These literary mappings of the peoples of the isthmus represent, in essence, the mastery of chronotopes at the service of a symbolic connection to Central America.

Human Cartography in Print

As models of terrain, maps combine science and aesthetics to represent the state and national boundaries, climate, natural resources, physical features, and human as well as social geography of a given area. At once functional and artistic, whether they be maps or novels, the print product of such endeavors is a narrative tool rife with ideological and ontological repercussions. Hegemonic cartographic projects conceal abstract notions of the locus of power over spaces as well as the practice of redrawing maps years after those social systems were altered. Maps that plot bodies over space and time challenge their innocuous appearance and highlight the processes by which the most innocent of symbols have an intended ideological effect. With their focus on the Central American experience of space and time, the human cartographies drawn in anti-imperialist narratives excel in articulating the features of the Caribbean coast and the Canal Zone where vested political and economic objectives keep the spaces hidden from the purview of the legitimate citizen. Who inhabits these areas, what they do while they are there, and what the driving forces are of a consistent migratory flow are key elements to the practice of mapping bodies in these hazy spaces. When *Canal Zone*, *Barro*, and other print media sketched the Caribbean coastal landscape of Panama and Honduras to deliver the anti-imperialist masterplot to readers, they brought into focus an area within these nations that had never before been part of national or regional isthmian literary traditions, which had limited their scope to the Pacific and interior locales of national and regional *folclor*.

In tandem with other anti-imperialist texts of the first half of the twentieth century, authors of canal literature and banana novels worked together to create a sense of legitimate [*mestizo*] belonging to the national imaginary. The West Indian tradition whose seedlings can be perceived during this same historical period—and which would be amply studied by Ian Smart in his monumental *Central American Writers of West Indian Origin*—was itself a response to the mapping and cataloguing of Afrodescendants as a liminal citizenry in the isthmus.[92] At this high hour of exclusion, isthmian intelligentsia endeavored to map ethnolinguistic privileges in such a way that Blackness could be plotted according to the physical boundaries of departments, districts, and autonomous zones on the Caribbean coast, always with a keen eye to linguistic belonging. Ultimately, the fictional human cartographic project at the crux of these fictions conditioned readers' sentiments about both geographic and racial fragmentations within singular national spaces. As I discuss in the next chapter, the discourses that further deepened the geographic split between legitimate and [Black] liminal citizenry were reinforced by narratives addressing Black/Indigenous divides within Central American nations.

Chapter 3

Mesoamerican Core, Kriol Periphery

Mesoamerica. The area that today encompasses southern Mexico, Guatemala, Belize, El Salvador, and parts of Honduras, Nicaragua, and Costa Rica. Mesoamerica. The area over which the Spanish and British empires laid borders that were succeeded by those of the Central American nations we recognize today. When Paul Kirchhoff coined the term "Mesoamerica" in 1943, his definition was based on "geographic limits, ethnic composition, and cultural characteristics at the time of the Conquest."[1] While this way of framing the region and its peoples has been superseded by new models focusing on economic relationships, the cultural links implicit in Kirchhoff's definition have had the deepest impact on the construction of Central American national imaginaries.[2] *Indigenismo* and *mestizaje* are central to the Central American Hispanophone cultural sphere, ensuring little if any relationship to Belizean cultural production emerging from a Creole imaginary and a Kriol lingua franca.

A Hispanophone identity unifies the countries where Spanish is the official language and the majority of the inhabitants claim their belonging in varying degrees to Indigenous, *ladino*, and *mestizo* groups.[3] Belize is an exception among its Hispanophone neighbors, since it is there that Afrodescendance, Creole identity, and Kriol language acquire the importance more commonly associated with Anglophone Caribbean islands.[4] Put another way, claiming a connection to a Maya past has been as critical to the Central American Hispanophone experience as claiming a Creole heritage has been essential to the articulation of Belizean identity. Guatemala has long been recognized as the country with the most solid claims to a Mesoamerican historical trajectory. Belize, on the other hand, has long been seen by the rest of the Central American community as an Afro-Caribbean nation fashioned by Great Britain at the expense of, first, the Spanish empire and, second, the Guatemalan government.

The Belize/Guatemala border dispute garnered a prolonged, unsettled, and transatlantic debate throughout the Cold War and in the very midst of the Guatemalan war (1960–1996) that resulted in a state-sanctioned genocide of Maya communities. Although Guatemala had sought international support for its territorial claim as early as 1939, it pursued an aggressive agenda for the disputed Mayan lands in the Cold War years. The United States concurred with the idea that Belize could become "a potential base for spreading subversion" due to its proximity to Guatemala's Petén region and what could be easy Cuban access to Central America.[5] With Guatemala poised to cite "security" as its primary concern, Belize's bargaining chip was Great Britain's security forces, which it said would remain in the country to safeguard its "independence and territorial integrity."[6] As a result, Belize was able to gain its independence in 1981, twenty years after Great Britain's offer to relinquish hold on the colony, and absorb Mayan lands and Maya peoples into its Creole fold. Though Maya people in Belize continue to be on the lowest rung of the economic, political, and social ladder of the country, they remain fiercely opposed to the threat of incorporation into Guatemala even as the land dispute has continued into the twenty-first century.[7]

The masterplots and chronotopes of the print materials examined in this chapter are distinct, yet all offer fruitful data on the sharp divide established between Blackness and Indigeneity in Mesoamerica as well as its dissolution in the latter years of this critical historical juncture. This chapter examines the Black/Indigenous divide cultivated primarily in Miguel Ángel Asturias's *Mulata de tal* (1963) and decolonized in David Ruiz Puga's *Got seif de Cuin!* (1995). The first two sections of the chapter bridge the discussion of Blackness in banana novels set in Guatemala's Caribbean coast with the discussion of Blackness in the Guatemalan highlands. The third section examines the designation of Blackness marked as linguistic difference as a metaphorical and tangible threat to Maya populations on the Belize-Guatemala border. As the chapter demonstrates, the Central American rhetoric of incompatibility between Blackness and Mayanness resulted in an unprecedented fictional representation of Blackness as distinct, divergent, and threatening to Indigeneity during this critical period in the isthmus's history, and in many ways acted as a smokescreen to a war that was known worldwide to specifically target Maya communities in the Guatemalan highlands.

From *Indigenismo* to the Negro/Maya Divide

Guatemala is the only Central American nation that has a Maya majority, and, as such, its political and literary discourses have highlighted its "Mesoamerican distinction" in Central America. Politicians and intellectuals alike have undertaken the task of negotiating and crafting an identity based on its connection to a brilliant Mayan past in what has long been considered the isthmus's sole *indomestizo* nation.[8] Whether they fall on the right or the left of the political spectrum, the notable thinkers of the isthmus have not underestimated the importance of cities like Tikal and Iximché, capital of the post-classical Kaqchikel Maya until 1524 when the Spanish invaded. Yet, while this past has been central to both the Guatemalan national imaginary and the regional imaginary, this reverence for an ancient Maya past did not extend to contemporary Maya populations during the Cold War. Consequently, Guatemalan intellectuals who defended Maya peoples understood the primary ethnic conflict in Guatemala to be between Maya communities and their exploiters, be they called *mestizos*, *ladinos*, or *blancos*. Miguel Ángel Asturias (1967 Nobel Prize laureate in Literature and a widely recognized emblematic figure in Central American letters), for example, is credited with a significant number of novels and essays focusing on the Mayan question in Guatemala. Penned during the era of military dictatorships in the country, his *indigenista* approach sheds light on ethnolinguistic questions during this critical period. Following Antonio Cornejo Polar, *indigenismo* can be understood as the ideological position adopted by [*mestizo*] supporters of Indigenous causes who responded to their nations' underdevelopment and dependency through the production of a "referent—the Indigenous world—[that] appears conditioned by a rural structure stained with feudal residues."[9] According to Cornejo Polar, *indigenista* authors purport to highlight a major conflict, the dismembered constitution of a society and a culture that still, after centuries of coexistence in the same space, cannot tell their story without the attributes of a conflictive and tragic dialogue. This difficult intersocial and intercultural dialogue constitutes the bedrock of *indigenismo*.[10] Implicit is the *indigenista* author's conviction that the Indigenous/oppressor dynamic has permeated social relations to such an extent that it overshadows any other conflict in the same nation. Attending to the Central American context, *indigenista* authors write about the Mesoamerican referent as a space that cannot be understood without comprehending the extreme dispossession of Maya peoples from the colonial period forward. Texts within this genre suggest that Afrodescendants are not victims in the central conflict at the heart of Mesoamerican identity. Consequently, even those texts that feature Black subjects fail to assign complexity to them when they are positioned in the Mayan context featured in *indigenista* literature.

Asturias's oeuvre followed an *indigenista* trajectory: his later novels opened a space for the discussion of Blackness in Guatemala through his banana trilogy (1950–1962) and his last novel, *Mulata de tal* (1962).[11] These novels leave behind the Indigenous cosmologies of Asturias's most celebrated novels and, as literary critic Arturo Arias observes, are a literary experiment that transgresses the author's previous literary achievements.[12] The settings and characters of these novels diverged from Asturias's earlier *indigenista* novels, but they were also unlike the *criollo* novel that was popular in Guatemala at the time.[13]

In short order, and quite unintentionally, Asturias gained a monopoly over the representation of Blackness in Guatemalan letters in the second half of the twentieth century. Written during the reformist presidency of Jacobo Árbenz (1951–1954)[14] and during the author's exile after the fall of this leader's progressive government, the novels appear at a critical period in Central American history. Árbenz was responsible for consolidating constitutional rule; extending voting rights to women, poor *ladinos*, and Mayas; establishing social security and health programs; putting an end to forced labor on coffee plantations; and, in 1952, passing an agrarian reform law that went beyond distributing uncultivated land to the landless.[15] The law diluted planter authority by instituting a system of rural power, which ultimately spurred a rapid growth of rural peasant organization among poor *ladinos* and Maya communities in the country. Guatemala's cultural and intellectual circles blossomed during Árbenz's government, giving a platform to the voices of writers like Asturias and Luis Cardoza de Aragón.

They, along with other writers, poets, and artists of their generation, were committed to working toward a democratic political culture and defense of Maya peoples.[16] They ushered forward the vision that had been so clearly articulated by Guatemalan president Juan José Arévalo, in 1945:

We believe that man, above else, desires dignity. To be man with dignity or to be nothing. For this reason, our socialism is not oriented toward the naïve distribution of material goods, toward the idiotic equalizing of men who are economically different. Our socialism seeks to liberate men psychologically, to return to them all of the psychological and spiritual integrity that was denied by conservatism and liberalism. . . . First we must invest in the worker with all his dignities as a man, destroying at the same time the many pretexts that have been used to keep him in humiliation and servitude. Spiritual socialism is a doctrine of psychological and moral liberation.[17]

Asturias and other intellectuals in his literary circle espoused a "spiritual socialism" that infused the concept of democracy with the solid objective of dignity through economic and social justice. Asturias himself turned to Guatemala's Caribbean coast and, specifically, to the working conditions of banana plantations.

Choosing this context for his banana trilogy allowed Asturias to widen his gaze beyond Maya themes contextualized in the highlands to include the Black and *mestizo* masses in the banana zones. The narrator of *El papa verde* describes them in the first pages of the novel: "Negros. Blancos. ¡Qué raros se miran los blancos de noche! Como los negros de día. Negros de Omoa, de Belice, de Livingston, de Nueva Órleans. Mestizos insignificantes con ojos de pescado, medio indios, medio ladinos; zambos retintos, mulatos licenciosos, asiáticos con trenza y blancos escapados del infierno de Panamá." (Blacks. Whites. How strange the whites looked at night! Like the Blacks during the day! Blacks from Omoa, from Belize, from Livingston, from New Orleans. Insignificant *mestizos* with fisheyes, half Indian, half *ladino*.)[18] The narrative voice continues listing, among others, *zambos* and mulattoes. They come from near and far—Honduras, Belize, Guatemala, and the United States—and together form a group, not a community, that ultimately makes the exploited tropical Caribbean coast their home. While all workers on the banana plantations are vulnerable subjects, the West Indian laborers depicted in this novel remain in a perpetual state of ambivalent wandering. Unlike the Maya and even the *ladino* subjects depicted in the novel, Asturias's Black characters lack the roots that bind them to the Guatemalan landscape. In a manner reminiscent of Demetrio Aguilera's *Canal Zone*, Afrodescendants in *El papa verde* lack a sense of belonging. This has direct implications for their development as characters in the novel, as they fail to embrace the spiritual socialism that gives purpose to the Indigenous and *mestizo* subjects in the same context.

Both *El papa verde* and *Los ojos de los enterrados*, the last in Asturias's banana trilogy, distance themselves from the highland-context Maya content of Asturias's prior novels.[19] In *El papa verde*, the lands of a group of mulatto families are expropriated by the "Green Pope," who extends his banana empire while the dispossessed Afrodescendant families are mired in poverty. Ten years[20] later, in the timescape of the same novel, readers encounter Juambo, the *Sambito*,[21] the Green Pope's loyal employee. Details soon emerge about this Afrodescendant servant: Juambo is a believer in Black Saint Benedict, he calls himself a tricky mulatto, and he "[obeys his boss] blindly and fear[s] him more than God."[22] As a Black male house servant, blindly dutiful to a high-ranking official in banana companies, Juambo is fashioned as an archetype in the banana novel genre. In these manifestos against capitalist intrusion in Central American affairs, as explained in the third chapter of this book, Black characters at best failed to challenge imperialism and at worst were in collusion with the owners of the means of production. While Juambo submits to his state of deplorable servitude, the Maya and *mestizo* subjects in Asturias's banana trilogy organize themselves against capitalist interests. The struggle against elites leads them through a meaningful spiritual labyrinth, while Juambo and other Black characters remain locked in a maze of dutiful servitude to their masters without an escape, echoing conditions of enslavement.[23]

Juambo joins a banana laborers' strike in *Los ojos de los enterrados*, but he remains in the background of the novel's generalized discourse of justice. The novels thus reduce Blackness to a purely anecdotal and trite element in a plot that undermines Black thought and experience. In these narratives, Maya subjects are singled out as the victims of colonization, repression, and imperialism. Blackness, on the other hand, is the marker of perennial alterity, a condition from which subjects cannot emancipate themselves. The novels indicate that although *indios* have been marked as subhuman by the hegemony, their awareness of their material and historic condition fuels their drive to challenge imperialism.[24] Afrodescendants are not rebellious characters fighting against exploitation and promoting consciousness-raising among the masses. The narratives thus reinforce archetypes of Uncle Tom–like characters at the same time that they posit a divorce between Black subjects and the spiritual socialist ideology that can transform the working masses into subjects and agents of history. In effect, these narratives stipulate the legitimate citizenship of Maya peoples while sharply dividing them from the Black peoples who are not portrayed as integral to Mesoamerica.

This *negro*/Maya divide does not only manifest itself in the Black male subjects of the aforementioned novels. The few likeable qualities that Juambo possesses are entirely subtracted from the Afrodescendant women in the same two novels. Toba, Juambo's older sister, makes her first appearance in *El papa verde* wrapped in the seductive embrace of a *mestizo*. The archetype of "the easy mulata" that she embodies is replicated in Asturias's *Los ojos de los enterrados*, in which Anastasia, Juambo's second sister, appears. She is: "Anastasia, sin apellido, ni reloj, ni calzón, todo al aire como la gente del pueblo, el nombre, el tiempo, el sexo" (Anastasia, without a name or a watch or underwear, everything out in the open like the people of the town, the name, the time, sex).[25] And while their mother declares that Toba is superior to Anastasia, both are poor, young mulattas living in the margins and whose sexuality is flagrantly displayed in the text. Neither of them can claim the same measure of dignity afforded to Maya women and, consequently, become consumed and subsumed in a narrative that makes multiple references to their promiscuity.

Furthermore, *Los ojos de los enterrados* highlights ethnolinguistic divides by contrasting the standard Spanish of *ladinos* and Mayas with the mulatto siblings' use of Creole Spanish. The folkloric depictions of Maya Spanish and rural *ladino* Spanish in *costumbrista* texts allowed readers to come closer to the daily realities of an exploited class, peasant farmers, and their communities. In this last novel of Asturias's banana trilogy, however, Creole Spanish surfaces as a technique to highlight the Black characters' unskilled use of the Spanish language and inability to communicate profound ideas. Instead of positing Creole Spanish as another linguistic variety in the isthmus (as *costumbrista* texts purportedly do with Maya and *ladino* varieties of Spanish), the use of Creole Spanish highlights the incomprehensibility of the Afrodescendant characters. In one instance, for example, Toba leads Juambo to their mother's house stating, "Vamos nosotros Juambo, donde está madre. Casa allá. Juventino señor entrar fiesta. Juventino señor bailar bailar mujer pintada. Nosotros regresar, regresar aquí, y Juventino volver Toba. Toba besarlo. No reclamarle nada." (We go us Juambo, where mother is. House there. Juventino man enter party. Juventino man dance, dance painted woman. We us return, return here, and Juventino return Toba. Toba kiss him. Not demand nothing.)[26] The text creates a Creole Spanish variety—which purportedly includes the use of infinitives, morphologic simplicity, and lack of agreement—specifically for Black characters. The features of this linguistic variety are not present in the speech of other characters; no others but the mulattoes in the narrative purportedly speak Creole Spanish.[27] While it is beyond the scope of this analysis to examine Creole Spanish varieties in Central America, it is imperative to nonetheless note that this linguistic otherizing establishes a marked difference between the intelligible Maya Spanish and *ladino* Spanish crafted for members of those groups and the *un*intelligible speech designated for the Black characters of the same novel.

Afrodescendance and Mayanness

Asturias penned his penultimate novel, *Weekend in Guatemala* (1956), in exile and openly dedicated it to his homeland: "alive in the blood of its student-heroes, its peasant-martyrs and sacrificed workers." President Árbenz, whose presidency Asturias had supported, was responsible for implementing the Agrarian Reform Act of 1952, aimed at large landowners holding over ninety hectares (224 acres) of land—a law that affected the vast holding of the United Fruit Company, which had benefited from concessions offered by previous Guatemalan presidents. After appealing to Washington, the United States depicted Guatemala as a Soviet satellite and approved a CIA invasion of Guatemala, Operation PBSUCCESS, from Honduras. Árbenz was forced to step down in 1954.[28] By the time *Weekend in Guatemala* was published, the CIA had already spent two years compiling lists of Guatemalans to "dispose of" following the coup.[29] The counterinsurgency funding and anti-communist ideology of the United States led to the reinstatement of authoritarian rule that foreclosed the possibility of "spiritual socialism" articulated by Guatemalan thinkers during this period. The United States supported a second coup in 1963 to prevent Árbenz from returning from exile and running for reelection. The CIA's compilation of lists of enemies continued throughout the Cold War and resulted in the capture, interrogation, torture, and execution of suspected communists and sympathizers.[30] The repression and extreme censorship during this period led to a surge in political analyses and literary texts by Guatemalan thinkers in exile.

Mulata de tal (1964), Asturias's final novel written in exile, was once viewed as "a potboiler whose content is not sex, but anger, anger at the loss of the family, the country, and political ideals," but as René Prieto poignantly states, it merits much more serious consideration.[31] The text demands a historically grounded reading because Asturias turned his exile following the fall of Árbenz into an opportunity to speak out against authoritarianism while evidencing the Nobel laureate's predilection for myth as an explanation for history. This is a novel "en la que Asturias exterioriza de manera explícita su intencionalidad intermestizadora al fabular mitos, leyendas e historias orales americanas en una textualidad poblada también de vertebrales tradiciones europeas" (in which Asturias exteriorizes in an explicit manner his *intermestizo* intentionality by spinning myths, legends, and American oral histories in a textuality peopled as well with vertebral European traditions).[32] The *mestizo* and Indigenous worlds form a single entity in the rural context where Guatemalan identity is molded. Asturias leaves behind the themes of both his early celebrated novels as well as his banana trilogy and, as Arturo Arias observes, dedicates himself to a literary experiment that transgresses his previous achievements.[33] Written during the author's exile after the fall of the Jacobo Árbenz[34] government, the novel's *indomestizo* approach directly challenges the anti-communist and anti-Indigenous postulates of the succeeding regime. Like his banana novels, however, it positions Indigeneity in contrast to Blackness.

In novel and metaphor—in fact, as a novel metaphor in the Central American literary context—the title character is a *mulata*, a racial alien in the Mesoamerican context. The title character's ethnic identification notwithstanding, the protagonists of the novel are Celestino Yumí and Catalina Zabala. They are poor and are described in a lengthy passage that calls attention to ethnically symbolizing details like the sombrero hanging behind Celestino's neck and Catalina's shawl over her right shoulder. Celestino and Catalina bear the symbols of Indigeneity, from the classic description of the Indigenous woman's light step to the way in which she sleeps next to her husband on a straw mat: "[Catalina], su costilla, dormía junto a él en el suelo, sobre un petate de tul, cada cual tapado con su cobija de lana colorida, colores y figuras contra los malos sueños." ([Catalina], his rib, slept next to him on the ground, on a palm *petate*, each one covered by their colorful woven blanket, with colors and designs to ward off bad dreams.)[35] Echoing passages from Asturias's earlier works, *Mulata de tal* replicates the same sentiment about the social, cultural, and political place of Indigenous peoples. Recalling the observations made by Darcy Ribeiro in *The Americas and Civilization*, they are "the plundered peoples of history" who face the challenge of negotiating the opposing

European and autochthonous ideologies they have inherited and who are "distinguished by the presence of values of the old tradition they have preserved and that have bestowed on them the image they present."[36] As Testimonial Peoples, their identities are a result of the sociocultural factors that frame their subjectivity: "centuries of subjugation or of direct or indirect domination have deformed them, pauperizing their peoples and traumatizing their whole cultural life."[37] Though they bear these signs of Indigeneity in the opening pages of the novel, the course of the narrative emancipates them from the socioeconomic factors that would render their experience painful. Gone is the forced labor on plantations, the cultivation of maize, the hateful *ladino* society, and the cult to the ancestors in the highlands of Guatemala. Asturias invites the reader to envision a world where "the men of maize" have ceased to be defined by the toil of their bodies.

The complex plot deserves to be divulged before exploring the novel's treatment of Indigeneity and Afrodescendance. In the first pages of the novel, Celestino agrees to sell his wife, Catalina, to the devil in exchange for the riches that will lead him out of poverty. He finalizes the deal and becomes the richest man in the village overnight. Shortly thereafter, he meets a mulatta who becomes furiously attached to him. Catalina and Celestino conspire to trap the mulatta—who never acquires any other name but "Mulata"—in a cave and proceed to enjoy their riches. They embark upon an odyssey that leads husband and wife through a supernatural quest that leads them to transform themselves into dwarfs, giants, wizards, succubi, and demons, before returning them to their state of "human beings," a saga that involves over thirty physical transformations. The only constant in the narrative is Mulata, who meanders throughout the novel with the comparatively banal desire of sexual consummation.

In *Mulata de tal* Catalina and Celestino bear the mark of Mayanness in dress and modest behavior. They exemplify true subjectivation[38] as they alternate between exercising agency and being subjected to socio-hierarchical forms of power. The stress on transformation and fluctuating identities is a precondition for being birthed anew after being tempted by the devil's riches. The deftness with which Celestino and Catalina assume agency over their transformations, however, stands in contrast with the unwavering yet compromised position of Mulata. Despite her capricious attempts at subjectivation, she exits the novel in the same lackluster pitiful condition in which she enters the narrative. The narrator describes Celestino's confident gaze over this Afrodescendant character:

"Se detuvo y la miró con la insolente seguridad de rico que sabe que no hay mujer que lo resista, menos aquélla, tan planta de infeliz, vestida con un traje amarillo que era tan baba de tan viejo y usado, sobre su cuerpo de potranca, que estaría en busca de dueño." (He came to a halt and looked at her with the insolent confidence of a rich man who knows that no woman can resist him, especially her, with such a miserable appearance, dressed in a yellow outfit that was so sodden from age and overuse, over her mare's body, in search of an owner.)[39] Mulata's clothing is a sign of her dejectedness, and her body is conceived as her sole bargaining chip. Her identity is fixed as *la fulana* from this point forward, and "Mulata" remains both her ethnoracial classification and her name. She brandishes a fiery, burning look and laughs at Celestino. Hers is a violent laugh, assures the narrator, like that of a dog brandishing its ivory teeth, stuck in livid flesh.

This is where the reader confirms Mulata's marked position. She is a doubly animalistic (mare and dog), racialized, and impoverished other, plagued with an evil from within that threatens to ensnare Celestino. Afrodescendance is hardly incompatible with Mayanness in the narrative, rendering any possible claim of transculturation between Black and Maya subjectivities obsolete.[40] Mulata embodies anti-values, when compared to Mayan cosmogonies or even *ladino* conceptions of morality and repentance. As a symbol, Mulata lends herself to a broader claim: it is impossible to know Blackness intimately. Catalina and the other "good" Maya women in his hometown stand in stark contrast to Mulata, who immediately demands that Celestino hand over his wallet to her before he can fondle her, essentially prostituting herself: "¡La cartera antes!—le repitió, imperiosa, refregándole todo lo que en ella había de raíz flexible, de raíz que estuvo enterrada siglos debajo de un palo de ébano, y ahora vestida de carne, tan pronto era culebra como mujer." (The wallet first! she repeated imperially, rubbing everything that in her was an inflexible root, a root that had been buried for centuries under an ebony tree, and now dressed in flesh, as much a snake as she was a woman.)[41] Mulata captivates Celestino because her avarice and sexual appetite surpass those of the chaste women he has previously encountered, and it is because *indigenas* and *mestizas* are polar opposites to the sole Mulata that this becomes part and parcel of that sexual experience. As Anabella Acevedo Leal indicates, "Lo interesante aquí es que las fuerzas del mal están personificadas dentro de la novela sobre todo por una mujer, la Mulata, cuya caracterización y cuya fuerza dentro del texto parece más concreta y más definida aún que la de Cashtoc y Candanga, los dioses del mal que se disputan el poder."

(What is interesting here is that the forces of evil are personified in the novel by a single woman, the Mulata, whose characterization and force in the text appears more concretely and more defined than even that of Cashtoc and Candanga, the gods of evil who vie for power).[42] Celestino ignores the signs that Mulata is in fact an enchantress, but it is crystal clear that ceding to his passion for her will guarantee him a dark fate.

To dismiss the centrality of the *negro*/Maya dynamic in the novel would be to ignore the fact that this is the first instance in which the *mulata* archetype appears in Central American literature. The character became engrained in Latin American literatures, especially in Cuban novels, in the nineteenth century following emancipation. The *mulata* was readily defined by intellectuals of all stripes, including Cuban doctor Benjamín de Céspedes: "There is no such civility, culture, beauty or flattery in the semi-savage type of the ordinary *mulata* who only possesses the art of moving her hips acrobatically."[43] This was the "visceral, non-sentient, threatening object" that invariably met a tragic demise in the national narratives of the period. While the archetype was well known in Central American literary circles (and Rubén Darío himself once penned a poem about a Black Cuban woman), the *mulata* archetype was absent from Central American narratives until the publication of Asturias's *Mulata de tal*. And, although Asturias declares that he fashioned this character himself, his own rationale hearkens to the recurrent literary prototype: "La Mulata en sí es un invento mío. La llamé Mulata para no usar la palabra Mestiza, porque no me parecía que la mezcla de sangre era suficiente en la mestiza. Evité Zamba, que habría dado una combinación de las sangres indígena india y negra, porque no creí que la palabra sugeriría la gracia de movimientos tan especial que tiene la mulata." (I called her Mulata so as to avoid the term *mestiza*, because it didn't seem to me that the blood mixing was enough in the *mestiza*. I avoided the term *zamba*, which would have resulted in a combination of Indigenous and Black blood, because I didn't think the word would suggest the special grace of movements that *mulatas* have.)[44] Asturias argues that, unlike the *mestiza* and *zamba* options, the *mulata* possesses an exotic, sexually appealing body. Not only does she promise to satisfy desires, she also remains connected to the mysterious, supernatural world. While Asturias states that his text explores racial mixing in female characters, he affirms that neither *mestiza* nor *zamba* conjure the image of the *mulitas*' unique supple movements recurrently seen in fictions about them. As Roberto Morales astutely indicates, however, the pivot away from the more typical

Maya/*ladino* central characters does not contradict the adoption of an *indomestizo* identity as the political, spiritual, and literary objective.[45] In Asturias's novel, Afrodescendance is a clear anti-value, a carnally driven subjectivity that purportedly destabilizes the more spiritually inclined Mesoamerican subjectivities.

The moralistic imperative that drives the battle between Cashtoc, the Indigenous devil, and Candanga, the *mestizo* devil, is an important driver of the novel. Cashtoc declares that the men of maize must be destroyed because they have abandoned their communal ways and have become egocentric and individualistic. Candanga doesn't see a need to destroy beings, observes Cashtoc, because his interest lies in prompting human beings to reproduce in order to populate his inferno with human flesh. At the height of the battle between Candanga and Cashtoc, a reference is made to Mandinga, a minor Black devil that concretely manifests Mulata's position at the crossroads of racialized and gendered tropes in the throes of hell: "Sabido es que entre los diablos se ayudan, y a Candanga, el demonio ladino, lo ayudaba Mandinga, el demonio negro que estaba siempre de fiesta, sudoroso, con un mondadientes en la boca, o el puro, rodeado de chulísimas hembras de ébano, mimbreantes antes y después de sus deshonestidades, con no sé qué de pírrico en los ojos, y artificio de fuego fatuo en los pezones y las caderas." (It is well known that devils help each other and Candanga, the *ladino* demon, was assisted by Mandinga, the Black demon who was always partying, sweaty, with a toothpick in his mouth, or a cigar, surrounded by hot ebony women, malleable before and after their dirty business, with I don't know what glint of pride in their eyes and the ploy of a conceited fire in their nipples and hips.)[46] The Mesoamerican rural landscape in which Celestino and Catalina live notwithstanding, the narrative voice centers on a timeless struggle for dominance between the Indigenous Cashtoc and the *ladino* Candanga, until the balance is tilted in favor of Candanga thanks to the help he has received from Mandinga, the Black devil. The mythology/fables that ground this novel thus echo archaic notions featuring *negros* pitted against *indigenas* in colonial color-coded spaces. The depiction of evil thus assumes that Blackness nourishes the evil in *ladinidad*. Not only does Mandinga assist Candanga, Mulata embodies the sadistic evil itself.

George Yancy observes that in hegemonic discourse, "Blackness is a congenital defect, one that burdens the body with tremendous inherited guilt. On this reading, one might say that blackness functions metaphorically as original sin. There is nothing that a black body needs *to do* in order to be found blameworthy."⁴⁷ Since the Black subject is sinful by nature of its existence, it is a coefficient of monstrosity when it is sexualized in a manner that does not subscribe to a heteronormative model. Mulata, who doesn't stop at being a seductress in the novel, also refuses to have children and rejects intercourse in the standard missionary position, demanding instead she always be sodomized. Anabella Acevedo Leal remarks that these transgressions are so aggrandized that they result in moral deformities that fix the *mulata*'s character as a monstrosity.⁴⁸ These "anti-values" are further heightened when the Indigenous female counterpart, Catalina, speculates that Mulata might be intersexed or otherwise sexually ambiguous. Specifically, she states that Mulata needs a "little something more" to be a man, though she has too much of a "little something" to be a woman.⁴⁹ Mulata remains a racialized, sexualized, and abject other throughout the novel and is featured as a dangerous and destabilizing force for the primary Indigenous characters in the narrative.

As Nicaraguan thinker Sergio Ramírez states with relation to discourses of belonging in what was once the Mesoamerican region, pride in a "simply double mestizaje" has been fixed as inoffensive adornment by Central American hegemonic culture, while shame in the one-dimensional designations of *negro* or *indio* is recurrent since the colonial period.⁵⁰ Perhaps most insidiously, the terms *mulato* and *mulata* are beyond shame—they are simply irreconcilable with conceptions of Central American identity. Even when words like *nápiro*, *picholo*, *negricillo*, *musuco*, *cerullo*, *murruco*, *trompudo*, and *chajuma* denote Blackness, "the word *mulato* is suppressed in daily language, as if just recalling it were enough to infuriate, and we prefer to recognize ourselves in the Indohispanic '*mestizo* pretext' in which the Indigenous component is less threatening."⁵¹ The literary enunciation of Blackness through the archetype of the *mulata* is a red flag that indicates a marked departure from the Mesoamerican cradle of identity. With rightful citizenship and the historical legacy of the Mesoamerican cultures posited as symbiotically related to place, Blackness becomes an empty signifier that can only be filled with the ideological material of abjection.

(Undoing) Indigenous Borders and Black Limits

Guatemala is an iconic gem in Mesoamerica with its twenty-one Maya languages and communities, in spite of the historical marginalization and continuous genocide of Indigenous peoples. While the country's Mayan past and present ensures its place in the Mesoamerican regional imaginary, Belize's Afrodescendant foundation excludes it from the purportedly shared historical trajectory of Mesoamerica and the larger isthmus. As Salvadoran novelist Jacinta Escudos observes, even the maps that schoolchildren use in Central America serve as ideological apparatuses that condition the sentiment that Belize is a "territory" that doesn't fit with the rest of the isthmus: "Un último recuerdo de infancia: cuando estaba chiquita y nos hacían dibujar el mapa de Centro América, la parte correspondiente a Belice o no se dibujaba o se coloreaba con franjas transversales para indicar que allí ocurría una situación 'especial.' Es colonia inglesa, decían mis profesores de primaria. Alguno pensará que estos recuerdos personales son inoportuna vanidad mía. Pero sirven para ilustrar el origen de algunos vicios actuales, como es el de excluir en el pensamiento regional a Belice." (Here's a memory from my childhood: when I was a little girl and we had to draw a map of Central America, the part that corresponded to Belize was either not drawn or was colored in with horizontal lines to indicate that there was a "special" situation there. It's a British colony, my primary school teachers would say. Some might say that it is vain of me to write about these memories. However, they help illustrate the origin of some of today's vices, namely that of the exclusion of Belizean regional thought.)[52] Central American citizens, from Guatemala to Panama, learn that Belize is a spurious anomaly in the region. While Hispanophone countries in the isthmus have all enjoyed over a century of independence from Spain, Belize is but forty years of age. Even after its independence from British colonialism, Belize maintained its connection to the former imperial power by remaining part of the commonwealth. Furthermore, it is the only country in Central America that has instated English as its official language. Even in formerly British areas and towns along the multilingual Central American Caribbean coast—places with names like Livingston, Guatemala, and Pearl Lagoon, Nicaragua—inhabitants are expected to speak Spanish. In addition, there is a keen awareness of the Creole identity in Belize and its Afrodescendant roots that contrasts sharply with the founding national ideologies of the other six countries. As if that were not enough to highlight Belize's "unassimilable" qualities in Hispanophone discourses of the region, the territorial dispute between Belize and Guatemala continues to lead to discussions about citizenship and belonging to this day.[53] In essence, the Mayanness of Guatemala and the Blackness of Belize are posited as incompatible.

While the Kekchi, Mopan, and Yucatec communities as well as Garifuna peoples constitute a significant portion of the population in Belize, the highlighted Anglophone Blackness of the country effectuates a different degree of belonging to Central America.

This legacy is the bedrock of the narrative of Belize's standing among the other six countries of the isthmus, and the matter was not ameliorated in the twentieth century with the Guatemalan government's reinvigoration of the country's border's dispute with Belize. As William Noel Salmon and I explain:

> While most former English colonies obtained their independence from the British Empire in the 1960s, Belize had to assess three interrelated factors before claiming its independence. It had to consider first the threat of a Guatemalan invasion of Belize during the former's civil war (1960–96); second, the brutal genocide against Maya populations across the border in the Petén region; third, the ongoing territorial dispute between the countries over the existence and precise location of the Belizean-Guatemalan border.[54] The factors remain salient, as their potential threat has not attenuated in the years since the end of the Guatemalan civil war. The territorial dispute is still very much alive, with the territory involved including the southern section of Belize District, most of Cayo District, and the entirety of Stann Creek and Toledo Districts, which are home to the Kekchi and Mopan Maya linguistic communities.[55] Importantly, this disputed territory also includes the entirety of the Maya Mountains.[56]

After Belizean independence and especially at the end of the end of the Guatemalan civil war when the Hispanophone government attempted to divert attention away from its genocide of Maya peoples, annexation became an important threat to Maya communities within the disputed area.

It is a conflict that lulls to a stop only to reemerge when the government attempts to divert attention away from itself. A map of the disputed territory appeared in a 2013 article entitled "Reclamo territorial" in the Guatemalan newspaper *La Prensa Libre* (figure 3.1). The bullet points highlight "differences" between Belize and the rest of Central America to the Guatemalan readership: "Guatemala claims 12,272 km^2 of Belize's

Figure 3.1. Belize-Guatemala Border Dispute. *Source*: Nelson Xuya for Prensa Libre.

110 | Black in Print

Maps 3.1a. Areas of Belize Affected by Guatemala's Land Claim. *Source*: U-Spatial.

territory and about a hundred islands; Guatemala has claimed this territory for more than 150 years; Belize has a monarchic system with a Prime Minister; agriculture is the main activity, followed by fishing, construction, transport, and tourism; Belize has 0.74 percent of Central America's population with some 311,000 inhabitants; Belize's economy is the smallest of the seven countries in the isthmus; and Belize is Anglophone, but many of its inhabitants speak Kriol. The currency is the Belize dollar." As Salmon and I continue to highlight and illustrate with maps 3.1a and 3.1b: "The disputed territory easily includes half the land of Belize, [which]

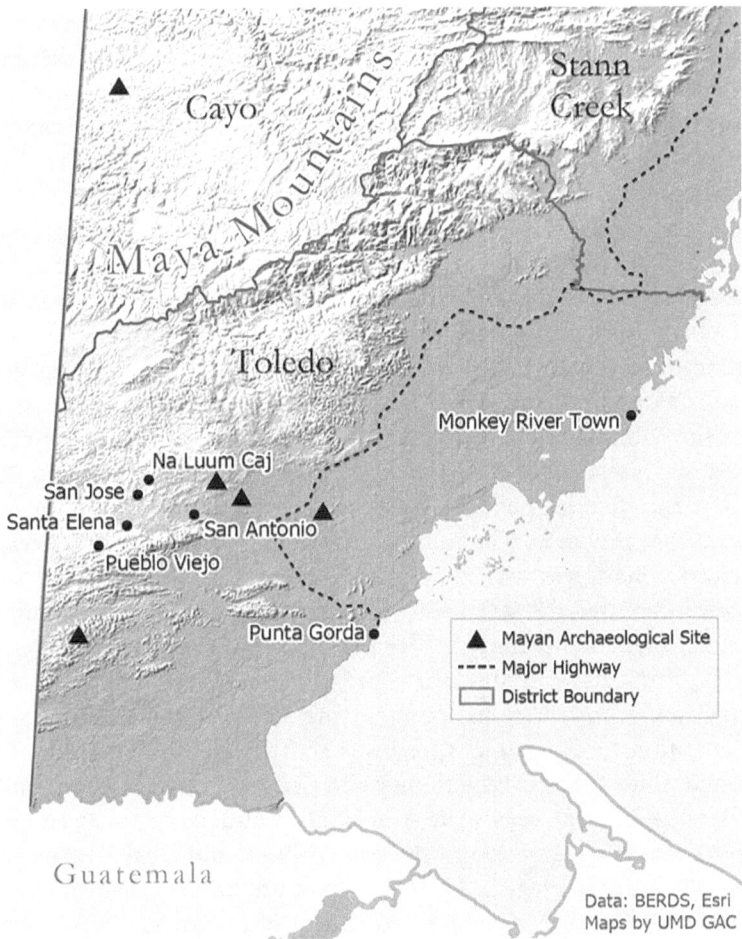

Maps 3.1b. Areas of Belize Affected by Guatemala's Land Claim. *Source*: U-Spatial.

includes valuable forestlands, coastland, and approximately one hundred islands; a large percentage of the country's agricultural sites; archaeological sites; and conservation zones, all of which are on ancient Mayan homelands."[57] Annexation would provide Guatemala with access to the Caribbean Sea and control over the highways transporting raw materials out of this lush landscape. With an eye to its natural resources and the Indigenous communities in the Maya Mountains, the Guatemalan government claimed that Belize would become prey to communists if it gained its independence.

David Ruiz Puga, one of the few Maya authors from Belize to publish a novel in Spanish through a Guatemalan press, argues that the culture clash arising from Belize's British colonial past and the binational border dispute has resulted in Belize's invisibility in the Central American realm of letters. He explains: "Por el hecho de que compartimos una historia política con el Caribe, y por tener el fantasma del reclamo territorial de Guatemala, ha sido ésta suficiente razón para aislarnos de Centroamérica." (Because of the fact that we share a political history with the Caribbean and because of the ghost of the territorial dispute with Guatemala, this has been reason enough to isolate us from Central America.)[58] As an outsider to hegemonic Central American discourse, a Belizean author like Ruiz Puga must draw parallels between his nation and that of others in the isthmus for his work to gain traction in the literary circles of the region. His novel *Got seif de Cuin!* (1995) received attention in the initial years after its publication, as it uncovered the direct impact of colonization and nation-building on a Maya community. Its treatment of Belizean Blackness was hitherto missing in Central American letters. The novel captured the sentiment of multiple Indigenous generations who witnessed Black Belizeans shift from being subjects of the Crown to free subjects of the new republic. In short, this novel was unlike any of the tragic Black representations found in previous Central American texts. This attention to *Got seif de Cuin!* was short-lived, however. Ruiz Puga's subsequent literary oeuvre, although focused on the Maya community of Old Benque (Belize), was written in English and, as of this writing, has received very little attention in the primarily monolingual Hispanophone literary circles of the region. He was, clearly, unlike any other Maya author in Central America. His complex treatment of Blackness as a subjectivity determined by time and place with distinct implications for Indigenous peoples, likewise affected by time and place, was clearly before its time.

Got seif de Cuin! was a challenge for Central American literary circles to better examine the epistemic borders and limits that have been erected in political and literary discourses. As the perceived beneficiaries of British and North Americans colonial histories, Black peoples are de jure citizens and de facto foreigners in the Hispanophone nations of the isthmus. The political disenfranchisement of Afrodescendants from Guatemala to Panama is notable.[59] Only in Belize have Black peoples enjoyed the privileges of inclusion into the body politic because, in contrast to its neighbors, the Belizean national imaginary is founded on its Creole cultural origins and the undeniable history of African slavery in the country. The Belizean government boasts, "Even though the Creole, the descendants of African slaves and European settlers of the colonial era, constitute only one-third of Belize's population today, they may be considered to be the most 'culturally influential group' in Belize."[60] This new country was conceived as a nation of New Peoples. Even before it claimed its independence, Belize announced it would be a melting pot of more than ten distinct cultures, including Mayan, Indian, Chinese, Palestinian, and German Mennonite. The linguistic consequence of this national imaginary is notable. Approximately 60 percent of the population in Belize considers itself *mestizo*, but the population speaks Belizean Kriol as the lingua franca.[61] Blackness and the Belizean Kriol identity are symbolically aligned with the Anglophone Caribbean literary tradition in the cultural sphere, while Mayanness, *mestizo/ladino* subjectivity, and the Spanish language are emblematic of Nuestra América, the intellectual tradition to which Central America generally subscribes.

Got seif de Cuin! takes readers to a relatively isolated town in the Tipú region on the edge of the Río Viejo. Naming is political: Anglophone Belizean readers will know it as the Belize River, but Central American readers will recognize it by its Spanish name. This detail is not to be dismissed, given the controversial nature of the Guatemalan/Belizean border. The river is navigable up to the Guatemalan border and has served as the main artery of commerce and communication between the interior and the coast well into the twentieth century, all facts that highlight its importance. The river charts its course along the northern edge of the Maya Mountains across the center of the country to the sea just north of Belize City, passing through a number of Mayan archaeological sites. These qualities make Río Viejo/Belize River a site of contestation as perceived by the British and Spanish empires and later, the Creole and the Guatemalan governments.

Nigel Bolland explains that when British logwood cutters were expelled by the Spanish from the Bay of Campeche in 1717, the British expanded their logwood trade along the Belize River.[62] The enslavement of African and Creole peoples from Jamaica and Bermuda on Mayan lands situated along the river continued from 1724 to 1838 and bolstered the British wealth that was garnered from logging mahogany. Colonial settlers requested colonial status in the mid-nineteenth century because they believed that British Honduras's designation as a settlement hindered their logging interests, which had depended first on Afrodescendant slave labor.[63] British Honduras drafted a political constitution similar to that of the Anglophone Caribbean islands in 1854, and the British Honduran Legislative Assembly sent a petition to Queen Victoria asking that the area be formally integrated into the empire as a colony in 1861.[64] The British Crown acceded to the settlers' request in 1862, formally declaring "British Honduras" its colony and the Afrodescendants therein its free subjects. Maya peoples were likewise claimed as subjects, though the Crown employed Anglophone Black subjects to spread the news to speakers of Mayan languages in the farthest reaches of the new colony.

Got seif de Cuin! tracks a history of foreign intrusion into and attempted ethnolinguistic conversion of Maya peoples along the Belize River into Anglophone *mestizo* peoples. The first representatives of the British empire described in the novel are religious men and women who intend to convert Maya peoples to Protestantism and insist on the use of the English language. One is a "blue-eyed priest with a turned-up nose who said he came to establish a school to teach everyone the language in which Her Majesty wished her subjects to speak."[65] This, in the context of a period in which—according to historical records—the British successively incorporated Maya and *mestizo* populations from the border areas with Guatemala and Mexico to manifest their settlement of the colony: population records were thus able to show an increase from a mere few thousand in the early 1800s to a total of 25,635 inhabitants at the first colonial census in 1861.[66] Maya and *mestizo* lands were important to the British, as they lay adjacent to areas in which mahogany extraction was the principal economic driving force. Although emancipated, Afrodescendant men continued to labor in logging while Maya men were recruited to work in chicle harvesting.[67] The presence of Anglophone white and Afrodescendant peoples on Maya ancestral lands announcing allegiance to Queen Victoria, Sovereign and Empress of India, had the same effect on the Maya as it had had centuries before when the Spanish claimed their lands property of the Spanish empire. The imposition of a European language and chain of command from across the Atlantic Ocean was incongruent with the practices of village elders, whom the narrator in *Got seif de Cuin!* describes as: "survivor[s] of the mystical city of the Tipú, lost in time, where there grew bountiful ears of corn and where Chaac descended to water the crops with crystalline drops of imperial Jade."[68]

The novel thus centers Mayas while highlighting coloniality as a condition that extends beyond Indigenous peoples to the Black subjects sent by the British Crown to enforce British rule. The Belizean Maya community whose ancestors have tilled and inhabited the land for centuries experiences disbelief when they are told that a white monarch has sent a Black messenger to enforce rule merely by proxy. The Maya community henceforth experiences what some scholars might call the consciousness of the borderlands.[69] Survival for the borderlands subject, observes Gloria Anzaldúa, depends on developing tolerance for contradictions and ambiguity.[70] Only by remaining flexible do they survive the demands placed on them for continuing to reside on ancestral lands at the boundary. Rather than instructing his borderland community to fight change, the community's elder, Don Enrique, leads his people in camouflaging the autonomy they continue to have over their ancestral territory.

The ethnolinguistic heritage of Maya peoples comes into contact with European traditions during this poignant moment in the community's history: "I have heard German nuns trying to teach Maya children using a book written in English that they had to explain in Spanish," wrote a governor who visited the colony and observed children speaking "Ispamal"—a mix of English, Spanish, Yucatec Mayan languages, and German.[71] Queen Victoria, the empress, never meets her Maya subjects, but she does continue to send Afrodescendants from her Caribbean colonies to enforce her sovereign authority. The narrator of *Got seif de Cuin!* describes an elder's reaction to a second enforcer by proxy sent by the monarch:

> Muy de repente alzó la cara y vio a las pocas personas a su lado petrificadas, con la quijada colgando, viendo hacia arriba. Don Enrique volteó los ojos y se encontró cara a cara con un gigantesco caballo, sobre el cual estaba un hombre, negro como el carbón e inmenso como las chatonas que bailaban en las fiestas de la Virgen. . . . Dio dos pasos atrás y dándole una mirada cortés al negro de guantes blancos, se inclinó y dijo: "¡Viva África!"[72]

> (Suddenly he lifted his gaze and saw that the few people at his side were petrified, their jaws wide open, looking up. Don Enrique turned and found himself face to face with a giant horse, over which there was a man, black as coal and as immense as the *chatonas* [giant dolls displayed in the festivals of the Petén Province in Guatemala] that danced at the festival

of the Virgin. . . . He took two steps back and courteously looking up at the black man wearing white gloves, he bowed and said, "Long live Africa!")

The Black man on horseback wears white gloves. Known as Cabo Saxo among the Maya villagers, he "belongs" to the colonial order. He ushers in a cavalry of twenty more Black officials who all wear similar white uniforms with gold polished buttons. The narrative thus establishes a contrast between these broad-shouldered Black men on horseback who appear in an official capacity against the typical representations of Afrodescendants in previous narratives that do not incorporate them into the national fabric. The destinies of both the Maya people and the Afrodescendants at the Guatemalan/British Honduras border are posited as a direct consequence of colonialism, though the fate of both ancestral and contemporary Maya peoples is linked in the narrative.

Ruiz Puga then brings into focus the battle between the British and the Guatemalan government, which results in the cessation of free transit between Río Viejo on the British Honduran side of the river and Fayabón on the Guatemalan side. Travel was prohibited under penalty of imprisonment and entire Maya families were affected by this measure. As stipulated in previous scenes of the novel, the law is enforced by an authoritative Afrodescendant officer who possesses "the body of a bull and the eyes of a ram." When Maya leader Don Enrique presents a request to visit family across the river, the officer gruffly responds in Kriol: "Dis da di Polees Stayshan . . . if Ah ketch enybady di go da Fayabón true riva, Ah wahn haffu lak ahn op!"[73] In the established hierarchy of the colony and the future Creole nation, Afrodescendants sent to British Honduras to enforce the laws are subaltern subjects of intermediate rank whose mandate becomes oversight of the border between Anglophone and Hispanophone contexts. The situation that manifests what Gayatri Spivak highlights as the problem of granting a voice to the subaltern is twofold: it assumes cultural solidarity among heterogeneous peoples and depends on an intellectual to speak on their behalf.[74] The Afrodescendant characters in Ruiz Puga's novel transcend the clichés of representation by reinscribing themselves as enforcers of policy, even when that enforcement hinges on settler colonialism on Maya ancestral lands. The Afrodescendant subjects in this novel—like those who ascended the military ranks in nineteenth-century Central America as explained in the introduction—can speak and are heard. Afrodescendant subjects occupy an enfolded position that is generally only afforded to *mestizo/ladino* subjects in the Hispanophone narratives of Central America. These Afrodescendant subjects will become known as Creoles and will insist on their rights as a people, as they begin to question colonialism and drive the movement to independence. Important to *Got seif de Cuin!* is the observation that Guatemalan officials, particularly the Guatemalan president himself, put into motion a plan to divide Black and Indigenous peoples in order to conquer Mayan land on the river.

The emergence of two options for British Honduras on the eve of its coming into being as Belize brings about the possibility of multiple nations within one Belizean nation, a prospect that does not exist if they form an allegiance with Guatemala. As Jeff Browitt notes, "A different perspective between the Maya townspeople and independence leaders is forged."[75] As history shows, Maya communities along the Belize River were ultimately absorbed into the Belizean nation (instead of Guatemala) due to the fact that Creole governments interfered very little with Indigenous autonomy in areas outside of Belize City. *Got seif de Cuin!* gives readers a glimpse into the political rhetoric used by independence leaders to sway Indigenous opinion. In one scene, two Black men and one "mulatto" visit the community. In broken Spanish, they put forth their proposal: Independence, the lead orator claims, will bring about a peaceful revolution for the entire community. They will all become "comrades" and together they will embody the concepts of a popular movement, liberation, progress, and the rights of all citizens. He declares that Belize belongs to Black *and* Indigenous peoples, not to King George or any British governor, and that self-government will entail a peaceful life with brethren in Fayabón. In order to break the chains of colonialism, states the mulatto orator, Mayas must become Belizean. The independence movement promises to "do away with the lanterns and bring them electricity, create better jobs for the workers, a better life for their families . . . education for their children."[76] These promises bear the stamp of racial equality—made manifest in the Belizean flag they unveil before this Maya community. The flag itself visually represents the dissolution of the *negro*/Maya dividing line: "Un susurro de estupor brotó de la asistencia al ver el pabellón de dos yardas de largo con un colorido escudo al centro. . . . 'Aquí están los trabajadores . . .' explicó apuntando a las figuras de los dos hombres, uno de piel negra cargando un hacha sobre un hombro y otro de tez clara cargando un canalete, '. . . las razas de este pueblo viviendo y trabajando juntos para construir el nuevo país de las Américas.'"[77] (A whisper of astonishment erupted among the audience upon the sight of the flag with the colorful coat of arms at the center. . . . "Here are the workers . . ." he explained pointing at the figures of the two men, one with black skin and the other with a lighter face carrying a paddle, '. . . the races of this nation living and working together to build a new country in the Americas.") The flag is meant to represent the Belizean [Black and Maya] peoples' past and future, providing them with decolonial rhetoric upon which the new national imaginary is founded.

Don Justo, Don Enrique's successor as leader of the community, best summarizes Mayan weariness with divide and conquer tactics as imposed by colonialism. Undressing the nation to its bare economic framework, he wisely states: "Qué es eso que los indios por un la'o y los negros por acá y los más negros más allá . . . el fuerte se da el lujo de hablar de la pobreza y la justicia, y no nos damos cuenta de nuestra triste realidá." (What is this about the Indians on one side and Blacks over here and the Blackest over there . . . the strongest can have the luxury of speaking about poverty and justice while we do not realize our sad reality.)[78] Siding with Belize implied the possibility of self-governance while the new republic's laws are framed, with the ultimate goal of the community rising from the economic precarity to which it was subjected under colonial regimes. This was important because few other inter-isthmian policy issues garnered as much prolonged and unsettled debate in the region as the border dispute between Guatemala and Belize during the Cold War. While Guatemala had sought international support for its territorial claim to Belize as early as 1939, it pursued a more aggressive agenda for the disputed Mayan lands in the Cold War period. It claimed that Belize would become prey to "Communists" if it gained its independence. Although Great Britain had declared by 1961 that Belize could become independent whenever it chose to, the presence of Mayan communities in the disputed area halted negotiations. The United States, for its part, remained invested in Guatemala and considered said region to be "a potential base for spreading subversion" due to its proximity to Guatemala's Petén region and what could be easy Cuban access to Central America.[79] With Guatemala poised to cite "security" as its primary concern, Belize's bargaining chip was Great Britain's security forces, which would remain in the country in order to safeguard its "independence and territorial integrity."[80] As a result, Belize gained its independence and absorbed the Mayan lands and Maya peoples into its Creole fold.

Ruiz Puga observes that pre-independence Belizean political and literary discourses were meant to contribute to the task of consciousness-raising for political independence, yet post-independence texts are oriented toward the ethnolinguistic dynamics of the new multiethnic Belizean society.[81] Belizean Maya communities face linguistic, political, and cultural challenges in this context—those in the Cayo district remain in the borderlands between Guatemala and Belize, while those in the Toledo district are largely isolated from the rest of the country. As *Got seif de Cuin!* highlights, Afrodescendants were able to maintain their agency as a result of that *negro*/Maya dividing line. With the advantage of hindsight and a literary archive to consult, it is possible to imagine that Afrodescendants in the Tipú region on the edge of the Río Viejo/Belize River would have become classified as *mestizos* if the region had become part of Guatemala in those critical decades preceding Belizean independence. It is even clearer what would have become of the Mayas residing in the Toledo district, perilously close to Guatemala's Petén region where so many cases of genocide were committed from 1960 to 1996.[82] The complex *negro*/Maya fracture in this narrative thus highlights the importance of space, time, geography, linguistic variability in defining the coordinates and outcomes of Blackness in a divided Mesoamerican context.

Mesoamerican Departures

The Central American cultural sphere presumes that the five original nations of the isthmus were bound by Hispanicization, first through colonization and second after independence. As with the US intervention in banana zones and the Caribbean discussed in the previous chapter, Belizean independence shook the interior, the center core, of Central America. Its print media shifted focus to new ethnolinguistic dynamics that threatened national and regional belonging anew. Mesoamerica has been understood throughout its history as the cradle of Maya civilization and, in this scheme, Mayas have been appropriated in Hispanophone contexts for national imaginaries and the folkloric cultural products emerging therein. Meanwhile, Belize fought for recognition as a multiethnic and Belizean Kriol-speaking nation wherein a Mayan past was critical, though not the sole defining feature of the young republic. The preservation of the Mesoamerican imaginary through paternalism toward Maya peoples was a fundamental ideological consequence of *indigenismo*, resulting in the problematic positing of *mestizo/ladino* writers as rescuers and Maya peoples as dispossessed victims frozen in time. As Mesoamerica entered the final years of the twentieth century and the first two decades of the twenty-first, it would turn its intellectual gaze to a new group of dispossessed peoples within its borders. Central American intellectuals cast a fresh gaze on Blackness with the philosophy of *indigenismo* as a guide.

The nearly seventy years of authoritarianism in Central America from the 1930s forward affected all levels of society and left its mark on isthmian print media. For almost seven decades, intellectuals positioned themselves with the voice of the people and against the oligarchies, military elites, and foreign intervention. As in previous key historical moments experienced by the region, debates as to who belonged in the isthmus, who would fight for the isthmus, and who should "inherit" it in the post-authoritarian future carried through to the end of the century. In the process, the rhetoric of a Black/Indigenous divide emerged in Hispanophone countries while Belize emerged as an exception to the print and epistemological rules of the isthmus. The sharp divide between Indigeneity and Blackness that had been present since the colonial period was thus refashioned and put in place with the concerns of the time: the decades-long genocide of Maya peoples in Guatemala and the sovereignty and autonomy of Maya peoples in Belize.

The Central American cultural sphere stipulates that the nations of the isthmus are bound by the Hispanicization that occurred through colonization and after independence. Belizean independence threatened the Central American imaginary since, among other things, it shifted focus from the commonly accepted ethnolinguistic dynamics that have served as the point of departure for discussions of nationhood and belonging. Mesoamerica has been understood throughout its history as the cradle of Maya civilization, and in this scheme Maya communities have been appropriated by Hispanophone nations as the basis for national imaginaries and the cultural products emerging therein. Meanwhile, Belize fought for recognition as a multiethnic and Belizean Kriol-speaking nation wherein a Maya past was critical, though not the sole defining feature of the young republic. The matter of preserving the Mesoamerican imaginary by keeping Maya peoples "shielded" from processes that threaten to turn them into a new people has been one of the fundamental ideological bases of *indigenismo*. It is a problematic position that posits *mestizo/ladino* writers as rescuers and Maya peoples as dispossessed victims frozen in time. Writers like Ruiz Puga, however, are precursors of a masterplot that imagines both Indigeneity and Afrodescendance as a part of the decolonized national fabric, a matter to which I will return in chapter 5 of this book. The Central American sense of incompatibility between Blackness and Mayanness was cemented and heightened throughout the Cold War. Debates about the rightful belonging of these groups crossed into the literary sphere during the most critical moments in Central American history, but they continue to be salient in Guatemala and Belize where the territorial dispute continues to make headlines in 2022, twenty-seven years after the publication of *Got seif de Cuin!* and nearly one hundred years since Guatemala first sought to incorporate Belize's Maya peoples and their ancestral lands.[83]

Part 3
Caribbean/Caribe

Chapter 4

Multicultural Plots

It was during the Central American revolutionary movements of the 1970s and the 1980s that there emerged notable Afro-Central American writers at both extremes of the isthmus, including Belizean Zee Edgell and Panamanian Carlos "Cubena" Guillermo Wilson, who captured the Black experience in their texts and became prominent names in their respective nations.[1] In the unlikeliest of Central American nations, one that has promoted the myth of whiteness for centuries, there emerged an author who broke the code of whiteness like no other. Costa Rican writer Quince Duncan developed plots based on personal experiences of discrimination in his home country, leading a Costa Rican readership to open its eyes to Blackness and racial inequity in this Central American republic. As Dorothy Mosby writes in the introduction to her translation of his novels *Weathered Men* (1971) and *The Four Mirrors* (1973): "Before the tendency in Costa Rican intellectual circles in the late 1990s and 2000s to interrogate national myth, which identified the country's whiteness, Europeanness, and absence of a past history of chattel slavery as paramount to its exceptional economic progress and stable democratic institutions, Quince Duncan was among the vanguard of intellectuals who questioned the veracity of these notions and who engaged in conversations about the power of national belonging."[2] Duncan's fiction and nonfiction writing today continues to be activist oriented, as it advocates across a wide range of modalities for racial equality on national, regional, and global levels. As the most prolific Afro-Central American writer of the 1970s–1980s, Duncan wrote novels that opened the floor to discussions about pigmentocracy and racial apartheid in the Hispanophone countries of the isthmus. His work was connected, Mosby reminds us, to a post-Boom Afro-Latin American generation of writers that "called attention to issues of Blackness, identity, history, and the construction of nation, while also calling out the erasure and invisibility of Afrodescendants, the historical impact of slavery and capitalism, neoliberal economic policies, and imperialism in their creative fiction."[3]

Despite the rise of Black authors taking the print word in those decades, the cultural production that is most often associated with the period is grassroots media, including local radio and testimonial print.[4] This media transformed the communication channels of the isthmus, and the print matter circulating during those decades captured the rise of marginalized voices, especially those of popular classes, women, and Indigenous people.[5] As Laura Barbas-Rhoden observes, the print material from this period sheds light on "the politics behind divisions such as elite/popular and literature/orality, and they bring into focus gendered dichotomies like public/private, passive/active, desired/desiring, which have been inscribed in the story of the past."[6] Cultural production had become an ideological weapon, a solid critique of *History* and its role in the subjugation of "others," but the plots that circulated the most widely in the isthmus and in global consideration of Central American letters tackled gender content, as in the case of Gioconda Belli's writing, or literary questions of truth and testimony, as in the case of the mediations involved in transmitting Rigoberta Menchú's story. While certainly being produced, Black writing in Central America did not enjoy the same distribution and consumption patterns of "other" print in the isthmus.

Print media since the 1990s has reflected regional and global concerns about Central American topics previously considered "taboo," including racism.[7] Two specific trends dominated the dawn of the twenty-first century. Though it is beyond the scope of this chapter to explore the themes of "mainstream" print, this strand focused on a variety of issues in the private sphere that were once taboo topics of discussion in "polite society."[8] This cultural production runs the tropes of pain, pleasure, death, perversion, and abuse, among others. As Beatriz Cortez asserts, "Contemporary fiction suggests that it is not morality but passion that moves the individual beyond reason or his consideration of values of any type."[9] The second strand of Central American literary production is multicultural in nature, as it is driven by a desire to reenvision Central American social and geographic spaces as historically pluriethnic and optimistically inclusive futures. Print matter like that of Anacristina Rossi and Tatiana Lobo, examined in this chapter, represent a radical departure from constructions of the national subject—*mestizo* or white, male, middle class—and his national history. Focusing on Costa Rica, which was constructed as a beacon for human rights and stability for over a century, allows us to examine a situation that has had a ripple effect throughout Central America. Indeed, the texts I focus on in this last chapter seem to respond to a question posed by Quince Duncan and the historian Carlos Meléndez in the prologue to their 1972 groundbreaking essay, "El negro en Costa Rica":

> ¿Existe una política definida que tienda a disminuir las distancias socioculturales entre el negro y el resto de los costarricenses? Diríamos que no. Esto no es conveniente, de manera que en un futuro, lo más próximo posible, ojalá, habrá necesidad de tomar medidas más efectivas para contribuir a demoler las barreras interétnicas que nos separan de estos otros costarricenses nuevos, que tienen tanto derecho como nosotros a gozar de los beneficios de la ciudadanía.[10]

> (Does there exist a specific policy attempting to reduce the sociocultural distance between Blacks and the other Costa Ricans? We would say that there is not. This is not advantageous; therefore in the future, quite soon, hopefully, there will be a need to take more effective measures that can contribute to demolishing interethnic barriers that separate us from these new Costa Ricans who are just as entitled as we are to enjoy the benefits of citizenship.)

As these thinkers signaled in their essay, racial discrimination in Costa Rica would not be eradicated until racism both in interpersonal relationships *and* institutional racism were acknowledged nationwide. Nor could the work of dismantling these issues be properly advanced without the recognition of full citizenship for the Black members of the Costa Rican nation—who did not become de jure citizens until 1949 and in 1972 were still far from being recognized as de facto citizens.

The Central American multicultural print media that I examine in this chapter situate readers in the Central American Caribbean geographies and position the concept of "ethnic plurality" as a narrative goal. This reflects an intentional departure from colorblindness and an investment in thwarting the institutional racism that was embedded in Hispanophone Central American literary circles since the region began to develop its regional canon. I follow this discussion with a focus on the manner in which these narratives bring readers from the loci of Central Americanness (the Pacific Coast) to Black sites along the Caribbean coast that enchant the reader/traveler with descriptions of ethnic and natural beauty. While often problematic for their exoticism, they establish a literary sensibility that dialogues with the politics of multiculturalism that Costa Rica espoused in the last years of the twentieth century. The texts take what they purport to be quintessentially ethnic ways of being, seeing, and knowing in order to show the cracks and crevices of the hegemonic Central American regional imaginary that has historically excluded "others." While by no means achieving the status of a radical masterplot to overthrow previous works, these novels did overtly pair themselves with multiculturalist policies developed in the political sphere. The chapter thus concludes with a discussion of the globally circulated discourse of multiculturalism and cultural difference that has put institutional racism under the microscope. With its insistence on political correctness, the print ushers in the rhetoric that highlights white/*mestizo* privilege in the region while making it possible to insist on the plurifaceted nature of Central American experience. What better place, then, to begin investigating this ideological turn than Costa Rica, a country known outside of its borders as a tranquil, culturally hegemonic nation.

A Neoliberal Trend in Practice

Like the novels explored in chapters 2 and 3, the novels examined here carry their reader over the large, fertile Central Plateau—a tectonic depression over which the most important cities in the country have been raised. Costa Rica attracted less European immigration after independence than it had hoped but, starting with the building of the railroad to the Caribbean coast in the 1870s, hundreds of Chinese and thousands of Afro-Caribbean laborers entered the country.[11] Since then, these groups have lived outside the Central Valley, where the majority of the Costa Rican population—the national electorate—lives.[12] Demographic and political imbalance, accentuated by ethnic difference, meant that the Central Valley also received a disproportionate amount of public spending during the twentieth century.

Writing about sites outside of the Central Valley, the cradle of what has been improperly termed "Costa Rican culture," is a political maneuver.

In the afterword to *Limón Blues*, Anacristina Rossi states her desire to reveal to the reader "un mundo que, por la barrera del idioma y la incomprensión y el racismo costarricense, quedó fuera del acervo cultural del país" (a world that, due to language barriers, misunderstanding and Costa Rican racism, remained outside the cultural heritage of the country).[13] Meanwhile, Tatiana Lobo asserts in a 2002 interview that her intent was to "dejar testimonio de cómo la cultura dominante está destruyendo la cultura de los pueblos del Caribe costarricense. . . . Con su desaparición el país está perdiendo la maravillosa posibilidad de diversificar la cultura de su territorio y esto nos empobrece a todos"[14] (leave testimony of how the dominant culture is destroying the communities of Costa Rican Caribbean. . . . With their disappearance, this country is losing the marvelous possibility of diversifying the culture of its territory and this impoverishes all of us). Following Abril Trigo's critiques of multiculturalism in Latin American cultural production,[15] these narratives highlight print media's intimate dance with neoliberal approaches to the exclusion of Black peoples throughout the hemisphere. Like the *proyectos de rescate cultural* that have been promoted by the Ministries of Culture and the Ministries of Tourism across Central America since the postwar (1979–present) period, however, the novels continue to reflect activities created for teaching outsiders.

Costa Rica's Black Heritage Festival, for example, developed as a result of the movement headed by the Teacher's Union in 1980 to establish August 31st as the "Día Nacional de la Persona Negra y la Cultura Afrocostarricense" on the school calendar; this was affirmed by Decree No. 11938, signed by then president Rodrigo Carazo.[16] After three decades of annual festivities, the Legislative Assembly voted on March 28, 2011, to make this date an official national holiday. Speaking on behalf of her Limón constituents, who have turned the event into a highly anticipated and well-organized event attracting tourists from Central America and the Caribbean, Deputy Elibeth Venegas stated that Afro–Costa Rican culture "ha tenido un impacto positivo en nuestro quehacer diario, porque hemos heredado su música, su comida, su ritmo y su alegría. . . . No hemos dejado de aprender de sus grandes valores y de destacados aportes en distintos ámbitos de la vida nacional. Esta iniciativa, va a permitir que el valor de la festividad se traslade a todos los centros educativos y sociedad en general, impulsando así el valor de la contribución de esta hermosa cultura"[17] (has had a positive impact on our daily lives, because we have inherited its music, cuisine, rhythm and happiness. We have not ceased to learn from its great values and distinguished contributions to national life. This initiative, will allow the value of the celebration to be transplanted to all the educational and social centers in general, propelling the value of the contribution of that beautiful culture). While these words are specifically relevant to the newly implemented law, they also confirm that the locus of enunciation for diversity and inclusion has shifted from popular sectors to the government. Moreover, forces external to the nation-state have tinged political rhetoric in the thirty years between the clamor for an initiative and the enactment of a law that validates Black experience in Costa Rica. I am referring here to the discourses of human rights ushered in by United Nations involvement in the peace processes of neighboring countries, the increasing NGOization that raised the status of women's groups and ethnic coalitions and a general call for governmental accountability to marginalized communities. In short, these past three decades mark the advent of a conceptualization of pluralistic Central American societies that appeals to both governments and civil society.

"Fostering cultural diversity, intercultural dialogue and a culture of peace" is one of the overarching objectives of the United Nations Educational, Scientific and Cultural Organization (UNESCO). Its mission is to create the conditions that foster the dialogue necessary to create the conditions for a dialogue through which the world can achieve "global visions of sustainable development encompassing observance of human rights, mutual respect and the alleviation of poverty."[18] The San José, Costa Rica field office is the responsible party for six of the seven Central American countries (the notable exception being Belize, which is under direction of the Kingston, Jamaica, office) and as such is the beacon that is expected to steer this critical dialogue in the direction best aimed to achieve the aforementioned goals and objectives. It is an active office that regularly posts on its website the initiatives that best reflect its adherence to the UN-established areas of greatest concern. On March 11, 2011, the field office announced a strategic plan between UNESCO and the Consejo Regional Autónomo del Atlántico Norte (CRAAN) to work collaboratively to bring about the development of six Afrodescendant and Indigenous communities in the country's Caribbean coast. Like the March 28, 2011, law enacted by Costa Rican legislators, these two initiatives are not coincidental. The UN General Assembly established 2011 as the

International Year for People of African Descent. This declaration is symbolically important in its aim to strengthen national, regional, and international cooperation so that Afrodescendants may attain "full enjoyment of economic, cultural, social, civil and political rights, their participation and integration in all political, economic, social and cultural aspects of society, and the promotion of a greater knowledge of and respect for their diverse heritage and culture."[19] A reversal of discriminatory practices dating back millennia is not expected in 365 days; what is anticipated is a string of "best practices" that can be displayed as exemplary strategies by those who advocate, as the United Nations does, for cultural rights and dignity of all peoples.

In the language used by the United Nations and the international community, "best practices" are defined as examples of successful initiatives that have a demonstrable and tangible impact on improving people's quality of life; are the result of effective partnerships between the public, private, and civic sectors of society; and are socially, economically, and environmentally sustainable. Furthermore, they are promoted and used as a means of improving public policy based on what works; raising awareness of decision-makers at all levels of the public of potential solutions to common social, economic, and environmental problems; and, sharing and transferring knowledge, expertise, and experience through networks and learning. I'd like to close with the proposition that the novels studied here, *Calypso* and *Limón Blues*, read like the literary blueprints for the "best practices" to be taken in the era of globalization in Central America. They clearly predate the 2011 International Year for People of African Descent, but they bear the signature stamp of the cultural clauses of the Universal Declaration of Human Rights and other international covenants that were designed to induce government and civil society to bring an end to discrimination. These novels endeavor to raise awareness about the historical injustices committed against Black peoples in the "Switzerland of Central America," to raise awareness of the challenges they continue to face, and to highlight the community's points of pride that can be shared with Costa Rican society at large.

West Indians were fully aware that they were third-class citizens in every engagement with white Costa Ricans. They responded by establishing a chapter of the UNIA (Universal Negro Improvement Association)[20] on Costa Rican soil, promoting economic self-sufficiency, and developing a literary/artistic tradition that promoted the notion of a unified Black world. Santiago Valencia Chalá observes that more than in any other

Central American country, West Indians in Costa Rica were politically mobilized since their arrival, establishing cooperatives and political organizations that still exist today. This is the world that Anacristina Rossi fictionalizes in the novel *Limón Blues* (2002). Set in Costa Rica's Limón Province in 1904, the narrative focuses on a Black couple, Orlandus and Irene, who meet at the height of Marcus Garvey's UNIA movement and raise their three children in Limón. As the years pass, Irene realizes that her children suffer from a lack of opportunities in their small community on the coast and that they must migrate to San José, where they will certainly be exposed to flagrant racism. In this way, the novel chronicles multiple generations of West Indians in Costa Rica. The novel itself is based on an arsenal of documents that track West Indians in Limón from 1876 to the early 2000s, thereby questioning what it means to be Costa Rican in the twenty-first century. Sofia Kerns observes that the novel becomes a space where "West Indians and female subalterns are represented in their different logics and motives but tied together by their political rebellion and empowered by their solidarity, thus undermining the myth of a classless, single-race, and strictly heterosexual nation."[21] As such, it details the Black community's desire for entry in the political sphere—as evidenced in Black newspapers that circulated in Limón—while effectuating a historical reevaluation of Costa Rican whiteness narrative.

The novel tracks the structural racism that restricted the earliest West Indian immigrants to an economically blighted Port Limón. The matter is solidly manifested when Orlandus recalls his mother Nanah's impressions of Limón when she arrived with her husband in 1876. They flee from starvation in Jamaica only to step foot on a dock that smells of urine and vomit. Nanah is struck by her new position in this foreign country and gazes first out to sea imagining her Jamaican homeland and then at the six rows of mountains behind the bay that mark the boundary between Limón Province and the "interior." Ultimately, the deplorable conditions related to railroad work lead to the couple's decision to return to Jamaica.[22] After all, the railroad seemed to be a "duppie factory" that claimed the lives of one man for every wooden railroad tie that was laid, a situation that was aggravated by the incidence of yellow fever to which the men were exposed. Years later, the possibility of owning a private parcel of land on which to harvest bananas for private profit lures a new wave of immigrants back to Costa Rica. Convinced that a bright future lurks on the horizon for the family, Nanah urges her teenage son, Orlandus, to try his luck in Limón. These opening chapters put in place a matrix

Multicultural Plots | 133

indispensable for reading the rest of the novel, highlighting the push-pull factors that caused two waves of immigrants to arrive on hostile Costa Rican shores. Through a plot that interweaves the voices of men and women in the community, the remainder of *Limón Blues* addresses the Costa Rican government's abuse of power and complicity in taking private parcels of land away from Black owners. Orlandus, in tandem with the reader, learns about historical figures like Minor C. Keith[23] and Marcus Garvey.

The voice of the narrator is often the voice of historical record: "La United Fruit tenía una fuerte relación con Minor C. Keith, la Northern Railways, el Ferrocarril de Costa Rica, el capataz yanqui del muelle metálico, la electricidad, el teléfono, el telégrafo, los cincuenta vapores de la Gran Flota Blanca, los transatlánticos de la Elders & Fyffes y muchas otras cosas, sucesos y empresas."[24] (United Fruit had a strong relationship to Minor C. Keith, the Northern Railways, the Railway of Costa Rica, the Yankee foreman on the metallic dock, electricity, telephone, telegraph, the fifty steamers of the Great White Fleet, the Elders & Fyffes liners, and many other things, happenings, and businesses.) Orlandus remains unassuming and *un*judgmental, becoming a vehicle through which the reader learns new details in the story of Costa Rican capitalism. Orlandus's character is much more complex than it might appear at first blush, however. Through the same circuits that taught him about Costa Rica, he learns about Marcus Garvey, who is becoming increasingly known as "Black Moses," leading his people out of the desert and into the promised land. A moving fictional letter addressed to Orlandus conveys the philosophy of the UNIA, founded by Garvey himself:

> Sabe que viví en Panamá y que conocí Honduras, Nicaragua y Guatemala. Ahora quiero contarle que llegué hasta Ecuador. Pasé por Colombia y por Venezuela. Y en todos esos lugares yo vi lo mismo: los negros somos el fondo, la hez, no sabemos organizarnos duramente y no tenemos líderes. Cuando ya no soportamos más la injusticia, hacemos incendios. Entonces nos persiguen y nos martirizan. Y viendo todo eso yo me pregunté: ¿Dónde está el Gobierno del Hombre Negro? ¿Dónde su Reino, su Presidente, su País, su Embajador, su Ejército, su Fuerza Marina, sus hombres de grandes negocios? No pude encontrarlos y entonces declaré: Yo voy a tratar de que existan.[25]

(You know I lived in Panama and that I visited Honduras, Nicaragua, and Guatemala. Now I want to tell you that I have traveled all the way to Ecuador. I passed through Colombia and Venezuela. And in all those places, I saw the same thing: we Blacks are at the bottom, scum, we do not know how to organize ourselves strongly and we do not have leaders. When we can no longer stand injustice, we set fires. Then they chase us and torment us. And seeing all this, I asked myself: Where is the Black Man's Government? Where is his Kingdom, his Country, his Armed Forces, his Navy, his businessmen? I couldn't find them and so I declared: I will try to make them exist.)

The missive is important. That Garvey recognizes Black communities across Latin America adds to his position as a thinker with keen knowledge about an experience shared by Black peoples in this hemisphere and beyond. The letter is inspired by documents written and speeches given by Garvey himself. Under his leadership, the UNIA supported many Black entrepreneurial projects, some of which are likewise established in Limón: Black businesses, Black churches and Black schools, Black organizations like the African Legion, Explorers, and the Black Cross Nurses, as well as a line of steamships known as the Black Star Line that bore the names of heroes like Frederick Douglass. After becoming part of the UNIA fold, the novel reveals, Limón rises as a Black town that demands racial and economic justice.

The Costa Rican government was far from sympathetic. In a letter dated December 23, 1919—lines of which are reproduced in the novel—the Costa Rican government declared that the UNIA was "a Universal Association that attempted to organize the entire Black race in the world for anarchist purposes."[26] The threat was in the attitude taken by UNIA members who single-handedly financed the association's activities and organizations of the movement. The threat was also in the bourgeoning pride in Afrodescendance expressed by members and expressed in the novel through an epigraph quoting Garvey: "So down the line of history we come. Black, courtly, courageous and handsome." Orlandus and his wife Irene, fictional characters representing the millions of UNIA members, dedicate their life and earnings to the movement. The intertextuality of *Limon Blues*, marked by its incorporation of fragments from print media published and remitted by key figures, highlights the importance of this critical historical period for the Black peoples of the province. Importantly, the use of primary documents challenges the claims made by nationalist historians who have catalogued the UNIA as an anti–Costa Rican association and vindicates the association. Through intertextuality, the reader is able to gauge the historical importance and transcontinental impact of the association.

While the novel's intertextuality results in a critique of early twentieth-century nationalism, it nevertheless invests in that national pride when it develops its dénouement on the critique of the UNIA's position on repatriation to Africa. These moments depend on the use of Irene's voice as motivator to emotionally divest from the UNIA and invest energy instead in Costa Rica: "Irene me hizo notar que en sus discursos Garvey hablaba mucho de la repatriación a Liberia y la liberación del África, y poco de cómo conseguir aquí y ahora una vida mejor. Otros también lo notaron, y en una de las últimas reuniones se formó una delegación para preguntarle qué había obtenido de Presidente Acosta relativo a que se les diera a los negros mayores derechos en Costa Rica."[27] (Irene made me realize that in his speeches, Garvey spoke a lot about repatriation to Liberia and African liberation, but little about how to obtain a better life here and now. Others also noticed it, and in the last meetings we organized a delegation to ask him what he had obtained from President Acosta with regard to giving blacks more rights in Costa Rica.) The transition from a diasporic, transnational Black identity to a Costa Rican–anchored Black identity is very direct in the preceding quote. It brings to bear the emerging consciousness of a population that saw their checkmate situation in Costa Rica, while forgoing the vision of a better future in Africa. Equally relevant to this aspect of the narrative is that several characters, including Irene and the editor of the former Black newspaper in Limon openly discuss Costa Rican racism: "Prosperaríamos si no nos discriminaran. Costa Rica nos gusta, es tranquilo, hay trabajo, hay tierra; pero no nos permiten ser propietarios; los hijos nuestros nacidos aquí no son considerados costarricenses; no ven con buenos ojos que vayamos a la capital ni a las otras comarcas; además nos insultan—maifrenes, chumecos—y aquí mismo en Port Limón ahora nos prohíben entrar en casi todos los hoteles, restaurantes y balnearios. Eso no es vida?"[28] (We would prosper if they did not discriminate against us. We like Costa Rica, it's peaceful, there's work, there's land; but they do not allow us to become landowners; our children born here are not considered Costa Rican; they don't think well of us going to the capital or other towns; besides, they insult us—calling us *maifrenes* and chumecos—and even here in Port Limón we are prohibited from entering almost all the hotels, restaurants, and swimming holes. What kind of life is that?) This pivotal exchange highlights the existence of geographic apartheid. Indeed, Edwin Zalas Zamorra affirms that Afrodescendants from the Caribbean coast were not allowed in Costa Rica's Central Valley; a law that was not repealed until 1949 explicitly prohibited the West Indian population from crossing Turrialba, a town in the Caribbean coast located sixty miles from the Central Plateau.[29] Speaking as an insider of the Central Valley, this critic explains that the *meseteño* has long conceived of the Black Caribbean subject as "a lustful vagabond, given to vice and unable to produce anything of value. Associated, additionally, with lack of hygiene and inclined to evil for no other reason than the color of his skin."[30] Per *Limón Blues*, Marcus Garvey's movement leads Black Costa Ricans to assess the domestic policies that have long excised them from the national imaginary as citizens of equal value. It is influential in demonstrating to them that they must fight for their visibility within Costa Rica's borders.

Orlandus dies in the last pages of the novel, leaving Irene a widow with three young children. She becomes the bridge between the first-generation West Indian immigrants who held steadfastly to their identities as members of the British commonwealth and their Costa Rican–born children. When their opportunity to claim citizenship emerges, Irene carries the symbolic burden of deciding what she will teach her children. A friend insists that she consider the protection that such a document will provide them all: "Será tu única defensa cuando no te dejen entrar a un cine o subirte a un autobús, o cuando alguien te insulte en la calle. En esta época de nacionalismos, al que no tenga un estado bajo el cual ampararse le puede ir muy mal." (It will be your only defense when they do not let you enter a movie theater or board a bus, or when someone insults you on the street. In this nationalist period, she who does not have a state to shelter her can find herself in a terrible situation.)[31] Irene accepts the importance of the document as uncontestable proof that, despite being an Afrodescendant, she belongs within the borders of the nation. These final moments evidence the political aspects of Black mothering that, as Dawn Marie Dow explains, bring to bear the painful fact of being unable to protect Black children from the viciousness of racism as they grow into adults.[32] Within the novel, discourse commands the next generation's smooth integration—legal and imaginary—into the nation. As

Irene's friend states, lightly code-switching between English and Spanish, with regard to her children:

> Look at me, I'm a staunch Britisher, y ese orgullo nadie jamás me lo quitará. Tenemos nuestras tradiciones, organizamos nuestros debates con emoción sabiéndonos herederos de Cambridge y Oxford. We are Britishers, decimos inflando el pecho cuando un costarricense nos humilla, y nos sabemos superiores a ellos en refinamiento. Pero tu hijo, ¿qué posee? Un idioma que no le sirve en esta república, más bien le impide integrarse, un idioma que no representa su nacionalidad porque él ya no es británico por más que quiera. Por esa razón esos golfos se vengan en el inglés, envileciéndolo, usándolo para decir palabrotas. [Hay algunos que] aman el inglés y se identifican con los valores de sus padres. Yo sólo me pregunto qué futuro tienen en esta república.[33]

> (Look at me, I'm a staunch Britisher, and no one will ever take that pride away from me. We have our traditions; we organize our own debates with the passionate certainty that we are inheritors of Cambridge and Oxford. We are Britishers, we say swelling our chests when a Costa Rican insults us, and we know ourselves to be superior to them in refinement. But your son, what does he possess? A language that does not help him in this republic, it actually keeps him from integrating himself, a language that that does not represent his nationality because he is no longer British, as much as he may want to be. That is why those Gulf people avenge themselves, vilifying him, using him to say bad words. [There are some young people who] love English and identify with their parents' values. I only ask myself what future they have in this republic.)

The novel closes with the certainty that Irene should leave Limón to seek better opportunities in San José, but that she should do so with passports in hand for herself and her children. There is no pretense of this being a solution to the challenge of belonging, but there is a yearning to make the transition smoother. While the early parts of the novel might have been archival-heavy in their intertextual engagements with historical records, the final pages of the novel resuscitate nationalism. As a pragmatic choice, it is far from the romantic nationalism of Costa Rican foundational narratives. However, the poignant conversation between Irene and her friend reminds readers that maternal figures in literary discourses serve an important function, particularly when what is at stake reconfigures the image of a nation as properly multicultural.

Black in the Tropics

Tatiana Lobo's *Calypso* (1996) situates the reader away from the British-influenced town of Port Limón, which has become iconic due to its importance for Afro–Costa Rican history. Enslavement, rather than migration, is at the crux of this novel and it is made explicitly clear in the epigraph that explains the title: "Calypso: ritmo caribeño que narra una historia. Se origina en los informativos clandestinos que los esclavos solían cantar y bailar para comunicarse las noticias del día y las maldades del amo." (Calypso: Caribbean rhythm that narrates a story. Its origins are the clandestine communications of slaves who would sing and dance to share with each other the day's news and the evils of their master.) The setting is a fictional fishing village in Parima Bay, and its protagonists are three generations of women from the same family who experience the changes brought about by the twentieth century in their hometown. The principal characters are Amanda, Eudora, and Matilda, though their female relatives are also critical to the narrative as it moves from 1941 to the 1990s. In the span of time that covers the lives of the principal female characters, roads are built leading to the town, villagers introduce eggs into their diet and acquire radios, electricity, and running water—all which were available to Costa Ricans in the interior of the country long before they were introduced in the Caribbean coast. As Werner Mackenbach observes, the novel could be criticized for its heavy reliance on one of the grand archetypes of Latin American literature by recurring all too often to a Macondoized portrayal fitted to a Costa Rican tropical landscape. Yet, he continues, Lobo seems to achieve a correct metaphor of the Caribbean in the era of "postcolonial colonialism." The enchantment of the Caribbean continues to be veiled.[34] Against the destructive force of "progress" that threatens to engulf Parima Bay, the women in *Calypso* maintain a connection to paradisiacal nature that is unquestioned and is forever theirs to safeguard.

Despite its marked differences with *Limón Blues*, *Calypso* shares with the first novel a concern with challenging the oft-repeated Costa Rican narrative of Costa Rican whiteness. Like *Limón Blues*, it takes its readers on a voyage to what is constructed as a thoroughly mythical and almost forgotten Black homeland on the Caribbean coast.³⁵ *Calypso* and *Limón* are both invested in the discourse of multiculturalism, and especially in taking the Costa Rican outsider-reader out of their comfort zone in order to deconstruct and reassemble the Costa Rican collective memory. Maurice Halbwachs's observation, "while the collective memory endures and draws strength from its base in a coherent body of people, it is individuals as group members who remember," is central in the expectations about reader reception.³⁶ The texts evidence the goal of reconciliation, which is understood here in the same terms established by contemporary international organizations: reconciliation is a "process through which a society moves from a divided past into a shared future."³⁷ To bring Black peoples into the Costa Rican fold, these contemporary narratives written by outsiders scavenge the Caribbean coast to symbolically rescue Black *his*tories from oblivion and integrate them into the hegemonic national imaginary.

Nature and beauty go hand in hand in the descriptions of the Black women in both novels, though the lack of historical documents informing *Calypso* results in markedly more reductive descriptions of tropical Black femininity. An association with Blackness, women, and mystical knowledge is present in the first descriptions of Amanda Scarlet, the point of origin for the matrilineal line: "Obra perfecta de la naturaleza, todas las artes del África negra se habían puesto de acuerdo en definitivo consenso: Amanda Scarlet era una estatuilla de Dogón, una pieza de madera de Yoruba, una escultura de Bambara, un marfil de Nigeria, estilizada tinaja de Manbetu, talla de Baulé, bronce de Benin, barro de Dahome." (Perfect work of nature, all the arts of Black Africa had reached a definitive consensus: Amanda Scarlet was a tiny Dogon statue, Yoruba wood, a Bambara sculpture, Nigerian ivory, a stylized earthenware jar from Manbetu, a Baulé carving, Benin bronze, Dahome clay.)³⁸ Should a Black female character in the story not be physically beautiful, her command of nature envelops the reader in total rapture. In one scene, for instance, the reader observes Stella, the sole albino in the family, repeat incantations that lead hundreds of butterflies to encircle her body in the night:

Morpho peleides limpida. Morpho theseres aquarius. Morpho peleides marinita. Morpho poliphemus catarina. Cantaba.

Entonces, desde el bastón central, un resplandor de plata se extendía dulcemente hasta alcanzar los pies descalzos que danzaban siguiendo la ruta de un círculo invisible. . . . Un tupido enjambre de delicados insectos de alas azules envolvía a la albina ocultando su fealdad ante los rayos del astro madre, hasta que ella se cansaba de danzar y entonces las mariposas espectrales se alejaban por el camino de la luna entre los árboles nacarados de placer."[39]

(Morpho peleides limpida. Morpho theseres aquarius. Morpho peleides marinita. Morpho poliphemus catarina. She sang. Then, starting from the cane in the center, a silver splendor extended sweetly until it reached her bare feet that danced following the route of an invisible circle. . . . A dense swarm of the delicate insects with blue wings encircled the albino woman, concealing her ugliness before the rays of the astral mother until she tired of dancing and then the spectral butterflies distanced themselves along the path of the moon between the trees pearled with pleasure.)

Parima Bay is far, not only in terms of distance but also culturally, from Costa Rica's Central Valley, the cradle of nationhood and the symbolic region of fertile coffee plantations. The novel's style does not assume common ground with Black characters. Rather, it cultivates an exoticist lens as readers traverse space and time in order to find themselves in Black tropical paradise where mystical Black women are links to past, present, and future.

Black women are likewise associated with syncretic West African religion and ritual. Like Emily, Amanda's sister-in-law, some are born with the gift of seeing spirits, "dopis." The use of Twi, a language spoken in the Ivory and Gold Coasts, to name the spirits of the dead with whom these women communicate connects them to a heritage unknown to the reader. The connection is naturalized to the extent that, without italics or an explanation to accompany the use of the term, the reader too acquires the terms that have passed into daily use among these strong Black women who have inherited a mystical tradition. In this context, the women become important agents of communication with the spirit world. They are part of a genealogy of women who reside on the Costa Rican Caribbean coast and bear the responsibility of ensuring the spiritual teachings of a world that cannot be learned in the confines of a schoolhouse. As Stella, the elder that introduces Eudora to the spirit world, reminds her initiate: "If one intends it, the world changes and can be made different at will; losing oneself is enough to be able to see a dopi and the things that are most transparent."[40] The narrative marks a Manichean comparison between Black mysticism and the sterile lessons on science, civics, and British grammar that Black children were forced to repeat until their "lazy local diction acquired rigidity and fitted tightly according to the Queen's corset."[41] *Calypso* manifests that Black characters' devotion to the spirit world cannot be carried out in any other place than the Caribbean coastal community they inhabit. In line with narratives that work with the concept of Black women's genealogies, most of the female characters in *Calypso* do not express any desire to leave their beloved Caribbean Sea for the Costa Rican Central Valley and its Pacific Ocean. The risk of cultural loss hangs over any Black character who considers leaving the community.

Eudora, for example, does leave, but she returns with the message that those in Parima Bay should join the Costa Rican national fold: "Hay que integrarse al país, hay que aprender el español, no podemos vivir como mi padre, siempre soñando con volver a Jamaica." (You have to become integrated in the country, you have to learn Spanish, we can't go on living like my father, always dreaming of returning to Jamaica.)[42] She, like others her age, witnessed the construction of a highway to connect Parima Bay to the rest of the country. With time, it took vacationers to virgin Caribbean beaches, cricket fields became soccer fields, the picture of the Costa Rican president replaced the image of Queen Victoria, and electricity finally lit the small homes in Parima Bay. The advent of electricity brought with it great changes to the landscape and to the inhabitants' everyday life: "Y como había sucedido con la inauguración del camino, la llegada triunfal de la luz eléctrica estuvo amenizada con encendidos discursos atiborrados de propaganda al gobierno.... Parima Bay perdía en encanto lo que ganaba en progreso." (And just as it had happened with the inauguration of the road, the triumphant arrival of electricity was made all the more pleasant with passionate speeches stuffed with government propaganda.... Parima Bay lost as much enchantment as it gained progress.)[43] While Eudora and others relished the changes, others continued to light their candles and kerosene lamps in defiance of the "progress" and intrusions brought to Parima Bay.

Calypso assures readers that the town will never be divorced from its mystical roots despite the changes it experiences. Even as drug trafficking and ecotourism assault their tropical paradise, the people of

Parima Bay remain firmly connected to the traditions and beliefs that distinguish them from Costa Ricans in the Central Valley. For Matilda—the last young woman in a long line of mystical women—the Caribbean Sea itself is what makes life and adventure possible. Not only does she delight in fishing for lobsters in these waters, her many trips out to sea are a measure of the degree to which she has matured. The most significant of these trips occurs on the heels of her step-grandfather's passing: "Matilda creció en ese viaje, maduró entre el oleaje encabritado, el mar fue todo suyo. El viento, el sol y el agua, castigaron su piel en lo que esta tenía de culpa por seguir viviendo. El abuelo y la araña Anansi la acompañaron hasta límites que jamás creyó alcanzar, jugando peligrosamente entre las aletas de tiburones, la mantelerías de las mantarrayas y los saltos de los delfines. Regresó agotada, las lágrimas confundidas con la sal, el corazón alivianado."[44] (Matilda grew up on that trip, matured among the swell of furious waves, the sea was all hers. The wind, the sun and the water, punished her body for fault in continuing to live. Her grandfather and Anansi the spider accompanied her until she reached limits that she had never dreamed of reaching, dangerously playing among the shark fins, the stingrays and the leaps of the dolphins. When she returned, she was exhausted, her tears confused with the salt, her heart light.) The ocean becomes a powerful metaphor for freedom as the young girl is released from the pain of irreplaceable loss by the furious waves and the creatures that circle around her. Parima Bay itself shields her from the unwanted "progress" occurring at an accelerated rate elsewhere in Costa Rica. The village is idealized as the only space in the country where she and other Black women can lead fulfilling lives. The novel's essentialist feminist approach thus privileges Afro–Costa Rican women's experience, though it circumscribes them within a space that must be forever marginal to protect its people. Like *Limón Blues*, its multiculturalist approach depends on the alignment of Blackness to the Caribbean coast. The socioeconomic specificities of both novels take the reader from the core of Costa Ricanness to Black times and Black places in the tropics, where the political and literary rhetoric meet in order to determine the Afro–Costa Rican diaspora's rightful place in the national imaginary.

Coda on the "Switzerland of Central America"

A peasant economy emerged in the early eighteenth century in Costa Rica's Central Valley as families of agriculturalists rose in social status to become an exclusive social group in the area. Coffee bean cultivation was initially concentrated around San José, but it rapidly extended to other areas of the interior. Ultimately, it "bent the entire country to its will," and between 1850 and 1890, coffee sales accounted for almost 90 percent of the country's export earnings.[45] Coffee transformed the image of the nation from a peasant economy to a transnational trader, and it quickly became the product most intimately tied to its future, leaving outside the national imaginary the citizens who were not part of coffee production. European immigrants flooded Costa Rica's gates in order to take part in the boom and establish themselves among the coffee elites concentrated in the Central Valley.[46] Due to its perceived ethnically homogenous white population, as well as its professed stability and its economic promise, Costa Rica was heralded the "Switzerland of Central America."

As the most exported of its legends, "whiteness" has its foundation in the patterns of colonial rule and neocolonial ventures in investment capitalism. Travelers to Costa Rica corroborated the myth of whiteness that circulated beyond Costa Rica's borders. Writing in 1844, a Scotsman named Glasgow Dunlop stated, "The inhabitants of the state of Costa Rica are almost all white, having not mixed with Indians as has been the case in other parts of Spanish America, and the few of color have arrived without a doubt from neighboring states."[47] So often was the narrative of whiteness diffused and repeated that Costa Rica became known for "its natural beauty, the mystical qualities of its coffee, the abolition of its armed forces, and its demographic stability in a region of political violence," as Dorothy Mosby affirms.[48] As observed in chapter 2 of this book, print media were used in the early twentieth century to stress the ethnic homogeneity of Costa Rica. The response was as xenophobic as it was racist, given the plethora of texts published in response to the waves of immigrants arriving in Costa Rica from Jamaica and elsewhere in the Caribbean. An anonymous petition to the Costa Rican Congress in 1932 stated:

> I believe it is a principle of true nationalism that the companies that come to extract the juice from our land should be imposed on to respect and even adopt our language. The congress should begin to pay attention to this Jamaican race that is not only the owners of the Atlantic region but is also invading the interior of the country without anyone concerning ourselves with the fact, and when they do pay attention to it, it will be too late. Blacks, Chinese, Polacks [Eastern European

Jews], Coolies [South Asians], and all manner of undesirable scum who get thrown out of other countries or are kept out enter and exit our borders like it's nothing without the authorities showing any interest, and this has worsened the agonizing situation of workers like us.[49]

The author of the letter identified himself as an outraged citizen, aghast that the United Fruit Company would provide information to their Black workers as to the legal means of acquiring naturalized citizenship, for this would allow them to present themselves—"toda la negrada"—as Costa Ricans on equal footing with white Costa Ricans.

Today, such flagrant racism is unacceptable in political and intellectual circles alike. The multiculturalism espoused by countries like Costa Rica turns instead to pedagogical approaches and, in some instances, reductive essentialist representations of ethnic and racial others. Slavoj Žižek argues that liberal multiculturalism and its politically correct premise of respecting difference is hegemonic, since subjects continue to be absorbed into the homogenizing power of multinational capital despite the discourse that pretends otherwise.[50] The case of Central America brings to bear a region-specific approach to the integration of difference that has become an essential element of discourse since the Peace Accords were signed in Guatemala, El Salvador, and Nicaragua. Something akin to "peace" was institutionalized in that decade and proof of it was the ratification of the Dominican Republic–Central American Free Trade Agreement on July 28, 2005, and its final approval by Costa Rica on October 7, 2007. The scale of economic and cultural grievances arguably disturbs the notion of democratization that gives international credibility and ideological legitimacy to neoliberal policies, but this monumental agreement across the isthmus seems to gloss the social ruptures that it may have aggravated.

As William I. Robinson has indicated, the isthmus's cultural production in this period is faced with the "search for viable formulas of social and economic democratization, political empowerment and the construction of a counter-hegemony under new conditions of global capitalism."[51] Whereas Central America has consistently relied on international markets for the circulation of its cultural texts, the present neoliberal moment with its rhetoric of multiculturalism responds to and indeed *satisfies* the desire for texts that speak to these "newly discovered" pluralist societies themselves. Stated differently, Central American cultural production caters to an isthmian readership that is key to our regional authors' very viability. Their reputation precedes the novels, for the Internet provides a forum for a vast array of readers who can attest to the transformative power of these novels in their blogs and social media posts online.[52] Furthermore, the Costa Rican government itself has played a role in promoting such narratives as a historical/literary document for its citizens.[53]

The national imaginary is being reconstructed from multiple points, including personal discoveries and official mandates. Thus, the process of making diversity in print a best practice is a result of the need, indeed the desire, to use the neoliberal rhetoric of multiculturalism to fill the cracks and crevices that separate two worlds—that of the liminal citizenry and the long-heralded rightful citizenry—in the discourse of the nation. If reconciliation in the former warring countries was achieved through the institution of tribunals and truth commissions, Costa Rica emerges as that classic mythically ethical nation that is ready to address the grievances caused to its Black citizens.[54] An observation from *Reconciliation after Violent Conflict* provides us with deeper insight into what is at stake in today's neoliberal period: "We promote democracy and reconciliation for pragmatic reasons. There is a moral case to be made that reconciliation is the right thing to do. But there is also a powerful pragmatic argument to be made: positive working relationships generate the atmosphere within which governance can thrive, while negative relations will work to undermine even the best system of governance."[55] The act of multicultural reconciliation is indeed strictly pragmatic, since in both the literary and governmental worlds in the context of global connections, words can stand for themselves as "best practices." The power of neoliberal discourse in Central America cannot be denied, for it even taints today's print material in circulation. It has become imperative to reshape and revise official discourses, both literary and political, to recognize Blackness within Central American borders. Contemporary literary and political practices can allow outsiders to become responsible citizens and tourists who engage in a "ethical ethnotourism"—in order to revisit the Black times and Black places of the multicultural nation to vindicate Black experience. Thus, in this chronotope of Blackness in Central America, readers see an ethical imperative pushed by the global gaze, which has itself been prompted by Central America's turn to neoliberalism.

But that is not the end of the story.

In May 2018 Carlos Alvarado Quesada won the presidential election in Costa Rica, but it was his running mate, Epsy Campbell Barr, who caused the greatest stir. As an economist, politician, cofounder and president of the Citizens' Action Party, and deputy for the San José province in the Legislative Assembly, Vice President Campbell's credentials met and exceeded those of past candidates. The remarkable detail about her, however, was not only her professional background but also the fact that she had become the first Black woman to ever be elected to the office of vice president anywhere in the Americas.[56] Despite the long-standing and well-documented presence of Afrodescendants in this hemisphere, not a single Black woman had ever been elected to public office.[57] With the colonial *casta* categories' disintegration in the post-independence period into colorblindness, as discussed in chapter 1 of this book, Afrodescendance ceased to be quantified in all but the Anglophone contexts of the Americas. During her campaign, Vice President Campbell herself emphasized political identities, urging readers and viewers on Facebook and other social media to vote under the hashtag #EsPorCostaRica (It's for Costa Rica). A Facebook Live video featuring the statue of an Indigenous leader on the right side of the frame, directly behind her, centered Vice President Campbell as she spoke of an "inclusive Costa Rica, a Costa Rica where we have a place" and of "all the historically marginalized communities dreaming of a government that would ensure rights for everyone and for all people."[58]

Throughout her tenure as vice president of Costa Rica, she remained in the public eye, subjected to writings about her as much as she made herself the subject of her own writing on various social media platforms. Her use of social media mirrors that of her constituents, allowing her to better connect with potential voters. In their analysis of social media use as political communication, Waisbord and Amado remind us that there is a difference between the use of legacy and new media in the Latin American political sphere: "Since the early days of social media, political campaigns and government communication thought Facebook and Twitter as suitable platforms for candidates and officials to engage in direct interaction with citizens. In contrast to conventional one-way messaging through legacy media, social media facilitated personal, interactive conversation."[59] In keeping with her tradition of clear and direct communication with her constituents, Vice President Campbell posted a note of gratitude and farewell in Facebook Video form in May 2022. In that video, she reflected on her election and the role that the memory of her ancestors played in turning the page on mediated narratives of Black peoples in Costa Rica and beyond:

> For many people, [my election] was a historic moment. For me it was an event that should have occurred in the last century, but it finally became a reality in 2018. It was when I saw myself in the news that I understood how my election represented a great victory for those who were behind and finally saw themselves at the forefront, for those who were last and finally saw themselves first. The day I raised my hand to faithfully swear to protect and serve my country, it was raised with those of my ancestors. Since then, their strength has accompanied me during my administration, and their legacy has helped me to stand up, to walk firmly and with my head held high to overcome obstacles as they did. All of us who belong to communities that have suffered discrimination through generations, carry in our blood not only strength, courage, and conviction; but also love and hope from all people who fought before in order to be treated with dignity. . . . I was always willing to bear the cost, to silently trace, as my ancestors did, a path for the girls and boys who come after, for all the people who dream and work hard, to forge the foundations of a future of solidarity and prosperity, with equality, justice and inclusion.[60]

Vice President Campbell's term in office and presence online highlighted the importance of turning narratives about Blackness in the twenty-first century into an irrefutable national fact. She made it clear in her public speeches and in her use of legacy and new media that, like the Indigenous peoples of the isthmus, Afrodescendants in Central America are an ineffaceable group deserving of national and regional accountability, recognition, and new narrative strategies today. Black communities are rising and, with them, analyses of the narratives that have sustained the disenfranchisement of Afrodescendants from the nations they inhabit.

Vice President Campbell's election was a pinnacle moment in the struggles that have been waged in the isthmus, and throughout the Americas.[61] Writing about the regional panorama, Jean Muteba Rahier observes: "Since the late 2000s and early 2010s, a new reality of Afrodescendant participation at the higher echelons of state institutions has emerged. New Constitutions finally acknowledge Afrodescendants' existence and declare the nation-state to be diverse and multicultural. Constitutions and newly adopted special laws give Afrodescendants collective rights and some protection against racist crimes."[62] Central America went from being a place where there were purportedly no Black people, to one that was happy to have festivals and holidays called Día del Negro (Day of the Black Person), to the legislative revision to constitutions that led to countries such as Guatemala and Honduras where Black communities have the status of *etnias autóctonas* (autochthonous ethnicities) in equal measure to Indigenous peoples of the same nation-state.[63] During the same period, the Americas saw a proliferation of print material about, by, and for Black communities. Out of these two tributaries there has emerged a flow of narratives in which readers can perceive what, as Jan Hoffman French observes with respect to Brazil's northeast, and which can be applied to Central America's peripheral Caribbean region: "new legal identities are combining with the lived experience of ethnoracial identification and contemporary discourses of Black and Indigenous consciousness to change the concepts of race, ethnicity, culture, and law."[64] These identities highlight creative processes and cultural configurations that result from rights claimed for entire communities, and they circulate in both analog and virtual realms. To that presence of Indigenous Blackness in digital media is where I turn in the fifth and final chapter of this book.

Chapter 5

From Caribbean Sea to Digital Shore

Print culture underwent an indelible shift in the twenty-first century with the arrival of digital publishing platforms. Until then, the making of recognizable Central American authors and the welcome reception of their texts largely depended on their access to intellectual circles where intermediaries like international presses, national presses, and *ferias del libro* (book fairs) in the isthmus's capital cities facilitated the circulation and promoted the readership of a curated slice of published volumes.[1] These were, until very recently, predominantly monolingual Spanish-language venues generally presided and attended by white- and *mestizo*-presenting reading publics.[2] The 2012 Feria Internacional del Libro de Costa Rica (International Book Fair of Costa Rica) honored Black literary contributions, featured special guest Nobel Prize Laureate Derek Walcott (St. Lucia, Caribbean), and marked a turning point as the call to diversify these spaces began to draw attention to decades of exclusionary practices in the Central American literary world.[3] Yet, as chapter 4 illustrated, multicultural overtures alone cannot reverse a national tradition of problematic print representations. Neither can they eliminate the structural barriers that have historically prevented Afro–Central American writers from participating in such events, including their residence in Caribbean coastal locales far from the presses and book fair hotspots of their countries. Virtual spaces presented an alternative for the historically excluded Black writers of the isthmus, as it was increasingly understood as "a narrative exercise inside an accelerated and interconnected space of unlimited growth, relatively free and uncontrollable, made possible by digital technology, and information and communication systems."[4]

New media became the means of circulating Central American Black thought from digital shores when, despite the discursive openings of the 1990s, the space available to Black writers remained limited to celebratory multiculturalism.[5] Through a combination of chance and strategy, these narratives reached audiences and had the joint effect of diversifying the Central American literary archives through a process of anti-racism and decoloniality that derailed its historically exclusionary practices. Interfacing with technology became for many Black writers a way to not only weave transnational social networks in order to resist erasure and launch into cyberspace narratives of Blackness hitherto uncirculated in proper intellectual circles. This chapter examines the cyber-distributed oeuvre of two Afro–Central American poets, Wingston González and Carl Rigby, with special attention to their defiance of expectations in producing and circulating their work. Both poets hail from marginal Black communities on the isthmian Caribbean coast and work with themes that diverge from those published and popularized in academic circles, literary conferences, and book festivals. As such, their work is less likely to circulate in the "serie de actividades y agrupaciones tradicionales y nuevas que contribuyen a definir, canonizar las expresiones literarias, tales como las sociedades profesionales, la crítica literaria, las editoriales, las bilbiotecas, las ferias de libro, los encuentros de escritores y los premios literarios"[6] (series of activities and traditional as well as new gatherings that contribute to defining, canonizing literary expression, such as professional societies, literary criticism, presses, libraries, book fairs, writers' symposia, and literary prizes). Defying what Ángel Rama once called "the lettered city," Guatemalan Wingston González's 2006 poetic anthology first became available on his personal website and Nicaraguan Carl Rigby's posthumous documentary *Antojología de Carl Rigby: primer tomo de los que vienen* (2019) available on YouTube.[7] These projects have not only opened spaces for wider circulation of their work, but have also nourished digital reading publics outside of Central America.

In tandem with taking up the pen, the mouse, and the trackpad, Black writers have also availed themselves of digital spaces to produce, distribute, and consume each other's work. These actions are intimately tied to the proliferation of new media in the lives of literary creatives and their audiences. The tools developed within and through cyberspace facilitate the diffusion of knowledge and communication between peoples in different geographic points. Like the electrical technologies in the nineteenth century, new media are factors in wider social change that become quickly embedded in the social context. The term "new media," argues Terry Flew, takes into account "the wider transformations in work, lifestyle, identity and culture, as well as politics, global affairs, and forms of interaction" correlated with the magnitude of its social impact.[8] New media and media convergence in general (the interlinking of computing and IT, communications networks, media content enabled by digital technologies, and the convergent products, services, and activities that have emerged as a result) transformed Central America, its inhabitants, and its diaspora.[9] Maritza E. Cárdenas notes that large-scale migration from the isthmus to other spaces as well as technological advances in the late twentieth century, including satellite television and the Internet, created the need and ability for Central Americans to remain connected across vast distances.[10] As the digital footprints of the poets studied in this chapter indicate, social networks and global digital access have transformed the production, circulation, and reception of Black writing. In the face of heightened scrutiny with respect to their content and ideology, creative output and capricious distribution cycles, Black writers in Central America and beyond are substituting the regional trend of writing about Black Central American experience with the practice of issuing their own self-styled print from digital shores in the information age.

[Black] Wording on Digital Interfaces

Wingston González is a poet whose work defies mainstream expectations of Black Central American writing. By positioning himself as neither a Guatemalan author nor an Afro-Guatemalan author, he highlights himself as a creative with a passion for poetic themes that span the arc of personal identity as well as abstract reference.[11] Adding a factor of complexity to his classification, González is a member of the Garifuna Afro-Indigenous community in Livingston, a community across the bay from Puerto Barrios. Both Garifuna oral histories and colonial accounts locate the roots of Garifuna culture on Yurumein (now known as St. Vincent). Kalípona was the language spoken by many families on St. Vincent, some of whom called kin the African men who escaped enslavement when the vessels that carried them as enslaved male cargo were shipwrecked near the coast of Yurumein.[12] Kalípona became the second language of the former speakers of Indigenous West African languages and, consequently, it became the first language of their children. This practice of calling kin those who married into the Kalípona community had already been established through the ancestral intermarriages of Arawak and Carib speakers. Unburdened by the racial tropes in vogue in Europe, phenotype carried little significance within the Kalípona community in Yurumein. Remarking on this fact, one French settler remarked in 1666: "They are passionate Lovers of one another; and though they are born in different Countries, and sometimes, when at home. Enemies one to another, yet when occasion requires they mutually support and assist one another, as if they were all Brethren."[13] Thus, the language spoken in homes and the language that children used in the community and in play, regardless of the ancestral origin of their fathers, was that of their mothers: Kalípona.

Unlike the enslaved West Africans who were trafficked and sold by Europeans in the Caribbean and elsewhere in the Americas, the African members of the Kalípona clans were not forced out of necessity to produce pidgin languages. Neither did their children suffer the linguistic colonialism that led to the transformation of those pidgin languages into creole languages consisting of European substrates—like English or French—and West African lexical and morphological elements.[14] The babies and tots who learned Kalípona did so through their unfractured and unenslaved kin networks, well outside of the system of enslavement that is commonly associated with pidgins and creole languages. The unencumbered linguistic and expressive culture transmission remained the case until the French and British imposed their nomenclature by renaming the population "Caribs" and proceeding to exploit standing conflicts between families in order to carry out their program of settler colonialism. Along with the renaming of speakers of Kalípona, the French and the British subjected the community to the racial taxonomies in vogue in Europe, resulting in their classification as "Red/Yellow" or "Black" depending on their phenotype. As Peter Wade observes, "Indigenous people and Africans had different locations in the colonial order, both socially and conceptually. Indigenous people were, officially, to be protected as well as exploited; Africans were slaves and . . . the main concern was with control, rather than protection."[15] The population named "Charaibes Noirs" and "Karaib Negroes" was comprised of individuals who possessed a phenotype akin to that of the Africans enslaved by the British and French on Yurumein, and the Europeans proceeded to deal with this subset in a manner distinct from the way that they engaged with Yellow/Red Caribs. Nonetheless, within the Kalípona community, "the Black Caribs were quickly indistinguishable from the Yellow Caribs in terms of dress, diet, language and lifestyle—everything, in fact, except pigmentation and similar racial characteristics. They even adopted the Carib practice of head deformation."[16] Together and as one, they resisted European settler colonialism for multiple generations, leading Yurumein to become "the site of the last battle of people living a traditional lifestyle against European colonialists anywhere in the islands. It was here that the Caribbean saw its Little Big Horn and its Wounded Knee."[17] Chief Joseph Chatoyer, leader of the "Black Caribs" as he was known to the British, became a key figure in the oral histories and documents concerning the Kalípona war against Europeans. The Indigenous legacy and the power of a hero like Chatoyer is prevalent in Garifuna media, particularly in *Garifuna in Peril*, released on Amazon Prime in 2017.[18]

Garifuna ancestors were deported by the British from Yurumein in 1797. Describing the event, Christopher Taylor writes: "On Thursday 9 March the remains of the Black Carib nation caught their last glimpse of Youroumaÿn's green mountains as, unwilling passengers on the ships of their conquerors, they left their homeland behind for good."[19] They were deposited on the island of Roatán, and over time, they first established communities in Honduras before branching off into communities they founded in Guatemala, Belize, and Nicaragua. Yet they would not be deterred from their love for their personal and community's tradition of freedom. Captain Rossi and Rubi related the words of Jack, a Garifuna leader, in an article for the Gazeta de Guatemala in 1797, just months after their disembarking: "Yo no mando en nombre de nadie: yo no soy ingles, ni francés, ni español, ni quiero ser nada de esto: soy un caribe, un caribe, sin sujeción, no quiero ser más, ni quiero tener más."[20] (I do not lead in anyone's name: I am not British, nor French, nor Spanish; I do not wish to be any of this: I am a Carib, a Carib, without subjection; I do not want to be more than that, nor do I wish to have more than that.)

The communities founded by Garifuna ancestors after their disembarking were all on the Central American Caribbean course and are the same [Black] sites that appear on maps I.1–I.4 in the first pages of this book. Labuga (originally founded between 1804 and 1806) was renamed Livingston in 1831 by a decree issued by Mariano Galvez, chief of state of Guatemala, during the period of the Federal Republic of Central America.[21] Guatemalan officials hoped to end British influence in the Miskito Coast and other Central American Caribbean communities while encouraging to accept Guatemalan rule and "protection" from the government that tore them from their homeland of Yurumein. With very few white or *mestizo* Guatemalans interested in establishing themselves in the hot and humid areas of the district known then as Chiquimala, Garifuna culture and language thrived in Labuga/Livingston over the course of nearly forty years. With trade came speakers of other languages—Spanish, English, Creole, and Miskito—but without a top-down imposition of any single language, the linguistic vitality of Garifuna language and culture remained strong. The internal configuration of the Labuga/Livingston Garifuna community began to change from the 1870s forward as wage labor in Puerto Barrios's emerging banana industry drew Garifuna men away from their homes. It was then, as has been discussed in chapter 3, that Central American print like that of Paca Navas de Miralda depicted Garifuna peoples with cruel and eugenicist strokes. This world of isolation from the rest of Guatemala, of Garifuna-speaking matriarchs, and of mainstream racism toward the Afro-Indigeneity of the community is the ideological context from which González wrote when he first launched his 2006 website.

González left Livingston at the age of fifteen when he accepted a scholarship to continue his schooling in San Marcos, Guatemala. A member of what he calls a "trans nation," his leave-taking marked his initiation into what he calls his "traveler's vocation," a path taken by those who feel themselves to be nomads, persistent voyagers.[22] Yet González's identity as a Garifuna poet born in Livingston follows him as he moves from one page to another, from one interview to the next literary feat. His work is doubly scrutinized, for the literary world demands perfection in the craft as well as the sensibility of a cultural broker who will use his "vivid language and expressive force" to provide an account of a historically marginalized Guatemalan Garifuna culture.[23] In González's oeuvre, the demands for "ethnic authenticity" are met with references to the literary and extra-literary influences that have shaped the cyberpoet/digital poetic voice in the course of his travels. If the reader wishes him to conform, to settle, to remain chained to one way of rhythm, he has effectively problematized that expectation. He is at once a different configuration of tempos converging, and yet as equally complex an arrangement as the interlocutor.

The experience of belonging to a community with an age-old proclivity for managing many cultures at once, integrating the spirit world into the world of the living, expressing respect for maternal figures in the home while respecting the sojourning paternal figures, among other balanced concepts, appears in González's poem, "de pequeño las cosas que me nombrabanbambam [adán enumera infancias]" (as a child, the things they proclaimedclaimclaim [adam recites childhoods]). The poem, dedicated to his mother, was unpublished at the time it was uploaded to González's personal webpage and is one of ten poems that provide a glimpse into the origins of the poet behind the voice. González, who was raised by his mother and grandmother, captures the female voices of his youth and the memories he conveys in snippets are interwoven with the voices of the two women. Written in a stream of consciousness fashion, the poem moves from Spanish to English to Garifuna as the poetic voice conveys images from his household, from ThunderCat cartoons on television, cable television, and US rapper 50 Cent's music, to the daily rituals followed to ward off evil spirits, to admonishments, to the names of women he recalls from conversations overheard:

> Echa ajo que nos vamos a dormir. Los espíritus. Power. Power. Thunder thunder
> thunder thunder cats. Si esa es mi memoria. Las cajuelas de fósforos. Ponle agua al
> corazón de Jesús. Todos tus tías son brujas. Brujería. Negro. Todos los vecinos.
> No les hables te digo. No les hables. . . . en verdad COMEGENTE es la dueña de
> nuestros destinos. En realidad (¡oh comegente!) aunque mis versos suenen
> infantiles a ti te canto. ¡oh señora del mundo! La brujería y la Biblia. Las cajuelas.
> Tu bisabuela lucía. La seño Constanza. Esa sí era estricta. Si vas a esa fiesta no
> bailes con tus primas. Chutitia lau irahü le. Ayé. Liraü lando ani tiraü hesili.
> Madumerehatibusa garifuna? Mamá garífuna buguya wingston. Exilio. La
> brujería. Santa lucía y santa Constanza. Los dientes de la abuela. Los postizos
> recuerdos de la historia. Hubiera querido alegrarme. No iré a la procesión. Ponle
> agua al corazón de Jesús. Perdona a tu pueblo señor. Baba wicho. Belice city. No toques la comida de tus bisabuelos. HBO. 50 cent. Mama garífuna buguya brao. Figiaburu. Madumerehati garífuna. ¿dónde está la luz mamá?[24]

(Throw some garlic, we're going to go to sleep. The spirits. Power. Power. Thunder thunder thunder thunder cats. If that is my memory. The matchboxes. Leave some water for the heart of Jesus. All your aunts are witches. Witchcraft. Black. All the neighbors. Don't talk to them, I tell you. Don't talk to them . . . truly, DEVOURER owns our destinies. Truly, (oh devourer!) although my verses sound childish I sing to you. oh lady of the world! Witchcraft and the Bible. The little boxes. Your great-grandmother lucía. Ms. Constanza. She really was strict. If you go to the party don't dance with your cousins. Chutitia lau irahü le. Ayé. Liraü lando ani tiraü hesili. Madumerehatibusa garifuna? Mamá garífuna buguya wingston. Exile. Witchcraft. Saint lucía and saint Constanza. Grandmother's teeth. The false memories of history. I would have liked to cheer myself up. I won't go to the procession. Put some water out for Jesus's heart. Forgive your people, Lord. Baba wicho. Belize city. Don't touch your great-grandparents' food. HBO. 50 cent. Mama garífuna buguya brao. Figiaburu. Madumerehati garífuna. Where is the light, mom?)

The poem brings together the voices of González's mother and grandmother as the digital poetic voice explores the fine distinction between the voices of the spirits and those of the living, pop culture, and migration. The repetition of the word "comegente" (devourer) in the light gray background of the web document itself 198 times, and thirteen times in the text of the poem, with six instances in bold font, deserves mention. In Garifuna spirituality, the devourer is often seen as a spirit more powerful than the devil himself, for it has the power to take on the appearance of animals and focuses its destructive influences on the homes of its victims.[25] The verses "oh devourer!" and "oh lady of the world!" invoke the powerful force of the devourer in the midst of a context where the daily rituals to ward off evil spirits coexist with the boyish rituals of ThunderCat cartoons, HBO programs, and 50 Cent's rap music.

When it was uploaded to González's personal webpage in 2006, "de pequeño . . ." was one of ten poems that gave readers a glimpse of the poet behind the voice, and a glimpse into spatiotemporal conceptions of Black Indigeneity that continue to be central in his work. In the poem, the intrasentential and intersentential forms of code-switching between Spanish-English-Garifuna are used to invoke linguistic markers of identity that bridge the miles between Livingston and the Garifuna communities to which members of the community have migrated.[26] The strategy of repetition is deployed once again with "Belice" appearing abruptly as singular utterances six times in the poem as instances of disruption in the more fluid syntactic pattern of the poem, and in this same vein, it is not possible for the reader to overlook the reference to the US national anthem. Garifuna communities in the United States are arguably larger than those in Central America at the present time. In fact, most Garifuna residents living in Honduras have relatives that have immigrated to the United States and keep in close contact with them through new media.[27] The easy availability of new media contributes to community networking, as television and smart phones, Facebook and YouTube, are ubiquitous in Garifuna households. As Pamela Wilson and Michelle Stewart observe, "Media produced by and for Indigenous peoples, usually in their own languages and for internal consumption, under Indigenous control and funding, have come to exist alongside media produced in the media industries of the dominant society."[28] This means that, along with the Spanish-language and English-language dominant radio, television, and film produced in Honduras and the United States, respectively, Garifuna-language content has multiplied.

The digital poetic voice thus captures the multiplicities and flux of Garifuna experience at all levels and dimensions, covering the expansiveness of homelands and centuries of spirits in motion. In tandem with changes in hardware, González and other youth of his generation witnessed the introduction of Web 2.0 principles in new media. In Labuga/Livingston and beyond, the Internet became a platform upon which services could be delivered, collective intelligence could be harnessed, and open-source development practices would lead users to drive innovation and invent new purposes for the platform.[29] The fastest growing websites of the 2000s—Wikipedia, YouTube, Blogger, WordPress, Instagram, Pinterest, Facebook, Google, and Twitter—were all based on Web 2.0 principles. These, along with the proliferation of digital technologies and the growing array of digital platforms, led to a cycle of ubiquitous use of user-created content and user-led innovation of new media. As Gloria Chacón and I write in our introduction to *Indigenous Interfaces*, "A key driving force behind Indigenous interfacing with cyber technology is to advance the process of decoloniality and its attendant nationalist manifestations . . . interfacing with technology is not an end in itself but rather a means by which Indigenous people across generations can connect and build networks in the face of the onslaught of colonial and national pressures to lose culture."[30]

González's Labuga/Livingston is hundreds of miles away from any of Guatemala's presses and annual bookfairs and is a space in which travel guides are the most popular traded book.[31] His website, complete with the .gif images popular in the day, announced in an unintimidated voice facing clearly and directly the racial, geographic, and linguistic exclusion that would have snuffed out the voice of the Afro-Indigenous poet before the digital age. In "I, II y III," for example, the poetic voice erupts with confidence declaring:

> Ellos tienen un idioma y yo tengo varios, ¡bum! ¡bum!
> *Se siente mi flow por donde paso*, ajá,
> yo que nací en un caribe iluminado con linternas
> puedo conmover a cualquiera
> me dicen las bocinas que los tallos se siembran en los huesos quebrados de los viejos.[32]
>
> (*They have one language and I have many, boom! boom!/ My flow is felt where wherever I go*, uh huh/ I, who was born in a Caribbean illuminated by lamplight/ I can move anyone/ the sirens tell me that stems are sown in the broken bones of the elders.)

Taking this poem as a starting point, new readers experienced linguistic sleights of hand including the poetic voice's phonetic modification of "boom," fashioned to fit within the phonological rules of Spanish. His play with the word "flow" brought forth the intrasentential code-switching that highlighted the poetic voice's agility with both English and Spanish. "Flow" was a loaded word that evoked images of the spoken word poetry and rap music associated with Black poets and musicians outside of the Caribbean. These five verses, launched first and only in cyberspace for nearly a decade, were replete with juxtapositions that disrobed the sheltered and provincial Guatemalan literary scene for readers worldwide to see. As such, the verses were and continue to be a challenge to the isthmian literary tradition, which until recently prized only monolingual Spanish narrative and poetry. The enunciations of the young poetic voice disrupted the literary scene through its tone, its distinctly trilingual content, and its diffusion through digital venues. Despite having been raised in an often-ignored Caribbean context far from the literary epicenter of Guatemala, González was partaking in the cosmopolitanism of a subject in contact with worlds and influences beyond the boundaries of his nation-state.

The digital poetic voice's wordsmithing was successful in drawing online readership/followers because, in its very linguistic/transregional "flow," it remained grounded in the concreteness of Garifuna experience. Never far from the poet voice's purview was the conviviality of the spirit world and that of the living. In "I, II y III," for example, the bones of the elders are fertile ground for the fledgling stems that will grow in their place. In this poem as well as another poem from the same first online collection, the cyberpoet arranges long and short enunciations throughout the poem, bringing to life that moving "flow" he proudly embraces. "Escribe a la iglesia de Filadelfia: poema frente la estatua de Colón en Livinston" (Writes to the Church of Philadelphia: Poem before the Statue of Columbus in Livingston), from the same digital anthology, deploys similar techniques.[33] In doing so, it provides readers with images of the digital poetic voice's cosmopolitan reach:

> Think. I'm a rastaman, beautiful people; I'm a *Basta*man, I'm
> a nothingman. La eminente tribulación del android en
> que mis ojos se seca
> y salto loco de un imperio que no es de este mundo, *nohay-
> nadamalomalo endartecalorcalor*, angélico y vacío.

> (Think. I'm a rastaman, beautiful people; I'm an *Enough*man,
> I'm a nothingman. The imminent tribulation of the android
> in which my eyes dry/ and i jump crazily from an empire that
> is not of this world, *thereisnothingwrongwrong ingivingyou-
> warmth*, angelic and empty.)

Moving from English to Spanish, he uses the imperative mood to interpellate the reader to literally imagine the cyberpoet's body. His transfigurations—once again a demonstration of the fragility between the world of the spirits and the living, of specter and veracity—conjure up the exotic Rastafarian sought out by tourists who seek quintessential Blackness in Caribbean sites, the ethicist who contemplates the limits of the subject, and the robot from science fiction who bears the figure but not the affect of a human being. In doing so, the poetic voice highlights the "problem of indeterminacy," a philosophical question concerning the circuitousness of definitions and the need for approximations, a Kantian solution to the problem. Wordsmithing, particularly when it involves code-switching, provides a solution to the poetic voice's desire to convey an approximation of the self on a journey that begins on a digital shore and crosses spiritual, linguistic, literary, and geographic divides.

Mark Anderson explains that contemporary conceptions of Garifuna identity are based on "a configuration of indigeneity as marking a particular cultural status or condition, a mode of being more than a matter of blood."[34] Blackness does not preclude the state of being Indigenous; it is a simultaneous embodied experience. As Paul Joseph López Oro observes, "Garifuna communities throughout Central America and the United States disrupt notions of who, what, and where blackness, indigeneity, and mestizo Latinidad is to be situated. St. Vincent as an ancestral homeland, is an important social memory that marks diasporic Garifunaness, because it anchors a site of belonging, remembering, and maroonage to colonialism and slavery."[35] Tourists, however, do not arrive in the Caribbean seeking to learn the truth of Indigenous dispossession and its relationship to the transatlantic African slave trade and the displacement of Caribbean first peoples. "(o leleru Bungiu)," from the same collection, speaks assertively about this point. Tourists have not chosen a Caribbean fraught with the history of genocide and enslavement, but an exotic Caribbean where Black bodies perform to entertain them. Little do they care for the reciprocal exchanges made with members of kin along the coasts of Honduras, Guatemala, Belize, New York, and Los Angeles as they define themselves and their communities. Far less do they care about the history of survivance embodied by Garifuna peoples, whose foremothers cultivated cassava, yucca, bananas, and plantains and whose forefathers dominated the Caribbean Sea in canoes, and who are now a community stretched across social networks forged by processes of migration.[36] According to the digital poetic voice:

> los turistas quieren palmeras. once onzas. quieren negras
> en bikini y una voz que les diga tu plata que les diga
> lo que sea a cincuenta tiempo. dance hall o reggaeton.
> barroco o reggaeton. poesía o la animal historia del
> pueblo garínagu. el dios necesita un pueblo sin ombligo.
> uno que camine sobre las aguas hacia la miseria uno que
> sea el más turístico de una ciudad saqueda. *un freestyle*

cual esta maniática canción, ese es el ombligo, esta es la idea. . . . ellos no quieren saber que Haití es patria en América. me quejo. me quejo. suelo morderme en las fiestas y no bailar. me quejo. como una droga el cuerpo disperse en los cartílagos del niño que mira de lejos el exceso, paisajes ateos. ellos no son ángeles de Etiopía, quieren, un muchacho rasta que cante un mito, una estrella y un vaso de gifitti[37]

no vudú please
no chugu please
no palo mayombe
no garinagu please

no no no. me explota el poder. el tema. glacial consejo de hombres me niego: *mama garífuna buguya. no eres hijo de madre. mama garifuna buguya.*[38]

(the tourists want palm trees. eleven ounces. they want Black girls in bikinis and a voice telling them your cash your cash telling them whatever at fifty time. dance hall or reggaeton. baroque or reggaeton. poetry or the visceral story of the garinagu people. god needs a people without a bellybutton. one that will walk over water toward the misery one that will be the most touristic of a ransacked city. *a freestyle which this fanatical song, that is the bellybutton, that is the idea . . .* they don't want to know that Haiti is homeland in America. i complain. like a drug that disperses itself in the cartilages of the child that sees excess from afar, atheist landscapes. they are not angels from Ethiopia, they want, a young rasta man to sing a myth, a star and a cup of gifitti/ *no voodoo please/ no chugu please/ no palo mayombe/ no garinagu please/* no no no. power exploits me. the issue. glacial advice from men i refuse:/ *mama garífuna buguya. no eres hijo de madre. mama garifuna buguya.*

In this way, "(o leleru Bungiu)" engages directly with the racialization of Garifuna peoples while at the same time recounting the Garifuna cultural elements that connect the digital poetic voice to its homeland. These consist of the spiritual gifts of the ancestors: voodoo, chugu, and palo mayombe. With this, the poem reminds readers of Garifuna Indigeneity as the survivance of rituals and ceremonies learned in Yurumein prior to the deportation of ancestors to Central America. These are the rituals that connect living souls with spirits and kin across vast distances, even as the markers of language and identity are challenged by tourist dollars and the ahistorical conceptualization of Black Indigeneity held by tourist spectators.

A central premise of this work González published online, then, was that Black Indigeneity could not be frozen or static. The demands for "ethnic authenticity" led to poems launched into cyberspace ebbing with acrimonious verses like those of "Hahari Wagübürigu [something like *the spirit of our fathers*]" where the cyberpoet's transition from a lyrical tone to the mechanics of prose highlights the tension between such expectations:

> Un catedrático ebrio se me acerca y pregunta
> ¿es su madre feliz Wingston?
> y alguien responde por mí
> :no tienes madre hijo
> :no tienes madre hijo de la gran puta
> porque abruptos recuerdos me niegan
> me marcan
> con los símbolos de la ignorancia
> las contraseñas patológicas
> de estos malabares lingüísticos
> no tan garífunas como todos quisieran
> Así publico mi rencor:/
> Como un testamento contra todos
> /contra el fuego sobretodo/
> /contra las palabras sobretodo/
> /contra el reggaeton sobretodo/
> /con la propia catharsis
> de quienes rumian en español
> los cirios negros que el mar les negó[39]

> (A drunken scholar approaches me and asks/ *is your mother happy, Wingston?*/ and someone answers on my behalf/ :*you don't have a mother son*/ :you don't have a mother son of a bitch/ because abrupt memories deny me/ mark me/ with the

symbols of ignorance/ the pathological passwords/ of this linguistic juggling/ not very Garifuna as they would like/ I thus publish my rancor/:/ As a testament against all/ /against fire above all/ /against words above all/ /against reggaeton above all/ /against catharsis itself/ of those who brood in Spanish/ over the vigil lights that the sea denied them)

The undercurrent of the poem is announced in its title, which makes present the spirits of the ancestors in the daily lives of the living who utter prayers in a European tongue for the souls that the sea took from them. In addition, while the historical conditions of loss of language and the surviving veneration for one's ancestors is not lost upon the cyberpoet, the patronizing scholars who make assumptions about Black Indigenous culture miss the mark. The othering that occurs with the scholar's question about Wingston's mother is palpable, and the cyberpoet despises him and responds with his own insult in turn. Poignantly, he responds by giving way again to the lyrical style of his "pathological passwords" and his "linguistic juggling" that reveals itself to be "not as Garifuna as they all would want them to be." He moves from formal and informal registers of Spanish, but not without first asserting his Black Indigenous Garifuna identity, and second engaging with the linguistic debates surrounding the centrality of language in contemporary Garifuna culture as well as current discussions of language loss as cultural death.

In this online anthology, González affirms Black Indigeneity as palpable as the rhythm that imbues his verses with depth and meaning. The poems feature Labuga/Livingston as a context in which Blackness takes on the symbolic meanings associated with Indigeneity—tradition, rootedness in territory, and a special relationship to nature—with collective value and historic cultural value while engaging with the ways that conceptions of Blackness render the subject a racial-cultural other at the margins. As Claudia Cabrera notes, we feel the rhythm, the grittiness, images in succession that flow like a rifle in repetition and fill space, inducing us into a trance.[40] These are the verses of a marooned poetic voice on the shores of the twenty-first century, living in one temporality while being marked by the ancestral memory of time and space on Yurumein. Launched into cyberspace on an early website before they were committed to print media, these verses crossed the worlds of the living and the spirits, linguistic divides, and the geographic reaches of a transnational Garifuna nation with a soulful prayer for Yurumein.

González received the 2015 Luis Cardoza y Aragón Mesoamerican Poetry Award for his book *Translaciones* (Translations, a meaning defined in Spanish in the astronomical sense without punning on language translation), which was published by the Guatemalan Editorial Cultura that same year. Asked if he would like to add something at the end of an interview shortly after receiving the award, González reflected on the literary moment in Latin America. It was, he explained, an unprecedented moment because small presses outside of the mainstream were venturing into the publication of trailblazing texts. He went further, adding: "Para todos ellos este premio y para ir sacándonos las tonterías racistas con las que uno se enfrenta cuando tenés que pedir trabajo. Ahí te das cuenta que un garífuna puede dedicarse a cualquier cosa incluso a la escritura y aunque parezca un poco absurdo tener que recalcar esto hay que hacerlo y este tipo de premios sirve para evidenciar esas situaciones. Ojalá que también pueda server para enorgullecer a los garífunas que viven fuera de Livingston y que tienen que enfrentarse con todo tipo de prejuicios."[41] (This prize is for all of them and for us to begin wiping out all that racist nonsense one must face when looking for work. Only then can you see that a Garifuna can have a career in any field, even writing, and even though it might seem absurd to have to stress that, it has to be done and these awards help to highlight those cases. I hope that it will also help instill pride in Garifuna peoples living outside of Livingston who have to face all kinds of prejudices.) Seen in this light, González's poetry is timely: it coincides with the increasing recognition of Indigenous intellectual histories in Central America and, specifically, with Garifuna language and cultural rights movements across the isthmus. It also coincides with language and cultural revitalization projects taking place not only in Central America but also in the United States, where the new Garifuna heartlands have become established in New York City on the East Coast and in Los Angeles on the West Coast. González's publications and awards have drawn a new kind of attention to Livingston, markedly distinct from depictions of it as a Caribbean touristscape, as the coastal heartland of the Guatemalan Garifuna experience. He is the writer with an extensive online footprint whose followers leave comments like Palacios Martínez's "Felicidades. Orgullo Garifuna de Livingston" (Congratulations, Garifuna pride from Livingston), Ellington's "Estoy muy orgulloso por la entrevista, por ser Garifuna" (I'm very proud of the interview because you are Garifuna), and Nuñez's "Estoy muy orgulloso de vos Hermano. Ojalá que toda la gente de Labuga Livingston se den cuenta. Felicidades" (I'm very proud of you, brother. I hope all the people in Labuga Livingston notice. Congratulations). These are just three of the many comments circulating the virtual world on news sites, online literary collectives, YouTube, Twitter, and Facebook. González's sojourning out of Livingston, as well as the routes taken by his own works in traditional print and in the virtual world, have made him a household name and a symbol of pride in the transnational Garifuna nation.

Digitizing a Black Poetic Anthology

Antojología was envisioned as a digital mixed-media project funded by the Ródrigo E. J. Campbell Foundation to produce a documentary film and website, which would include research about the life and work of Carl Earlington Rigby, a photo gallery, a trailer for the documentary, and a digital selection of poetry by Rigby presented in both Spanish and English.[42] The project was the result of two years of conversations, poems, and monologues filmed in Rigby's home, a recording studio, and on walks through his neighborhood in Pearl Lagoon, Nicaragua.[43] Shot in black and white, with occasional archival footage in color, and with no immediately clear narrative arc to constrain it, the documentary straddles the border of experimental. Yet, it is far from such. As the title itself conveys, the film is a nod to poetic *antojos* (wants) while also a deliberate means of assembling a poetic *antología* (anthology). Departing from the anthropological documentary tradition that contributed to settler colonial projects while framing Indigenous peoples as a window into "pre-civilization," the film aligns itself best with the Cuban film style of *cine imperfecto* (imperfect cinema). In a similar way to the films of the genre, *Antojología* seeks to insert its audience into social reality through a film that presents a subject without the embellishments and technical achievements that are characteristic of commercial cinema. As Julio García Espinoza wrote in his landmark essay on this approach, "Imperfect cinema finds a new audience in those who struggle, and it finds its themes in their problems. For imperfect cinema, 'lucid' people are the ones who think and feel and exist in a world that they can change; in spite of all the problems and difficulties, they are convinced that they can transform it in a revolutionary way."[44] Obstacles to publishing are at the center of *Antojología*, and these are made explicit from the first frames of the film. The camera focuses on Rigby holding the bust of Rubén Darío (discussed in chapter 1 of this book), while asking for the literary giant's blessing so that he will not have to wait one hundred years to publish his first book. From this scene forward, the documentary captures a lucid Rigby who is as passionate about his writing as he is about sharing it with the people of Bluefields.

In a biographical entry, Thomas Wayne Edison writes that Rigby arrived in Managua from Bluefields "with a trombone and a passion to share the beauty of the Palo de Mayo dance tradition in the streets of Managua during public events. He began to write poetry during this period and honed his craft at a Bohemian-style cafeteria, *La India*, with other great poets of the day, such as Ernesto Cardenal, Juan Chow, Manolo Cuadra, Pedro Antonio Cuadra, and Joaquin Pasos. He [worked] as a radio host on programs addressing themes related to the history and culture of Nicaragua's Caribbean coast."[45] He remained a strong proponent of Sandinismo throughout his lifetime, leading early literary critics such as Ian Smart and Richard L. Jackson to state that Rigby (and David McField, another Afro-Nicaraguan Sandinista poet) did not address Blackness in their poetry.[46] However, contemporary scholars like Dorothy Mosby note that Rigby indeed addresses the literary themes of ethnic, regional, cultural, and linguistic alterity in conjunction with hemispheric Blackness that are manifested in the work of other Black writers of the region.[47] Rigby was, according to the *Antojología* website, "one of the pioneers of NiCaribbean spoken word poetry. His poetic work incorporates poetic elements, oscillating between social commentary and a critical dialogue with the Afro-descendant tradition of Central America. In more than half a century of intellectual work he produced a proliferative literary work scattered among unpublished poetry books, songs, tongue-twisters, and a *Palabrario* (word index) that included various neologisms created by the poet, in addition to what he called 'versions': poetic pieces that were memorized in order to be recited with variations."[48] The form and content of the digital project are fitting, then, given the range of Rigby's creative output and the extensive personal archives that he kept in his home and that he references in many shots of the film. It is also in keeping with Rigby's values from the Sandinista period (1979–1989) to allow the digital content to be freely available to any reader/listener/viewer perusing the photos, clips, and audio of his poetry.

Rigby's commitment to the ideals of the 1979 Sandinista revolution and his concomitant output of revolutionary poetry from his early years to his wise years is captured in the film. He is far from the stereotypical "Black poet." Writing for *Wani*, a periodical focused on the arts, culture, and politics of the Nicaraguan Caribbean coast, Carlos Castro Jo captured the enigmas that Rigby posed to critics attempting to decipher his work: "Rigby, 'nuestro gran poeta inédito,' . . . siempre ha peleado porque se incluya la cultura caribeña como parte de la cultura nacional, y esa cultura caribeña de la que él habla es negra y también indígena. Al mismo tiempo, él ha escrito sobre la necesidad de trascender la división racial para hacer un proyecto popular basado en la lucha de clases y la lucha contra el racismo simultáneamente."[49] (Rigby, "our great unpublished poet" . . . has always fought for Caribbean culture to be included in national culture, and that Caribbean culture about which he speaks is Black and Indigenous. At the same time, he has written about the need to transcend the racial divide in order to build a popular project based on class struggle and the struggle against racism simultaneously.) In line with his creative poetic persona, he turns what the directors envisioned would be a biopic into a poetic anthology in documentary form. His objective to make poetry that would reach people becomes central to every conversation he has with the filmmakers, whether the form it takes is a frame centering on a poem or a sequence in which he delivers spoken word, or a stroll past walls with spray-painted verses of his poems, or the digital project itself—making the entirety of his oeuvre accessible to a public far beyond his immediate circle. As he states in the first moments of the documentary, available in its entirety on YouTube, aesthetics matter as much as the defiant content. These precepts are revealed in the first poem reproduced in the documentary-anthology, "La beca del guerrillero" (The Scholarship of the Guerrilla). A poignant, yet beautifully arranged composition, its imagery conveys the urgency of a revolution in Nicaragua. The film pauses over the text, giving the viewer sufficient time to read the poem, the poet's signature, its title, and the year: 1969 (figure 5.1). It is a brief poem arranged in a manner that highlights the final words of each verse. The first is "huesodélica" (bone-delic) a neologism that brings together the images of bones and a psychedelic landscape. The second is a much briefer verse, ending with the word "robots," as an assertion of what a human cannot be. The final word of the third verse is the verb "escribo" (I write), which brings the reader back into the poet's fold as he states just what kind of humans exist in the landscape he describes: those who are dead and those who will "morir" (die), as he emphasizes in the very last verse of the poem.

 Rigby, like his comrades in other wings of the Sandinista revolution, recognized the value of video production as a means of sharing the goals

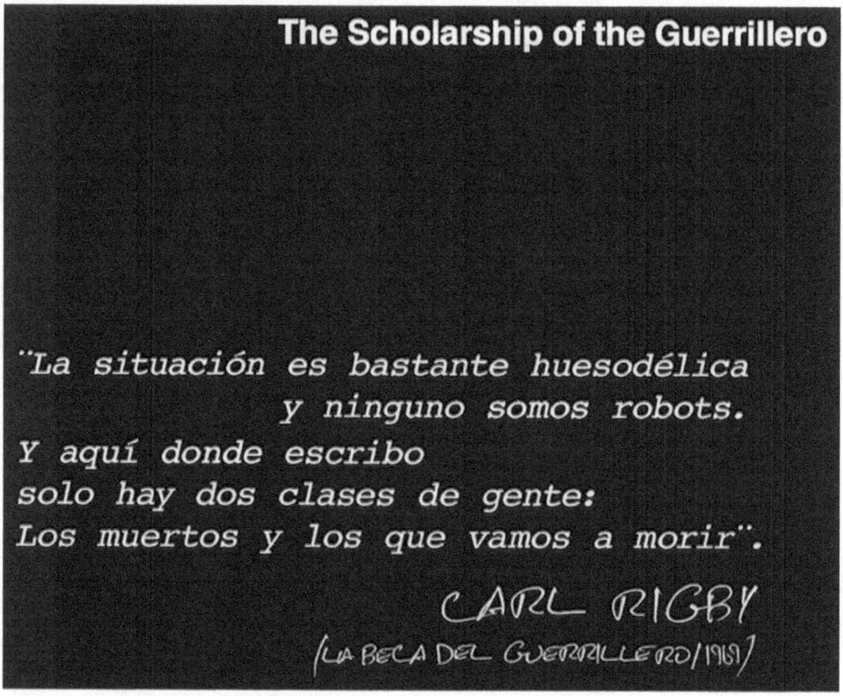

> **The Scholarship of the Guerrillero**
>
> "La situación es bastante huesodélica
>   y ninguno somos robots.
> Y aquí donde escribo
> solo hay dos clases de gente:
> Los muertos y los que vamos a morir".
>
> CARL RIGBY
> /LA BECA DEL GUERRILLERO/1989/

Figure 5.1. "La beca del guerrillero" (The Scholarship of the Guerrilla Soldier). *Source: Antojología*, directed by Eduardo Spiegeler and María José Álvarez.

of the movement with the people of Nicaragua. Susan Ryan writes in her review of Sandinista film production that it was "part of the larger project of popular media articulated by theorists and filmmakers of the New Latin American cinema. As a political act, popular media could convey the people's authentic experiences, rescue histories that had been obfuscated by official discourse, and challenge representations of the popular classes found in dominant cinema. Popular media performed a social function as a form of critical intervention, as well as provided people with a deeper understanding of the reality around them."[50] Drawing from the popular media thinkers of the region, especially those who had been engaged in the Cuban Revolution, Sandinista filmmakers saw in video a means of challenging the official discourses, dominant representations, and notions of high culture itself. The popular classes had a place as protagonists in film, they argued, as did the class interests and tastes of those who had been on the margins. Correspondingly, a documentary-anthology like

Antojología has the objective of overturning the rules of print publishing, by using mixed mediums and digital distribution to do the work that traditional presses were incapable of capturing. In a literary context where someone as productive as Rigby was unable to be published and where structural consequences were such that his legacy stood the chance of being erased, the digital project emerges to become the repository of what might have been forgotten manuscripts never incorporated into the artistic legacy of Black revolutionary Nicaraguan thought.

The digital turn led scholars to sharpen analyses of mediations, to uncover the means by which hegemonic discourses and narratives were fixed and transmitted within national spaces and entire regions across time. Following Omar Rincón and Amparo Marroquín:

> It became a way of thinking whereby the presence of the others is discovered, and other logics of communication, politics, and culture—what we call "the popular"—are read, understood, and revealed. This mutation implied decentralizing studies and moving from media communication to the social practices and mediations that articulate the experiences of individuals with media and political power. Thus, research studies moved their attention from media to practices and social uses. This epistemological turn also challenged the limitations of the empiricist effects approach and the Marxist approach, which were focused on media structure and power. The key issue was to broaden the understanding of media to cultures and to popular communication practices. The idea was to challenge and criticize media hegemony from the practices of individuals located in the territory.[51]

The roots of this epistemological shift can be traced to Jesús Martín-Barbero, whose theory of mediations became a map to explore the practices of media users, practices constituted by their political cultures, resistances, complicity with domination, and popular aesthetics, heeding the call "to understand media practices in and with people, to decentralize our way of looking at the media and their production logics, and to turn to what people do in daily life with what they consume and enjoy."[52] Following this track, it is possible to see *Antojología*'s availability on YouTube in contrast to the insular Central American publishing industry. Rigby's presence in the film and the poems he shared with the viewer represent a grassroots affront to the traditional print enterprise, particularly that which has omitted Black voices.

Following a chronological order in the poetic archive that Rigby presents in the film, the next composition in the documentary-anthology first appeared in a newspaper in 1972. The shot of the yellowed newsprint is available on the website and in the film; it is held in the frame for several seconds, just long enough for the title "Para los terremotólogos" (For the Seismologists) to be read and just long enough to serve as a backdrop for the voice-over of Rigby describing the first great catastrophe that prevented him from publishing a book (figure 5.2).

The poem itself plays with the image of passion for an object of desire. At times alluding to love for a woman, or love for a nation, or for poetry itself, the verses highlight the ardor of that love. Indirectly referencing what could also be interpreted as the revolution-yet-to-come, given that it was published seven years prior to the Sandinista triumph, the poem highlights the futility of measures like the Richter or the Mercalli to measure the force of that love, which stands firmer and more constant than any standing building. The poem was published just one month before the fatal earthquake in Managua that claimed the lives of over twenty-thousand people. Important to the notion of literary struggle

Figure 5.2. "Para los terremotólogos" (For the Seismologists). *Source: Antojología*, directed by Eduardo Spiegeler and María José Álvarez.

From Caribbean Sea to Digital Shore | 171

that is developed in the documentary, the earthquake claimed human lives as well as Rigby's first book in print, which he would have called "Lo rojoinegro de lo azuliblanco" (The Reddish Black of the Blue and White). This would-be title spoke directly to the Afro-Indigeneity of Nicaragua, so often represented by its blue and white flag.

Encoded in this film is the fact that Rigby passed on in 2017 without having ever published his long-dreamed book, while the matter to be decoded by the reader-spectator is that this documentary-anthology, available in its entirety on YouTube, and the poems available digitally on the website, are the sole (virtual) collection of writings published by Rigby; Antojología is, in effect, his long-dreamed poetic volume.[53] For that reason, the film includes direct dialogue with Rigby that details the obstacles that prevented the book from becoming manifest in traditional print. Some circumstances, like the earthquake, were unforeseeable. Others, like the fact that the Somoza dictatorship actively persecuted leftist intellectuals like Rigby, meant that for decades the poet's writings were endangered. Indeed, Rigby shares that a second book manuscript intended for publication was seized by Somoza's men and subsequently destroyed. The documentary-anthology shows him going through his stacks of papers to find his typeset poems and walking past brick walls adorned with his verses. Despite remaining an obscure poet in the larger

Figure 5.3. Rigby Admiring His Writing. *Source*: *Antojología*, directed by Eduardo Spiegeler and María José Álvarez.

Central American regional literary sphere, he has literally left his print on the walls of Bluefields and Pearl Lagoon.

Taking the spectator to these walls, Rigby smiles broadly as he reads his verses aloud and the camera rests on the print over the bricks. Many have, as in the case of those in figure 5.3, been extracted from longer poems written by Rigby.[54] The full composition contains references to Rigby as a child and to the lessons he learned from his parents about race, money, and class. The verses he selects for the public, however, not only revel in word play through the juxtaposition of parallel sound-images, like "blanquinegro" (whitish black) and "blanco y/o negro (black and/or white), but also reflect the literary figure of the poet himself as a voice that does not choose one shade over another in the color spectrum but one given to Bluefields as an undivided whole. The walls over which the camera pauses to consider Rigby's print are timeless, undated, and ever-present reminders of the structural inequality in Bluefields that remains as unaltered today as when Rigby was first interpellated by the Sandinista movement. Those conditions, like those of other [Black] communities described in chapters 2 and 3 of this book, include the isolation and disconnected state of the peripheral Caribbean coast in relation to principal Central American cities, as well as the higher rates of unemployment and the dearth of opportunities available for young people to thrive. In this way, the film highlights with great subtlety the linked themes between Rigby and older Black writers of the region, like Costa Rican Quince Duncan, as well as emerging Black writers of the Central American Caribbean coast, like Wingston González and Xiomara Cacho Caballero.[55]

The documentary-anthology digs deeper into Rigby's literary influences and the intellectual circles that he was a part of during this time. This memorabilia includes photographs and footage of the poet giving live readings, generally in the company of *mestizo* Sandinista poets. His exposure coincided with the increasing recognition by the Sandinista government of Blackness in the Nicaraguan coast.[56] It also coincided with language and cultural revitalization projects taking place by Sandinistas in this politically important area.[57] However, even as a well-connected poet known for his interventions in Sandinista poetry circles, Rigby was unable to print a book of his own. Presses remained concentrated in Managua, and, while a couple of university presses were established in León, the logistical challenges of publication remained a reality for Black poets like

Rigby.⁵⁸ That Rigby's writing was included in any Sandinista collections at all was nothing short of miraculous.

Sociopolitical poetry is not the only genre to grace the frames of the documentary-anthology. Rigby's anthologized work in the film also includes philosophical verses about his coastal home. As in the print that appears in yet another tagged brick wall, Rigby brings passerby readers and silver screen readers to contemplate the importance of water. The words in the frame tell us "es sobre el mar/ que debemos mirar/ si hemos de conocer/ la verdadera edad del HOMBRE" (it is over the sea/ that we must see/ if we are to know/ the true age of MAN). The content is aligned thematically with Rigby's impression of the Nicaraguan coast as his homeland, a cherished place overlooking the sea that holds truths to be deciphered. These verses, like other graffiti examined elsewhere, exist at the crossroads of textuality and audiovisuality.⁵⁹ The brevity of the syntax makes the verses ever more poignant, as the affront to convention is relayed to readers/spectators through its very position over an untraditional surface. In both digital productions (the YouTube film and the website), even graffiti is legitimized as a form of prized Black print.

From the book of poems that was destroyed by the earthquake, to the verses that were destroyed by paramilitary troops, to the fact of living in a disenfranchised Black and Indigenous community on the [wrong] coast, Rigby faced challenges that resulted in either the destruction of his folios or his typescript remaining on pages without ever going to press. Such is the case with the poem "Constancia" (For the Record) over which the camera lingers just long enough for the spectator to follow Rigby's finger and voice as the poet reads the verses aloud (figure 5.4). The poem is a summative reflection of the poet's experience after the revolution, as intellectuals who headed the movement were obligated to retreat. The short syntax of the first verse "desde entonces" (since then) punctuates the beginning of a new experience, captured in the equally brief syntax of the second and third verses "todos mis diás/ son formulas de dios" (all of my days/ are formulas from God). The sense of planning, of careful organization, even of passion, is absent in these verses. The verses are penned by a poet made all the wiser by time itself. The semicolon that opens the way to verses four and five provides the punctuation that manifests the lucidness of the thoughts they contain.

Rigby makes clear for the record, ": cuando la muerte se dio cuenta de mi vida/y había todo un pueblo con quien compartirla" (: when death

Figure 5.4. "Constancia" (For the Record). *Source*: *Antojología*, directed by Eduardo Spiegeler and María José Álvarez.

noticed my life/ and there was a whole community with whom to share it). Indeed, it was not with an intellectual elite that Rigby shared his poetry, but with the passersby who read his verses on the brick walls of Bluefields and Pearl Lagoon as they walked—to school, to work, to church, to the shore.

As the documentary-anthology approaches its final scenes, it opens a space for Rigby to reflect about his place in the Nicaraguan literary sphere. With Rigby on the left edge of the frame, the camera holds still over a framed certificate hanging on one of the walls of his home. While the small print is difficult to read, two lines stand out in this shot: the poet's name and the phrase Living Human Treasure. The certificate was presented to him by the Instituto Nicaragüense de Cultura (Nicaraguan

Cultural Institute) in 2011. As part of its "2011: Unidad Para el Bien (Unity for Good) campaign," the institute held the *Africanto* gala at the Rubén Darío Theater in commemoration of the International Year of Afrodescendants. It was at this event that the institute recognized Rigby for "revitalizing and enriching Nicaraguan culture with his literary and musical arts." Momentous as the occasion in Managua was, however, to Rigby, what remains important are his people. Hence, as if it were one of the poems captured in earlier shots of the documentary containing his notes and edits, the spectator sees that Rigby has added an important exclamation in the left corner of the certificate, just under the name of the awarding Institute: "El pueblo, Presidente!" (The people, Mr. President!)

This official recognition notwithstanding, the last minutes of the documentary-anthology reflect what Langston Hughes might have called Rigby's "dream deferred."[60] The 1951 poem by Hughes meditated over a common theme in Black experience, specifically what happened when racism and classism together worked to prevent the realization of a Black subject's dreams. There are many possibilities embedded in the poem, from its withering away to its explosion, and the manifest hypothesis that it sags like a heavy load over the dreamer. This last possibility is applicable to Rigby, as the poet returns often in the documentary-anthology to the circumstances that prevented publication. Yet, despite the dream's multiple deferrals over the course of his lifetime, we see in the final sequence of the documentary-anthology that the joy of the day he sees his own volume in print makes his eyes spark with delight. It is in these last seconds, as he touches the bricks of a wall by describing it, that the documentary-anthology comes back full circle (figure 5.5).

The powerful nature of this sequence cannot be understated, as it is charged with the spectator's knowledge that he never lived to see *Antología*, his only literary anthology. Martín Barbero's observation that (our) consumption of media is not just "the reproduction of meanings, but also a process of giving objects a social form that registers the demands and forms of action of different cultural competencies" is important to mention here.[61] The documentary presents to the viewer Rigby's negotiation of his position in the regional publishing industry, and leaves her the decoding of the digital audiovisual record of his writing in place of the dream repeatedly deferred. The frames that feature Rigby's body next to his print media become an integral part of his poetic legacy. He remains in these images a poet whose work deserved much more recognition than it received during the poet's lifetime.

Figure 5.5. Rigby's Anthology. *Source*: *Antojología*, directed by Eduardo Spiegeler and María José Álvarez.

The documentary-anthology thus deploys this last sequence as an afterword that could very well be found at the end of a standard published poetic anthology. Carl Rigby's writing emerged as a negotiation of the liminal position of Afrodescendants in Nicaragua, at precisely the moment when the Sandinista government sought support from Caribbean coastal communities. As Sandinista-led linguistic projects took form, so too did state-sponsored fieldwork about linguistic shift and recovery, which itself changed the demand for prescriptive usage and increased descriptive appreciation for linguistic variation.[62] Yet neither those conditions nor the literary environment after the Sandinista revolution changed the obstacles faced by poets like Rigby. This afterword sequence reminds its silver-screen readers that Rigby challenged the *mestizo* Nicaraguan literary tradition throughout his lifetime, both through the content of his writing and his defiant perception of himself as a writer for the people of the Nicaraguan Caribbean coast. It throws into relief the instances in which even scholars specifically focused on anthologizing Sandinista poetry overlooked his work. Poignantly, however, it manifests Rigby as a prolific poet on a digital shore whose legacy remains on virtual interfaces as well as in graffiti print on the walls of his hometown. The presentation of his poetry as anthologized via new media further brings spectators to question the processes of production, circulation, and consumption of Black writing in the region.

[Black] Central American Narratives Today

Despite the increased attention to Black lives across Central America in this century, there remains a glass ceiling for speakers of Creole, Garifuna, and other Indigenous languages that makes it virtually impossible for them to publish in mainstream venues. Not only do they generally hail from communities in the Caribbean that have been historically excluded in sociopolitical and humanistic matters, but these communities are multilingual. To date, publishing in Spanish remains an implicit requisite for narratives to circulate within Latin America. Those rules, however, are less enforced in digital realms. The rules of circulation for Black narratives are different in cyberspace, owing to the fact that the content that circulates on platforms such as YouTube, Facebook, Twitter, and other venues sees little if any intrusion from censoring bodies of the nation-state or the intellectual elite. In the same way that isolation and disconnection of Black communities has led the "lush languages" of Central America to thrive, so too has the perception of narratives in cyberspace as low culture enabled digital narratives to achieve a wider circulation than print media has ever allowed Black writers.

When the Central American literary tradition was established by Rubén Darío and members of his generation (discussed in chapter 1), they reinforced Spanish as the official language of the isthmus's intellectual production. Negative language attitudes with respect to Black—as well as Indigenous—languages and their speakers have prevailed across the middle and upper classes of these countries. Two centuries after Independence, the taste for mainstream representative national and regional narratives remains the same. Yet circulation and reception beyond the isthmus's borders extends the reach of Black narratives that do not conform to expectations of Black authors and their writing. The works of Black writers like Rigby and González launched from a digital shore are critical to preserving a myriad of approximations into Afrodescendant experience for generations. Both Rigby, now deceased, and González, who continues to publish his print in traditional as well as digital venues, were effective navigators of the cultural waters. In a literary trajectory where few passageways were open to Afrodescendants, they were trailblazers in the digital documentation of their work.

Black Central American writing has arrived at a time when Afrodescendants in the isthmus and beyond are invoking the status of Indigenous peoples with a claim to ancestral lands and protections, as guaranteed by Article 13 of the UN Declaration on the Rights of Indigenous Peoples. Principal among the provisions is the guarantee to communication rights and cultural self-determination: "Indigenous peoples have the right to revitalize, use, develop and transmit to future generations their histories, languages, oral traditions, philosophies, writing systems and literatures, and to designate and retain their own names for communities, places and persons."[63] Afrodescendant grassroots activism has contributed to the greater visibility of Black Caribbean coastal communities in the isthmus, while its writers have energetically sought to measure tides on the digital shore. More powerful yet—and what makes this literary moment a superb challenge to the narratives about Blackness that were devised from 1821 forward—is the multiplatform diffusion of that body of work. After all, incorporation into the world of Central American letters has long depended on the interests of Spanish-speaking *mestizo* intellectuals. Availing themselves of the discourses of language rights and the global attention to the cultural patrimony of Afrodescendants, as well as the grassroots linguistic and cultural revitalization efforts headed by Black peoples in the isthmus and beyond, Rigby's and González's digital footprints present a formidable challenge to the monolingual and monochrome Hispanophone-lettered cities of the isthmus.

Conclusion

The Battlegrounds of Central American Identity

Print, even that involved in the technical writing of censuses, has always been a battleground for Central American identities. A review of the most recent censuses from the seven nations can illustrate this issue. The 2010 Belizean census lists its five principal "ethnic" groups in descending order as: Mestizo, Creole, Maya, Garifuna, and Mennonite.[1] The 1994 Guatemalan census listed three categories: *indígena, no-indígena,* and *ignorado* (Indigenous, Non-Indigenous, and Unknown) but by 2002, it included a list of four possible ethnicities: *maya, garifuna, xinka,* and *ladino.* The 2001 Honduran census asked individuals to indicate which "community group" they belonged to and included *garifuna, miskito,* and *negro inglés* (Garifuna, Miskito, and English/British Black) among its options. It remains to be seen if a latter census will employ similar terms. The 2007 Salvadoran census experimented with the racial categories established in 1930 (*blancos, indios, mestizos, amarillos, negros, otros;* White, Indians, Mestizos, Yellows, Blacks, Others) and, after eliminating "Indian" as a race, replaced it with "ethnic groups"—better suited to the multicultural jargon of our present historical juncture—in order to account for Indigeneity. Despite keeping "Black" as a racial category, a footnote to the table with demographic data assures readers that any Black individual in El Salvador is a foreigner. Nicaragua refers to its Creole and Miskitu communities as "ethnicities" in its 2005 census. Costa Rica used the terms *negro/afro-costarricense* (Black/Afro-Costa Rican) as "ethnicities" in 2000 and included both of these, as well as *mulato,* in the category of "ethnic-racial self-identification" in 2011. Of all Central American countries, Panama is the only country to list five different types of Black identities on its 2010 census: *negro colonial, negro antillano, negro, negro-otro*, and *negro-no declarado* (Colonial Black, Caribbean Black, Black, Black-Other, Black-Undeclared). While the first two categories mark the Afro-Panamanian subject's historical entry into the nation, the last three reflect more of what we have throughout our long *parcours* of these census categories—ambiguity, denial, and uncertainty in the official print of the isthmus. The usage of these terms indicates the isthmus has, for the most part and at least officially, shifted away from biological to cultural perspectives on Blackness. As progressive as the isthmus's shift to a cultural lens might appear, however, framing Blackness as such assumes a connection to a historical context (colonial period or British rule, for instance) that has long ceased to exist. What is certain is that mainstream forms of print continue to locate the Black citizenry of Central America within discursive systems of power.

Perhaps most importantly, however, the harnessing of the power of print media, traditional and digital, by Black communities throughout Central America evidences the devising of a critical panorama over a constellation of multiple points, changing coordinates, identified as guiding stars giving form to the navigable seas of national identity. This need to trouble the waters remains as critical as ever, as Lorein Powell Benard explains in her interview for the podcast episode "Cocorí" for *Radio Ambulante*. The episode recounts her experience as an undergraduate student driven to write a thesis on the representation of Black peoples in Costa Rican literature. It was written in the 1980s, not a century ago, but even then her professors deemed her analysis *impertinente*, uncalled for, out of line. It was, as Luis Fernando Vargas, the narrator of the podcast, imagines her professors thinking:

> LUIS FERNANDO: Uncalled for. Because what business did she have—a young student, searching for uncomfortable things in the Costa Rican literary canon. It was like a lack of respect for our national history. Her team of readers asked her to review fewer books. Ten were too many, it would be an endless thesis, but she believes there was another reason behind this request.
>
> LOREIN: The hope was that by concentrating on a few works, the issue of racism would end up watered down.

LUIS FERNANDO: That it would feel more like a coincidence than something systematic. Three works can be ignored, but ten . . . that's more difficult.

LOREIN: That may have been the first time there was any talk of . . . of racism in the literature, right? And it was an Afrodescended person who was talking about it, you know? Racism was talked about, but never in the literary context.[2]

Pressed to select a smaller number of texts, Powell Benard was forced to select only two canonical texts for her thesis: *Mamita Yunai* by Carlos Luis Fallas and *Cocorí* by Joaquín Gutiérrez.[3] Both texts were canonical Costa Rican texts, written by figureheads in national and regional literary networks, and Powell Benard found that both reproduced stereotypes of Afrodescendants as bad, lustful, primitive, and beastlike.[4] Yet, with this came the attention of Joaquín Gutiérrez, who was still alive at the time that Powell Benard was undertaking her research, and he responded defiantly toward the young student. Knowing that the book continued to serve as required reading in public schools despite displaying such clear stereotypes, she and her thesis advisor, Quince Duncan, approached a *mestizo* writer with an equally valued literary reputation to speak with Gutiérrez about his book. Despite the attempt in their joint efforts at bringing the author to recognize the racist content of his book, Gutiérrez only agreed to change the white Costa Rican girl's statement after she sees the Black Costa Rican boy for the first time. Editions published after 1983 would have the white child say, "Mom, look, how strange!" instead of the original "Mom, look, a little monkey!" phrase. *Cocorí*, initially published in 1947 by one of the country's most respected writers, had been granted canonical status as required reading in the public schools of Costa Rica, and, had for thirty-six years highlighted a white voice's comparison of a Black child with a monkey.

It was—like the texts examined in the first three chapters of this book—a product of Costa Rican society and its willful denial of personhood and citizenship to the Black peoples within its borders. Even as an undergraduate student facing a literary master, Powell Benard tried to explain the gravity of *Cocorí*'s racist representations to Gutiérrez. She urged him to recognize the historical national racism that shone through the seemingly benign text:

Luis Fernando: The exchange of articles [between them] ended with one from Lorein. A large part of this last text is about what she calls "social programming," which is a bit abstract but can be boiled down to this:

Lorein: Writings are the product of an era. And whatever it is about, superheroes, or worms, or aliens, the worldview of that society is presented.

Luis Fernando: That is, of the society in which the work is produced. Lorein says that an author cannot escape the surrounding reality.

Lorein: I am going to reproduce my world, my view of the world, the worldview of the dominant society of my time.

Lorein: I don't know how Martians think, and if I write about Martians I'm going to make them think like Lorein Powell . . .

Luis Fernando: Or like the society Lorein grew up in.

Lorein: I am not responsible for the training I received. But I am responsible for becoming aware of who am I and why am I this way.

Luis Fernando: Now, this social programming thing is a theory, a way of approaching literary analysis, and like any theory, it can be debated; it is not an absolute truth. But what is interesting here is that Lorein doesn't really care if Joaquín Gutiérrez was racist or not. It is not about demonizing the author. This goes further. What matters to her is that *Cocorí* was written in a society that, in her opinion, is racist, and this is reproduced in the text.

When someone says there is racism in Costa Rica, many Costa Ricans get annoyed or uncomfortable, or, as we say here, their hair stands on end. In part I understand it; it goes against that mythology that Costa Rica is exceptional. That this country, the Switzerland of Central America, is beyond the problems of the rest of the region, a land of peace, without an army. That we are full of life, as Daniel [the host of the podcast] said at the beginning of the story. How can there be racism in the land that is full of life—that expression that denotes total enjoyment, good vibes to the maximum?

This book has interrogated print media to better pinpoint the coordinates of Blackness that have emerged over the course of Central America's history as a group of independent nations. Plenty of barriers have been erected in Central America to shield "rightful" citizens from the "discovery" of Blackness in their own nations. These range from a lack of integration of Atlantic coastal areas into the national framework to revolutionary declarations of sameness. Representations of Blackness emerge in the form of the occasional cluster of narratives in response to catalysts that rock the core of Central Americanness. These narratives prompt questions that require answers and changes in the valuation of mainstream print media as an authoritative source accounting for Blackness. Key to their renegotiation is the production, circulation, and consumption of traditional and digital media curated by Black communities in Central America to counter their historical position of liminality in the region.

As Tanisha Swaby Campbell, daughter of former vice president Epsy Campbell, explains in her discussion of the negative impact of *Cocorí* on her as a child and about the hateful reactions of fellow Costa Ricans during her struggle to have it eliminated from the list of required readings at school: "The issue is that you are Costa Rican, but not as much as they are. Being an Afro-descendant means you are really always in what is called a citizenship deficit, and what we can call the elite, or the majorities—the *mestizo*-White majorities—are always in that constant denial of citizenship."[5] By questioning the legitimacy of their citizenship, many of the narratives authored by *mestizos* have turned Black subjects into intrusive entities encroaching upon spaces designated for the "rightful" citizens of nations across the Americas. So arduous has that struggle been that it has reached the United Nations Commission for the Eradication of Racial Discrimination (CERD) in 2015–2016, leading to a series of recommendations that the state of Costa Rica remove this book from the school curriculum. In 2017 the case was analyzed in Costa Rican courts once again, and just as she had done when she was a twelve-year-old girl, Tanisha delivered her testimony:

LUIS FERNANDO: . . . She talked about how *Cocorí* affected her self-esteem and her identity formation when she was a child, and why she filed the protection appeal.

TANISHA: When I was in the room that day, it was really shocking for me to think how time had passed and how people of African descent in this country would not be able to win a battle against a fictional character. That seemed very sad to me.

LUIS FERNANDO: The thing is that this issue had been an important part of Tanisha's life for twenty-two years by then.

TANISHA: We are talking, in this country, according to the last census, about 8 percent of the population—we know it must be a bit more than that—whose voice doesn't count any more than a character in a book.

LUIS FERNANDO: Some four hundred thousand people whose voices don't count any more than *Cocorí*, according to Tanisha.

TANISHA: That is precisely what I told the magistrates, that I could not believe that twenty-two years later, I was fighting for the same thing and that now it was not for me, but for my son.

LUIS FERNANDO: He was two years old at the time. So that he would not have to live the way thousands of Afro-descended children have lived for decades in Costa Rica. A month after that testimony, in May 2017, the Constitutional Court issued its ruling. The appeal was declared to be without merit. *Cocorí* would continue in the Costa Rican education system . . .

In Central America, as is the case throughout our hemisphere, the cultural sphere is a battleground in which struggles are fought and the demarcations of dominance are drawn. They are platforms designed with the overall intention of wielding power over subjects outside the hegemonic order with the authority of images wrought from words. The battle is for recognition of Blackness as an integral and historically relevant feature of Central Americanness. Due recognition cannot be won, however, unless narratives about national belonging are traced and the coordinates that have framed Blackness over time are understood as a constellation that reveals the entirety of representational schema.

Print media encodes the ethnolinguistic and geographical divides that designate Pacific coastal stretch as the location of Central Americanness and its inhabitants as the "legitimate" citizens of the isthmus. The chapters in this book have treated the primary texts examined here as documents that mark a geographic, linguistic, and ethnic divide leading to the severing of Central America into three distinct areas: the *mestizo* Pacific coast, the Indigenous highlands, and the Black Caribbean coast. While the highlands prefigure in the Central American imagination as spaces of Indigenous autonomy and rebellion, Black zones are excised from isthmian national imaginaries. As the privilege of "rightful citizenship" is unequally distributed, mainstream print media became a vehicle for transporting Pacific mestizo readers to the Caribbean strip. For centuries, mainstream print has defined Afrodescendants as a "liminal citizenry," subjects who possess an uncontested citizenship status in the isthmus but are conceived of neither as the trustees nor the true inheritors of national legacies. The tension between notions of rightfulness and liminality are palpable in this body of work, since, being issued in the course of critical historical junctures, they complement political discourses with respect to Central American national patrimonies.

Impertinence and Accountability

In bringing to the table Blackness in Central American print media, this book participates in the discussion about national and regional accountability for the stereotypes that remain in print without due revision and critique—however "impertinent" that might be perceived. Across Central America, it is Afrodescendants living and residing in the isthmus whose rightful belonging has been questioned for nearly two hundred years. The grand narratives of nation-states have not been based on units of exactitude, but rather on ideological "fit." Notions of rightful belonging presupposed on perceptions have been compiled as an imagined register of Afrodescendants' contribution to the cultural patrimonies of the isthmus. The periods of socioeconomic transition I have explored in this book—Independence, the formation and dissolution of the Federal Republic of

Central America, the conversion of Central America into "banana republics," foreign investment in the building of the Panama Canal, the rise of military dictatorships and the processes of globalization—prescribed the demarcation of the territory to be considered Central America and definition of who is rightfully Central American. The debates about the relationship of citizenship were transposed to literature where its instrumental role becomes a means of providing an inventory of legitimacy and liminality.

The objective of *Black in Print* has been to shed light on the authorship of narratives that have historically framed Afrodescendance from 1821 forward, and to emphasize that they cannot continue to be overlooked. Authority rested for nearly two hundred years in the hands of white and *mestizo* storytellers. The narratives devised for those two centuries contributed to the erasure of Central American's involvement in the slave trade and to the formulation of a romantic disappearance of enslaved Black peoples. This is the first issue that distinguishes Central American narratives of Afrodescendance from those written in contexts like Brazil or the Caribbean. Afrodescendants were absorbed into the principal cities of Central America on the eve of Independence at the same time that the categories "Black" and "mulatto" that had existed in the colonial period became irrelevant to the forefathers of the region and they oversaw the elimination of such categories from censuses altogether. Since then, the census became, as it has been for other nations in the hemisphere, "a symbolic site where the nation is defined and a political tool for charting the path toward future national prosperity."[6] With the use of this quantifiable measure eliminating accountability to Afrodescendant citizens, early narratives constructed a fiction in which Black peoples in the isthmus simply did not exist in the region. This, despite the wealth of archival documents from a colonial government that counted and classified their subjects as "Black" or "Indian" in order to execute and rationalize regimes of systematic extraction, dispossession, and social control.[7] This would include the ancestors of all members of Afrodescendant communities in the isthmus, including formerly enslaved and emancipated Black peoples, West Indian migrants, and Garifuna peoples who have historically resided in the isthmus. Out of the newly forged capitals of the isthmus, literary circles became intermediaries facilitating the production, circulation, and consumption of narratives by and about the young Central American nations.

Intellectuals such as Rubén Darío and Francisco Gavidia were key in fashioning the [colorblind] narrativized cultural patrimony of the isthmus. Their texts advanced the myths that Black peoples did not exist in the isthmus, denying them a place in the then-present and future of Central America. Darío positioned them across the Atlantic in Orientalist locations, while Gavidia wrote a romantic disappearance for them after they were no longer needed in the independent republics. Both plotlines resulted in Afrodescendants being divested of their roles and contributions to their newly independent nations in the nascent print tradition of the region. Once fictionalized as inhabitants of the Orient instead of Central Americans or former slaves who vanished into thin air, print media made it possible for its readers to turn a blind eye to the Afrodescendants remaining in the cosmopolitan nations or to Black communities in peripheral areas of the nation. Quite literally, print media provided the sightlines to take in a view of desirable citizenry. Turning a blind eye to the role of geography in structuring the coordinates of Blackness over time, scholarship on ethnolinguistic processes has failed to recognize print media as maps that provide close-ups of Hispanophone *mestizos/ladinos* closer to the Pacific coast. This, at the expense of the multilingual populations closer to the Caribbean coast.

Banana novels and canal literature made clear the extent to which print media in Central America became a battleground in which ideological struggles about race, identity, and belonging were fought. The early twentieth-century fictions written by Paca Navas de Miralda, an author with a personal history of living in the polyphonic and multiethnic Caribbean coast, and Demetrio Aguilera Malta, an author who was an outsider but, during his time as a journalist in the Canal Zone, allowed the myths of *mestizaje* as belonging to gain ground. They also nourished nationalist concerns about the place of outsiders in eminently foreign-controlled areas of Central America, while in tandem enhancing the narratives with eugenicist discourses. The narratives that appeared in print media were designed with the overall intention of wielding power over Black subjects outside the hegemonic order with the authority of images wrought from words. The mid-twentieth-century narratives of Miguel Ángel Asturias and David Ruiz Puga abandoned the eugenicist imperative of previous decades in print history, though they retained the same distinctions between Black and Indigenous communities that had been evidenced in the past. Importantly, these fictions positioned

Indigenous peoples as legacy "others" while designating Afrodescendants as interrupters in the worlds of Indigenous characters.

At every critical historical juncture in the isthmus's print history, Blackness has been a moving target with its distinct coordinates for framing its belonging, expulsion, appearance, and disappearance according to shifting sociopolitical and economic factors that give its coordinates meaning. In the last two decades of the twentieth century, the demand for recognition of ethnolinguistic minorities within the isthmus was accelerated by grassroots movements demanding state accountability for centuries of oblivion. The narratives written by Tatiana Lobo and Anacristina Rossi were distinct from those that had been written in decades prior, as they were put in line with the discourses of multiculturalism increasingly embraced by the intellectual spheres of the region. Whether written with romantic nostalgia for a once-isolated Black community that was on the brink of incorporation into the national fold or with an extensive excavation of hitherto ignored Black histories, the narratives were committed to revising the history of the region as one in which Black peoples had always belonged while experiencing exclusion. That tender longing for the past is absent, however, in the narratives by Afrodescendants in the first decades of the twenty-first century. In lieu of a celebration of multiculturalism and bringing the Caribbean into the fold, narratives by Black writers such as Carl Rigby and Wingston González take a stance on Blackness from a position of cautious involvement. They do not request entry into the literary milieus of Central America, but rather avail themselves of video and digital media to launch writings that would not have otherwise gone to press. Like other Afrodescendants living in Central America, these writers are attuned to the narratives about Afrodescendants that remain in place and continue to promote problematic attributes to Black peoples in the isthmus.

In Central America a plethora of texts have been written outside of hegemonic literary scenes, particularly through independent publishing platforms, both analog and virtual. Afrodescendants in the twenty-first century are forging independent avenues for the transformation of narratives about Blackness by asserting their ancestral belonging to the Central American landscape. The battlegrounds of Central American identity are as much in the political sphere as they are in print culture. In both arenas, the nation's citizens partake in the grand narratives that allow them to claim belonging. These stories, however, are also protectionist gatekeeper myths. As this book has shown, they have historically excised Black peoples from national discourses, leaving them on the shores of their nations or in isolated language islands within the country's borders both literally and figuratively. Moments of socioeconomic shift have led the body politic to contract or expand to accommodate the reevaluation of the coordinates that designate the point of belonging to the national field. The wide variety of narratives examined here—from traditional print to digital print—have served to map the coordinates of Blackness in Central America from 1824 to the present, a period of just under two hundred years.

Turning the Page

Debates about Blackness in Central American are not, as critics and ethnographers in the last century argued, evidence that these communities have been submerged in silence and powerlessness. Rather, these debates reflect and actively intervene in complex and contradictory processes of reaffirmation of Black Central American identities accomplished through national and global recognition. The very presence of Afro-Central Americans forces politicians, economists, historians, and entire nations to recognize Afrodescendants as a constitutive citizenry of the Central American nations at moments of critical political and economic significance. As such, it has been intended to highlight Blackness as the Achilles's heel of Central American mediations and intellectual history from Independence through the twenty-first century. Examining print media allowed me to consider how the political discussions regarding the rightful belonging of Afrodescendants in Central America could be gleaned in the fictions of the isthmus. The focus on literature allowed me to achieve an analysis of transformation of narrative modes and cultural identities as Afrodescendants grew to include colonial descendants of Black slaves, and West Indian and Afro-Indigenous communities. Like the Indigenous peoples of the isthmus, they are an indelible group that has demanded accountability and recognition. Never fully forgotten nor fully recognized as citizens, Afrodescendants constitute a liminal citizenry that has been reinforced as such in the print history of Central America. In my analysis, literary discourse is the proverbial "ball and chain" that keeps the Black peoples of Central America shackled to the representations, secured and prevented from escaping so long as the print media produced emerge from the hegemonic spaces of lettered cities.

The first chapter demonstrated that paradigmatic authors negotiated the crisis of Central American nation-state formation by embarking upon a project to produce written works of art wherein Blackness was given an ornamental place, establishing the otherworldliness of Blackness—an element that would henceforth always be located on any other shore but that of the Pacific Ocean. The second chapter brought us to the mid-twentieth century and the discourses of eugenics and mappings of an unchartered Atlantic coast. Both West Indian and Garifuna communities within Central American borders were construed as enemies to legitimized citizens. The third chapter addressed the importance of Mesoamerica as a reference point for national imaginaries across Central America and its signature importance to Guatemala. It explored the metaphorical friction between Black and Indigenous peoples in one work and extended the discussion to the Belizean/Guatemalan border, pointing to the tensions of ethnolinguistic borders and decolonizing approaches to the divide. The fourth chapter explored two contemporary novels whose common point of articulation is diversity and inclusion, highlighting the rhetoric of multiculturalism that all too often fails to ignite structural change. The fifth chapter assessed external digital forces that have tinged print production and created new production, distribution, and consumption circuits at the behest of not just young Black Central American thinkers but also an older generation for whom writing by and for the community resonates with conceptions of local and popular media as understood in the isthmus. In all cases, the chapters have examined the mediations of Blackness as defiantly unfixed moving targets in Central America across time and space.

Print media are produced to be circulated and are circulated in order to be consumed by their intended readership. These phases of cultural production have designated print as perhaps the most elitist of forms, and lettered cities as counterparts to the Caribbean coastal areas in which Blackness in Central America is often restricted. In Central America, as is the case elsewhere, literature is the battleground on which ideological struggles are fought and the demarcations of dominance are drawn. It is a site fraught with conflicts designed with the overall intention of wielding power over subjects outside the hegemonic order with the authority of images wrought from words. With few exceptions, the literature examined in this project took a historically grounded approach to the inventory of "rightful" and "liminal" citizenry. As the case of Afrodescendants in Central America demonstrates, liminality is not solely predicated on alterity. Indigeneity *could* be as "other" as Blackness.

A central distinguishing factor is, as *Black in Print* posits, the multiple points of origin and articulation allotted for in the Black Central American experience. The perceived core of indigeneity finds its place in the highlands of Central America, in the cultural practice of tilling the land and in the experience of a plundered and decimated people. The liminal quality of Black experience is inherent in its escape from such constrictive geographic, socioeconomic, and experiential estimations. Writings of the colonial period tracked Blackness spilling over into prestigious positions in both rural and urban contexts; texts in the aftermath of Independence located Blackness in the Orientalist motifs of an array of the great literary masters; early twentieth-century novels designated the Atlantic coastal strip for the instrumental plotting of Blackness; other works allowed Blackness to upstage Indigeneity in a deft maneuver aiming to highlight its inapplicability to a isthmus heavily invested in its claim to a Mesoamerican grandeur; and more contemporary works find in Blackness a key element for investment and attraction for capital development and tourism. The five chapters of this book, then, have demonstrated the extent to which Blackness has historically been a liminal element in national and local imaginaries. As key socioeconomic shifts bring these imaginaries into crisis, cultural memory is activated and so too are the means of entrapping Blackness in isthmian print.

The representations of Blackness from Independence to the contemporary period begin to answer a question of key importance in the field: Why should print media by and about the isthmus be reexamined today in the twenty-first century? The overlapping mediations of polyphonic Caribbean, Latin American, Black Atlantic, and Black hemispheric literary and cultural traditions have left their mark on the narratives we tell, the print we share and follow, and the media we consume. In our century, it is critical that we evaluate discourses of Blackness emerging and transiting both traditional print and digital realms, as well as their impact on contemporary national discourses that continue to design sensibilities of belonging to Central America. After all, to write about ethnicity in Central America—a narrow isthmus that is sometimes considered an extension of the North American continent, on occasion conceived as a strip of Caribbean nations, and nearly always imagined as a peripheral Latin American region—is a venture into a rich terrain of cultural dynamics. It is a journey that, admittedly, most Central Americans have been hesitant to take. The national imaginaries that were constructed by the *criollo* elites in the wake of Independence posited Guatemala, El Salvador, Honduras, Nicaragua, Costa Rica, and Panama as an economic union of culturally and linguistically hegemonic states. Crossing the fissures and crevices of this terrain leads us to the unsettled soil of a Central American identity. It dares us to sift through Central American ethnolinguistic identities to answer, with the rich evidence of Black legacies that we have before us: Who is Central American? Who belongs in Central America? Who *is* there? Who has been *allowed* to feel and be defined as Central American? Sifting through the cultural debris of the last two hundred years reveals that the exclusion of Black experiences is a common feature of a *trans-isthmus* Central American intellectual tradition, but the next page need not be.

Appendix

Transcript of the "Cocorí" Episode on *Radio Ambulante*

"Cocorí" aired on *Radio Ambulante* on February 8, 2022. The episode tells the story of Joaquín Gutiérrez's *Cocorí*, published in 1947 as a children's story and incorporated for many decades in the curriculum of Costa Rica's public school system. The episode brings together the voices of Lorein Powell Benard, one of the first scholars to challenge the book's racist depiction of Black children; Quince Duncan, renowned Afro–Costa Rican writer and human rights activist who joined Powell Benard in the challenge; and Tanisha Swaby Campbell, who was a child litigant and, twelve years later, an adult witness on the two separate occasions that the challenge reached Costa Rican courts. Included in the episode as well are the reactions of the white author, Joaquín Gutiérrez, who adamantly defended his depiction of Black Costa Ricans, and sound clips of *mestizo* and white Costa Rican readers who just as staunchly fought to defend the book, despite its embedded racism. In conversation with these voices is episode host Luis Fernando Vargas, who untangles what this Costa Rican classic means to Costa Ricans—all Costa Ricans—and to the foundational myths of the country. The powerful narrative arc and reflections of Powell Benard, Duncan, and Swaby Campbell poignantly bring to bear the deleterious effects of a fictional character that continues to be protected and valued more than the Black citizens of the country.

With its attention to debates in homes, schools, national and international courts, television, airwaves, traditional print, and digital print forms, "Cocorí" is a key piece of evidence that print media remain a battleground of Central American identity, with the fight against racist, anti-Black fictions alive and well in 2022. We recommend that you cite the English transcript of "Cocorí" as follows, should you need to quote from it on any forum: Daniel Alarcón and Luis Fernando Vargas, "Cocorí: Translation," *Radio Ambulante*, NPR, February 8, 2022, https://radioambulante.org/en/translation/cocori-translation.

"Cocorí"

DANIEL ALARCÓN: This is *Radio Ambulante*, from NPR. I'm Daniel Alarcón. And I am here with our editor, Luis Fernando Vargas. Hello, Luis Fernando. How are you?

LUIS FERNANDO: Very well. How are you?

DANIEL: All good. *Pura vida*. Where are you located? Where are you greeting me from?

LUIS FERNANDO: From San José, Costa Rica.

DANIEL: Costa Rica. Very well, Luis Fernando. OK, then . . . Today you wanted to talk to me about a book, right?

LUIS FERNANDO: Yes, about the first book I ever read. Or at least, the first book I read consciously. Meaning, one I read from start to finish. I understood it. Or at least, that's what I thought. Or at least, I got a notion of what the book was about.

DANIEL: How old were you?

LUIS FERNANDO: I'm ashamed to say it, but I was about ten years old [laughs]. I mean, before that, my dose of stories was Nintendo and Dragon Ball.

DANIEL ALARCÓN: Very well, very good. Classics.

LUIS FERNANDO: Exactly. I read it in school, the book. It was part of the curricular program, that is, I didn't even read it for pleasure, but I was forced to read it. But I can say I have a lot of affection for the book.

DANIEL: Tell me a little about this book and what it's about. What the title is, etc.

LUIS FERNANDO: The book is called *Cocorí*. For most people who are listening to us, it won't mean anything, but in Costa Rica it's considered a classic. It was written by one of our leading, most important authors, whose name is Joaquín Gutiérrez Mangel. He wrote it in 1947. Basically— and I'll explain a complexity in a minute—it's the story of a boy named Cocorí, who lives on a beach that borders the jungle, in what is supposed to be like the Costa Rican Caribbean. It's a very, very rustic town. And one day, a ship arrives in the morning, a large ship, with passengers. Cocorí goes along with his neighbors bringing fruit as a gift in a little boat. They board the ship and Cocorí meets a girl. To him, she is the prettiest girl he has ever seen. And the girl gives him a rose that the boy considers as beautiful as she is. But the next day, the rose dies and the girl leaves. And Cocorí, very sad, wonders why beautiful things last so little and why ugly and bad things, like the dangerous animals in the jungle and the carnivorous plants where he lives, last what seems like an eternity. He then goes on an adventure into the heart of the jungle to ask old and supposedly wise animals to try and figure this out, right? Why is the weather so inclement?

DANIEL: Jajaja! OK, so . . . I'm laughing because it seems very dark to me, which doesn't match the *pura vida*, the full-of-life Costa Rican culture I know about, brother. So, all of this seems very surprising to me, but I don't know if that is the complexity you mentioned or if there is something else, but it still seems very strange. I don't know if you want to explain it to me or maybe I just misunderstood all these good vibes you have been telling me about Costa Rica for so many years.

LUIS FERNANDO: The complexity is that Cocorí is of African descent and the girl is White, and that begins to give everything meaning. In other words, the girl is the most beautiful thing Cocorí has ever seen; she looks like a rose. And Cocorí, on the other hand, on the first page of the book, is compared to a *caimito*, which is a tropical fruit with a dark skin that is not very popular, that is, it is not an apple, and this is the beginning of the idea that what is external, what is not from Cocorí's home, is better, more beautiful.

DANIEL: This fairly clear symbolism, let's say, of the ... the rose, the White girl and the Afro boy and the jungle, and the value system as seen from our point of view—or from my point of view—as you have explained, is quite racist. I imagine you overlooked that at the age of ten. I mean, you didn't realize it.

LUIS FERNANDO: It went over my head, obviously, and it was never explained to me in class that *Cocorí* had racist elements. Racism in *Cocorí* is never mentioned in schools, or at least when I was in school in the early 2000s. Now I see it, and it seems very problematic, and it creates a conflict for me because it's the first book I ever read, and you know I like to read, and it's hard for me not to love it.

DANIEL: I guess that's what we're going to talk about today.

LUIS FERNANDO: Yes, that's what we are going to talk about today—about Costa Rica's relationship with this book, and especially about people who argue that *Cocorí* does more harm than good and that there is no room in schools for this text.

DANIEL: Very well, Luis Fernando. So let's take a short break and we'll be back.

[Break]

DANIEL: We're back, and now I leave you with Luis Fernando.

LUIS FERNANDO: Let's start with her.

LOREIN POWELL BENARD: My name is Lorein Powell Benard, sociologist. I'm an English teacher.

LUIS FERNANDO: In the early 1980s, she was also a young literature student at the National University of Costa Rica, in Heredia, a province near the capital, San José. At that time, Lorein was looking for a topic for her undergraduate thesis. She is of African descent and, curious about her identity, she was interested in understanding how Black people were portrayed in the nation's literature.

LOREIN: So I reviewed a number of works. The first version of my thesis, I think, included ten works, something like that.

LUIS FERNANDO: And just as she was starting the literature review, even before she had written anything, problems started coming up.

LOREIN: The topic wasn't well accepted. The topic of searching for racism in Costa Rican literary works was not well-liked. I remember one of my thesis readers wrote that my thesis was uncalled for.

LUIS FERNANDO: Uncalled for. Because what business did she have—a young student, searching for uncomfortable things in the Costa Rican literary canon. It was like a lack of respect for our national history. Her team of readers asked her to review fewer books. Ten were too many, it would be an endless thesis, but she believes there was another reason behind this request.

LOREIN: The hope was that by concentrating on a few works, the issue of racism would end up watered down.

LUIS FERNANDO: That it would feel more like a coincidence than something systematic. Three works can be ignored, but ten . . . that's more difficult.

LOREIN: That may have been the first time there was any talk of . . . of racism in the literature, right? And it was an Afro-descended person who was talking about it, you know? Racism was talked about, but never in the literary context.

LUIS FERNANDO: Lorein decided to keep two texts in which the stereotypes of Afro-descendants were more evident. She wanted there to be no doubt—as the readers of her thesis demanded—that there was racism in those works. The first book she chose was *Mamita Yunai*, one of the most important novels in the national literature, written by Carlos Luis Fallas and published in 1941. That text portrays the social injustices experienced by workers at the banana plantation of the United Fruit Company in Limón, the Costa Rican Caribbean.
And the second one was *Cocorí*.

LOREIN: It was shocking the way . . . the way Afro-descendants were described in the two works I kept . . .

LUIS FERNANDO: The Afro-descendant was bad, lustful, primitive, and beastlike. Lorein also had problems with her thesis directors. She decided to move forward alone for a while and then turn to one person, the one who seemed most appropriate to deal with racism in Costa Rican literature . . .

QUINCE DUNCAN: My name is Quince Duncan. I am a writer. A human rights activist, especially for ethnic rights.

LUIS FERNANDO: Of people of African descent . . .

LOREIN: I did my work, and one day I went to Quince's office, since he was the director of the Institute of Latin American Studies, and I brought him the ton of pages, and I said to him, "Quince, take a look at this. If you think it's OK, if you agree with what I say, please, I want you to be my thesis supervisor."

LUIS FERNANDO: Quince was familiar with the work of Joaquín Gutiérrez, of course, as well as *Cocorí*. In 1975, Quince published a book titled *The Negro in Costa Rican Literature*, which covers the history of the integration of people of African descent in the country.

He devoted just one paragraph to *Cocorí*. It's strange how he talks about the novel there. He doesn't point out anything explicitly racist. He says the characters could just as well have been Chinese, but not much more. It is as if he had checked himself in what he was going to say. In fact, when I spoke with Quince, he told me that if there was one book he would like to reedit, it would be that one. Anyway, Quince agreed to read Lorein's work.

QUINCE: That was how I became aware of the seriousness of the text, especially since the book was being used for children. So I said, "No, that can't be right . . ."

LUIS FERNANDO: And he agreed to be her thesis director.

Carlos Luis Fallas had died in 1966, but Joaquín Gutiérrez, the author of *Cocorí*, was alive at the time. Lorein decided she wanted to talk to him, and ask him a few questions about the book. They were almost neighbors, and Lorein got his phone number. So she called him in February 1983.

LOREIN: He wasn't very friendly [laughs]. He was a very grumpy man, well . . . well, I only met him that one time, and I asked him for an interview, and he asks me, "What are you trying to prove?" I tell him, "No, I just want you to answer some questions about . . . about *Cocorí*." "Well, but what?" "Well, for example . . ."

LUIS FERNANDO: For example, at the beginning of the book in the early editions—and this will change later, I and I'll tell you why later—, when Cocorí goes to the ship and meets the girl, she reacts to his presence by telling her mother, "Mom, look, a little monkey."

LOREIN: "For example, that sentence; I want you to explain it to me." And he goes, "When you see a Black man for the first time, don't you think of a monkey?" And I say, "No, I think of a person, it's a person of the Black race," and he hung up the phone.

LUIS FERNANDO: Here I want to mention Lorein's laughter, because I think it says a lot about what it must be like to deal with being of African descent in Costa Rica. It sounds like a defense mechanism, a protection against a society that, although it is not going to enslave you, by telling jokes it will treat you as a second-class citizen, as the object of mockery and ridicule. And it is a laugh designed to avoid conflicts, something very Costa Rican. A laugh that makes everything seem lighter, unimportant. Because being confrontational, especially about issues of racism, makes you . . . uncalled for. So . . . Who was Joaquín Gutiérrez Mangel, that grumpy man whom Lorein described?

Here is some biographical information about him. He was born in 1918, in Puerto Limón, facing the sea, on the Costa Rican Caribbean. That is where the second largest Afro-descendant population group in the country is concentrated . . . More than fifty thousand people, according to the 2011 census. Joaquín Gutierrez was not of African descent; he was *mestizo*, like most Costa Ricans, and he died in 2000. He published six novels, three collections of poems, four travel books, and one memoir. He translated four works of Shakespeare into Spanish. His books, in turn, have been translated into twelve languages. One of those books is *Cocorí*, which was so successful that it has been published in French, German, Russian, Polish, and Portuguese, among other languages. He was a member of the Costa Rican Academy of the Spanish Language and winner of the National Culture Award; he received an honorary doctorate from the University of Costa Rica; and one of the most relevant newspapers in the country declared him a Person of the Century in national literature.

Joaquín Gutiérrez is also remembered as a man committed to leftist struggles. He was a member of the Costa Rican Communist Party. He traveled to Vietnam during the war to write chronicles, and worked in China as a translator of the works of the revolutionary Mao Zedong. He was a candidate for the vice presidency of the country twice in the 1980s, with the *Pueblo Unido* coalition. He did not win either time.

One of the main themes of Joaquín Gutierrez's literature is life in the province of Limón, although he only lived there for the first nine years of his life. He moved to San José and later to Chile, where he lived for more than two decades and wrote several of his books, including *Cocorí*. As a member of the Left, he left the country only after Pinochet's coup.

But back to the book: the character Cocorí lives on a beach with no name, no location. But it can be inferred that it is Limón because of the author's personal history and because all the inhabitants there are Afro-descendants. During the telephone interview in which the author hung up on Lorein, he told her that *Cocorí* was a love song to the Black child. It is an argument that will be heard more than once in this story.

A few months after the short conversation between Lorein and Joaquín Gutiérrez, in September 1983, she and Quince were invited, along with other people, to a television program to talk about racism in Costa Rica. The topic of *Cocorí* came up during the discussion. Unfortunately, I have been unable to obtain the recording of the program, but in the days that followed, Joaquín Gutiérrez published an article in the press responding to the accusations of racism made on television. After that, Lorein also replied in an opinion piece, and an exchange of several texts was put together that reconstructs the main arguments stated by Lorein and Quince on the problematic issues of the book.

Some of these elements are details, scenes. For example, the one at the beginning of the book: Cocorí is in front of a puddle of water in the middle of the jungle, crouches down and sees his reflection. And he is frightened, say Lorein and Quince, as if he was surprised to be Black.

QUINCE: The only human beings he knows are all Black people, so he can't be scared to see his face in the water.

LUIS FERNANDO: But there are also structural things. Elements completely rooted in the story being told. The most relevant thing is the relationship that exists between Cocorí and the girl.

LOREIN: The primitivism that the boy represents versus the civilization represented by the girl.

LUIS FERNANDO: Cocorí, who lives in the jungle, among wild animals, versus the girl who comes on a ship, a symbol of civilization. And then the symbolism of the rose—that rose the girl gives to Cocorí, and that the boy considers as beautiful as her.

QUINCE: The subtle scent of that pink cloud of enchantment that comes with the rose, symbolizing what is good and how civilization is useful to eradicate the useless evil that are the bad thoughts of the jungle, is a clear case of a European imperial imposition on our culture . . . And it is an incredible Eurocentrism.

LUIS FERNANDO: And the flower even makes Cocorí good. The book explicitly says so. Although it is nowhere indicated that Cocorí was ever a bad boy, what *is* inferred to be bad is the jungle, full of dangerous animals and ugly plants.

QUINCE: There is a moral salvation: In this case, some members make them better and the rose raises the IQ of the locals. It makes them intelligent. Cocorí and his friends dance for joy, but it is also a spiritual salvation. They have found meaning in their lives.

LUIS FERNANDO: In other words, to summarize: What is European—which is what is beautiful—came to save the Afro-descendants who live in the jungle.

In the exchange of articles between Lorein and Joaquín Gutiérrez, the author defends himself against accusations of racism. In a response to Lorein, he focuses on the meaning of *Cocorí*: "*Have you ever considered, miss philologist, what the theme of* Cocorí *is? I am going to tell you: It is his discovery that a rose—beauty, truth—has a precarious life in this world of ours, while arrogance, presumptuousness, and the abusive domination of evil forces thrive comfortably and lastingly*." He then answers regarding the scene in which Cocorí gets scared when he sees his own reflection in the water . . . "*Didn't it ever occur to you that anyone is amazed when they see themselves in a mirror for the first time?*" The exchange of articles ended with one from Lorein. A large part of this last text is about what she calls "social programming," which is a bit abstract but can be boiled down to this:

LOREIN: Writings are the product of an era. And whatever it is about, superheroes, or worms, or aliens, the worldview of that society is presented.

LUIS FERNANDO: That is, of the society in which the work is produced. Lorein says that an author cannot escape the surrounding reality.

LOREIN: I am going to reproduce my world, my view of the world, the worldview of the dominant society of my time.

LOREIN: I don't know how Martians think, and if I write about Martians I'm going to make them think like Lorein Powell . . .

LUIS FERNANDO: Or like the society Lorein grew up in.

LOREIN: I am not responsible for the training I received. But I am responsible for becoming aware of who am I and why am I this way.

LUIS FERNANDO: Now, this social programming thing is a theory, a way of approaching literary analysis, and like any theory, it can be debated; it is not an absolute truth. But what is interesting here is that Lorein doesn't really care if Joaquín Gutiérrez was racist or not. It is not about demonizing the author. This goes further. What matters to her is that *Cocorí* was written in a society that, in her opinion, is racist, and this is reproduced in the text.

When someone says there is racism in Costa Rica, many Costa Ricans get annoyed or uncomfortable, or, as we say here, their hair stands on end. In part I understand it; it goes against that mythology that Costa Rica is exceptional. That this country, the Switzerland of Central America, is beyond the problems of the rest of the region, a land of peace, without an army. That we are *full of life*, as Daniel said at the beginning of the story. How can there be racism in the land that is *full of life*—that expression that denotes total enjoyment, good vibes to the maximum? And that hurts. It's our identity. It's the way they raised us, thinking that we are all equal here.

But there is evidence that things are neither so simple nor so pretty. Let's talk about Limón, which, as we said, is the province with the second largest Afro-descendant population in the country. There, all human development indexes—which include categories such as life expectancy, schooling, electricity consumption and material well-being—are below the national average, although the difference is not abysmal. Perhaps for the same reason, Limón includes the municipalities with the highest rates of insecurity and violence in the country. But let's go back to Lorein and Quince. After the last article was published, Fabián Dobles, a writer who is also famous and is recognized nationally and internationally, called both of them . . .

QUINCE: And we explained to Fabián what the matter was. Fabián said, "Well, I'm going to talk to Joaquín, because there are things there that really should be changed, eh?

LUIS FERNANDO: Fabián spoke with Joaquín Gutiérrez. According to Quince, the author of *Cocorí* was very upset and decided that of everything they had pointed out in the book, he would change only one thing: When the girl sees Cocorí for the first time, instead of saying, "Mom, look, a little monkey," she would say, "Mom, look how strange."

QUINCE: So in later editions, after that date . . .

LUIS FERNANDO: That is, from 1983 onwards . . .

QUINCE: You will see that the book says, "Woah, how strange," but that doesn't solve anything, because our children were not strange, either.

LUIS FERNANDO: And that is the only change that has been made to *Cocorí* since 1947.
Lorein published her thesis in 1985 after a fair amount of wrestling with her readers. A two-volume document was the result. I saw the thesis. It is really huge . . . A total of 670 pages.
And there is another detail that seems crazy to me: A lot of people coming to hear the defense of a thesis.

LOREIN: There wasn't room for all the people. It was a tiny lounge, but people were listening from outside. Because there had been a lot of controversy before the defense, it caught the attention of a lot of people.

LUIS FERNANDO: But the thesis was accepted. She graduated and the matter seemed over. Time passed; she moved to the United States to study at Michigan State University. She sent her little son to school there, in a very inclusive, very diverse environment . . .

LOREIN: In the child's mind, that was the United States, right? He didn't know the other side . . .

LUIS FERNANDO: The terrible history of slavery, which ended only with a war . . . But much more . . . A systemic social exclusion designed so that African Americans could not exercise political power or accumulate capital, under constant threat of violent reprisals. The problem persists to this day: the part where you can die at the hands of the police just because of your skin color. They were in Michigan for five years and returned to Costa Rica. It was hard for him, who considered the United States his home.

LOREIN: Here he suddenly found himself in a very racist society from the moment we arrived at the airport. The person who carries the suitcases said, "Black girl, shall I take the suitcases?" and he said, "Mom, why do you let them treat you like that? They must respect you." Right? Why do you allow them to treat you like this?" And inside I thought, "Okay. We are back in our piece of land" [laughs].

LUIS FERNANDO: And in 1995, when Lorein's son was twelve years old, *Cocorí*—that book that had been forgotten for a time—was once again very much present in the life of her family. That year, the Ministry of Public Education decided to include it as compulsory reading in schools, specifically in the sixth grade of primary school, the grade that Lorein's son was in. When Lorein's son's class read it, they quickly began to compare him to Cocorí. But at school, the teachers told her:

LOREIN: "But everyone loves this little Black boy; they call him Cocorí out of love . . ."

LUIS FERNANDO: But to Lorein, it didn't make much sense to complain to the teachers because of what we were talking about a while back, about social programming:

LOREIN: Their view—they couldn't have a different perspective. To them, it was fine, and they patted him on the head, you know? And how nice, that shiny hair, how nice. And the child rejected all that, but they were not able to respect him.

LUIS FERNANDO: I tried to talk to Lorein's son, but he prefers not to remember that difficult stage in his life. And I understand, because I saw those things happen in my own school a few years later. I come from a public school where most of the children were *mestizos*. There was only one Afro-descendant schoolmate. I remember when *Cocorí* arrived, the shouts began at recess: "Cocorí! Come here, Cocorí!" And I also remember that my schoolmate's expression was different from the fun everyone else was having. A look that I couldn't quite identify, but now I imagine it was anger, frustration. Although it seemed normal to all of us. I probably called him Cocorí once or more than once. And I was one of the shy kids.

And I point out what I saw because I was never given the tools to understand that the book hurts others. The book reproduces racist stereotypes, it presents a relationship of inequality and submission that has lasted for centuries. And if someone had told me, would I have understood? I don't know, but it is something that creates contradictions in my mind. On the one hand, it doesn't seem healthy to underestimate children and their power to empathize. But at the same time, it seems naive to think that a child like me at the age of ten would have clearly understood the weight of centuries of slavery and social exclusion.

It's a question I asked everyone I interviewed for this story. About six people. And I discussed it with acquaintances and friends. Can a child deal with the historical burden of *Cocorí* at the age of ten? Some people said "yes," the majority of them *mestizos*, but the same number said "no," all of them Afro-descendants. I think it is important to emphasize this. Because for a *mestizo* to say it is not the same as for an Afro-descendant to say it. The truth is that we *mestizos* can say, "yes, let's teach *Cocorí* with a guide to critical reading of the text" from a comfortable position. Where no harm can be done. But for an Afro-descended child, this can mean a blow to their dignity. Being an object of study can never be pretty. And in a certain way, it would be to perpetuate the idea that we, the *mestizos*, are one kind, and Afro-descendants are another. The truth is that Lorein felt she had to do something to fight back against the bullying her son experienced.

LOREIN: So, I say, "Well, we'll take the legal path" . . .

DANIEL: Lorein and her son would take *Cocorí* to court. We'll be right back.

[Break]

DANIEL: We're back with *Radio Ambulante*. Before the break, we heard the first controversy that emerged around *Cocorí* and the claims of racism in the text. The discussion ended with the change of a single sentence in the book. But now another discussion would begin, and this one would involve state authorities. Luis Fernando continues the story.

LUIS FERNANDO: Lorein contacted her lawyer and explained her son's situation: his classmates compared him to Cocorí, and the boy felt uncomfortable with this, hurt. He felt that the comparison with a character that was seen as strange, like a *caimito*, was a mockery. She proposed to file an appeal for protection with the Constitutional Court of Costa Rica. An appeal for protection is basically a legal action that anyone can take if they feel that their constitutional rights are being violated. The objective of Lorein and her lawyer was to have the book removed from schools, to demonstrate that its reading was a violation of the rights of Afro-descended children. Specifically, they claimed the book violated the article of the Constitution which says that every person is equal before the law and that no discrimination contrary to human dignity may be practiced. Also, that reading the novel was against the law in the Convention on Children's Rights, which deals with freedom of expression and free access to information, except when it damages the reputation or the rights of others. Finally, they claimed that it also violated the Convention on the Elimination of All Forms of Discrimination.

The protection appeal would be filed by Lorein's son, who was only twelve years old. But he was joined by another girl of the same age.

TANISHA SWABY CAMPBELL: My name is Tanisha Swaby Campbell. I was born in San José de Costa Rica in 1984.

LUIS FERNANDO: Tanisha also read *Cocorí* in school. And she remembers a feeling.

TANISHA: That book, first of all, made me feel very ashamed, which was something that directly contradicted, let's say, all the messages that I had received from my immediate family circle.

LUIS FERNANDO: In her maternal family, Blackness was always treated positively. An ethnic awareness, says Tanisha, which came from her grandparents.

TANISHA: And I always think it was as a way of responding to what my grandparents knew my mother and her brothers and sisters were going to have to face in a society where they would be constantly receiving negative or pejorative messages about Blackness. So in the family, they presented it to us as a very important thing, as a source of pride, etc.

LUIS FERNANDO: It was humiliating for Tanisha to read *Cocorí* and for her classmates to start making fun of her.

TANISHA: Because first, all the Black boys and girls became Cocorí; and second, the traits of that character, his attributes, were attributes that personally, even at ten years old, made me feel very ashamed.

LUIS FERNANDO: The afro hair, the thick lips . . . and Tanisha attended a private school in Limón, but the children were mostly *mestizos*.

TANISHA: That shame I experienced at that time, you know? And that depersonalization that *Cocorí* has generated for decades among the Black boys and girls of this country. I took it home.

LUIS FERNANDO: And here we must explain who Tanisha's mother is. Her name is Epsy Campbell Barr, a politician who has fought against racism and for the rights of people of African descent for decades. She has led several anti-racist organizations and has been a member of the National Congress for the Citizens' Action Party. Since 2018, she has been vice president of the Republic of Costa Rica, the first Afro-descendant woman to hold a position of this stature in Latin America. So it's no surprise that Epsy was interested in joining the appeal proposed by Lorein. Of course, an appeal for protection is a concept that hardly any twelve-year-old boy or girl understands. But Tanisha understood the basics: This was about defending her rights and removing from schools that book that caused her so much shame. Now, there is an issue here. And it is whether removing *Cocorí* from schools is censorship or not.

TANISHA: In that context, there was never talk of removing *Cocorí* from all the libraries. Anyone who wanted to read *Cocorí* could always go and get it anywhere in this country.

QUINCE: The fight is not about censoring the book or stopping its publication, or if anyone wants to buy it. Just like so many other books out there . . .

LUIS FERNANDO: Just like *Mein Kampf*, by Hitler, says Quince . . .

QUINCE: If you want to buy it, read it, and give it to your children, that's up to you. But it cannot be that the State is promoting a text where poor Cocorí, in addition to other things, chews on thoughts darker than his skin. How can you teach that to a little fifth-grader?

LUIS FERNANDO: The Constitutional Court issued its ruling the following year, in 1996.

TANISHA: If you see the magistrates' ruling—it was a unanimous decision on the 1995 protection appeal. If you read that ruling with today's eyes, it makes you want to cry.

LUIS FERNANDO: Cry with sadness. The appeal was dismissed.
TANISHA: What the magistrates really did was an act of complete hubris and arrogance, saying that *Cocorí* was pretty much a favor to the Afro-Costa Rican people in this country, that it was a beautiful representation of what we were. Always from that perspective of "you don't know what is happening to you" or "you don't understand who you are."

LUIS FERNANDO: The magistrates said they found no discriminatory or racist elements in the book, and if there was any kind of reaction against Afro-descendant children, it could be avoided by educating the teachers of each school. The ruling was a big blow to Lorein's son.

LOREIN: It was devastating for him. So he would say, "Let's go back home. Hey, why did you bring me here? This is a horrible country. Let's go home." He couldn't understand.

LUIS FERNANDO: From then on, the controversy around *Cocorí* flares up again almost every ten years. All is quiet for a while, and then a bomb drops and the same argument starts all over again. It seems like the story of a country that refuses to see its history. In the year 2000, for example, the Ministry of Public Education eliminated the concept of compulsory texts and replaced it with book suggestions. In other words, recommended readings that can be done in the classroom. But this goes completely unnoticed in the media. It was not until January 2003 that a statement signed by the Vice Minister of Education at the time, Wilfrido Blanco Mora, stressed that *Cocorí* was not required reading in schools.

The vice minister said the statement was put out in response to questions asked by members of the Caribbean Project, an organization that considered *Cocorí* racist. One of its members was Quince Duncan.

QUINCE: By that time, we had made arrangements with the President of the Republic, who was Mr. Abel Pacheco, and his minister Astrid Fischel, to have the book removed from the school curriculum, alleging precisely that it was not an appropriate book for fifth-grade children.

LUIS FERNANDO: In April of that same year, a Costa Rican writer named Rodolfo Arias Formoso published an article questioning whether *Cocorí* was racist.

QUINCE: The point is that Mr. Joaquín Gutiérrez wrote it. And since he is a leftist ally, etc., etc., it is not possible for him to have committed any sins.

LUIS FERNANDO: He said that what the book *did* contain was racism against Whites, since it makes fun of how one of them seems to have burnt his hair because he is a redhead.
On April 26, 2003, six days after the article by Rodolfo Arias, then-President of the Republic Abel Pacheco published an article saying that for a large group of the Afrodescendant community, *Cocorí* contained unacceptable messages. Although he did not specify which messages.

A study by Dr. Marianela Muñoz-Muñoz, a professor at the University of Costa Rica School of Philology, Linguistics and Literature, says that in the four months that followed, there were at least fifty written or illustrated reactions to the *Cocorí* controversy. The majority favored the book. Over time, things calmed down again. Until 2015, when they completely exploded.

TANISHA: The National Symphony Orchestra decided to stage a show about Cocorí. They were going to present it at the National Theater and there was a giant billboard about Cocorí.

Luis Fernando: That was Tanisha. The *Cocorí* billboard showed him the way most Costa Ricans my age know him: with a big head, round eyes, thick lips, an open shirt, and shorts. Without shoes. Walking through the jungle with a titi monkey on top of his head, and with a scared look on their faces.

Tanisha: This—let's call it—pictorial racism shows the image of a stereotypical Black person, with excessively large lips, very much in the style of the racist caricatures of *Memín* and all that, where Afro-descended people are always drawn in close proximity to primates and that kind of thing, right?

Luis Fernando: The image was created by Hugo Díaz, who has since passed away, and is part of a series of illustrations that have accompanied the story since 1984.
　　The musical was to be financed by the Ministry of Culture and Youth. This event raised a flag for Epsy Campbell and Maureen Clark, who were members of the National Legislature at the time. This is Campbell on the floor of the Legislative Assembly on April 14, 2015:
(Archive sound bite)

Epsy Campbell: The children of many people in this country cannot feel identified with a character who today is on the facade of the National Theater dressed in rags, with a little monkey on his head, and calling him a little hero.

Luis Fernando: Then she says the following:
(Archive sound bite)

Epsy Campbell: There are no White children in this country, there are no *mestizo* children, there are no Indigenous children who want to be Cocorí.

Luis Fernando: The financing of the musical caused the Legislative Assembly to summon the Minister of Culture, among others, to a hearing before the Special Permanent Commission on Human Rights, of which Epsy Campbell was a member. Pressure from the Human Rights Commission ended in the minister's withdrawing funding for the *Cocorí* musical. And this, in turn, triggered another public debate about *Cocorí*'s belonging in schools and whether the book is racist or not.

It must be said that what you heard on most of the media was this. (Archive sound bite)

PERSON 1: This means that the work of Costa Ricans is silenced. It is unheard of; it is reprehensible, and it tells us that we need to mature as a country.

PERSON 2: I have children and they have all read it. And I don't think it is racist at all. I think the Legislator may not have read it well, or she didn't enjoy it.

PERSON 3: Removing something that is historical, that works, and that belongs to us. There is no reason to remove it.

LUIS FERNANDO: During April, May, and June 2015, twenty-nine notes and thirty-one opinion articles on the subject were published by six national media outlets. At first, the vast majority defended the book, according to the study by Marianela Muñoz-Muñoz. These were some of the headlines in the press:

HEADLINE 1: Cocorí is not to blame for being Black

HEADLINE 2: Cocorí: the price of denying history

HEADLINE 3: Cocorí, victim of complexes

HEADLINE 4: The silencing of Cocorí

Then came the violence on social media, an element that was not present in the previous controversies. This is Tanisha again:

TANISHA: I have had to put up with a lot of violence aimed directly against me and violence directly against my family. Many times, in the figure of my mother, who has taken on the *Cocorí* lawsuits, because Costa Rica is a very violent country on a symbolic level, let's say, and on an interpersonal level.

LUIS FERNANDO: They would say things like, if she didn't like Costa Rica, she should go to Africa, or more subtle things, like how pretty she looked with straight hair. This is something Tanisha has thought about a lot.

TANISHA: The issue is that you are Costa Rican, but not as much as they are. Being an Afro-descendant means you are really always in what is called a citizenship deficit, and what we can call the elite, or the majorities—the *mestizo*-white majorities—are always in that constant denial of citizenship.

LUIS FERNANDO: She experiences it, even in things that seem harmless.

TANISHA: Six times out of ten, when I enter the country, some person, or someone in the line, or one of the officers tells me I'm in the wrong line when I am in the line for citizens.

LUIS FERNANDO: And as Tanisha told me, these comments, which seem minor, are things that go through your body. They are more than abstract notions. You feel them. Reporting on this story, over and over I have come across an idea that is linked to this denial of citizenship: To be of African descent in Costa Rica is to live in a borrowed world. But if your land is not your land, where are you from? And that goes straight to the heart of the conflict with *Cocorí*: How can you have some kind of respect for a book that, while being part of the country's history, is not written for you, and treats you like a foreigner?

The harassment of Epsy Campbell, Tanisha's mother, became too overwhelming. She had to shut down her social media, and the Ministry of Security even offered her protection because of the threats she received.

In parallel with the insults, several protection appeals were filed. One of them came from Legislator Epsy Campbell and other members of the Acción Ciudadana party. The demand was for *Cocorí* to be removed from recommended reading lists in schools. There was another with the same purpose, presented by the Ombudsman. And one was also presented, but this one was against the Minister of Culture, Elizabeth Fonseca, for limiting freedom of expression and applying censorship by cancelling the financing of the musical.

YASHÍN CASTRILLO: This forced way of educating is exactly the opposite of what education should be, which is to stimulate critical thinking on the part of students.

LUIS FERNANDO: This is Yashín Castrillo, a constitutional lawyer and one of the two people who filed the appeal against cancellation of the financing of the musical. To Yashín, cancelling it was to impose a certain understanding of what it is to be Costa Rican. Something authoritarian. And to him, it is counterproductive.

YASHÍN: Eliminating a book from the curriculum because it contains some expressions that we consider racist today does not eliminate racism.

LUIS FERNANDO: In other words, according to Yashín, it would be like covering the sun with a finger. To him, the book should be a tool to teach that reality is complex.

YASHÍN: To teach students what really exists so that, if that reality is deformed, they can build a better reality with the guidance of their teachers, not denying the existence of reality, but improving it.

LUIS FERNANDO: Yashín won the protection appeal. And the State had to indemnify the musical's producers. Things calmed down over the months. During that time, Tanisha and the Center for Afro–Costa Rican Women collected all the insults that Epsy Campbell and Maureen Clark, the other Legislator involved, had received during the discussion.

TANISHA: And we take them to the Commission for the Eradication of Racial Discrimination, the CERD.

LUIS FERNANDO: Of the United Nations. It is a group of experts that watch over the implementation in all signatory countries of the International Convention on the Elimination of All Forms of Racial Discrimination. The collection of insults was to support the entire case that *Cocorí* was racist and harmed the Afro-descendant population.

TANISHA: And that's when the CERD issued a series of recommendations in which it specifically recommends that the State of Costa Rica remove this book from the school curriculum.

LUIS FERNANDO: The recommendation was made at the end of August 2015. But the Ministry of Education did not comply. What they did do, almost two years later, in 2017, was to transfer *Cocorí* from the list of suggested readings for the second basic education cycle to the third. This means that the age at which children can read *Cocorí* went from ten or eleven years old to between thirteen and fifteen approximately. This is because the institution considered that the book should be analyzed by a more mature student population.

That left only one loose end: the appeals for protection filed by Epsy Campbell and the Ombudsman. In April 2017, a hearing was held to analyze the case once again. Tanisha was invited to give her testimony in front of the magistrates. She talked about how *Cocorí* affected her self-esteem and her identity formation when she was a child, and why she filed the protection appeal.

TANISHA: When I was in the room that day, it was really shocking for me to think how time had passed and how people of African descent in this country would not be able to win a battle against a fictional character. That seemed very sad to me.

LUIS FERNANDO: The thing is that this issue had been an important part of Tanisha's life for twenty-two years by then.

TANISHA: We are talking, in this country, according to the last census, about 8 percent of the population—we know it must be a bit more than that—whose voice doesn't count any more than a character in a book.

LUIS FERNANDO: Some four hundred thousand people whose voices don't count any more than Cocorí, according to Tanisha.

TANISHA: That is precisely what I told the magistrates, that I could not believe that twenty-two years later, I was fighting for the same thing and that now it was not for me, but for my son.

LUIS FERNANDO: He was two years old at the time. So that he would not have to live the way thousands of Afro-descended children have lived for decades in Costa Rica. A month after that testimony, in May 2017, the Constitutional Court issued its ruling. The appeal was declared to be without merit. *Cocorí* would continue in the Costa Rican education system. One of the arguments was that it is not proper for a constitutional court to censor or prohibit a literary work. Also, that there is no technical study, a survey for example, showing that the book negatively affects the Afro–Costa Rican population.

But there was a small victory for Tanisha: the votes of two magistrates who said that it fuels racial bullying and that it affects the self-esteem of children. And that due to the structural racism present in Costa Rica, it is necessary to establish a form of education to combat it—although they did not say what that might be. There are seven magistrates in all, and rulings are decided by the majority, so the votes in favor of the book being eliminated from the school curriculum did not change anything. But for Tanisha, they did show some progress in the fight. More awareness. More empathy.

During the last few months, I have asked myself several times what *Cocorí* means to Costa Rica.

The answer cannot be reduced to any one thing. It is the legacy of a beloved and admired author, the legacy of a good man who fought for social justice. It is also an easy narrative for a large part of Costa Rica's *mestizos*, one where Afro-descendants are different from them, more alien, more primitive. I've also thought about it this way: What would I be if I hadn't read *Cocorí*? It is not an exaggeration to say that it changed my life, because after that reading, I did not stop reading, and without books there is no doubt I would be a different person. I don't know if better or worse, but different. Now, is this worth more than the damage that book caused to my classmate, who was bullied by us? Well, no. I don't think so. It is difficult for us to hear that something we love hurts others. Because we, the *mestizos*, never want to admit that we can be the bad guys in the story. Aren't we the heroes? And what are we without our myths?

DANIEL: Luis Fernando Vargas is an editor at *Radio Ambulante*. He lives in San José, Costa Rica.

Thanks to Roberth Pereira, Silvia Chavarría, Bernardo Montes de Oca, Estefanía Fresno and Gustavo Quirós for lending their voices for this episode. This story was edited by Camila Segura and me. Desirée Yépez did the fact-checking. The sound design is by Andrés Azpiri and Rémy Lozano, with music by Rémy. The rest of the *Radio Ambulante* team includes Paola Alean, Nicolás Alonso, Lisette Arévalo, Aneris Casassus, Emilia Erbetta, Fernanda Guzmán, Camilo Jiménez Santofimio, Ana Pais, Laura Rojas Aponte, Barbara Sawhill, Elsa Liliana Ulloa, and David Trujillo. Carolina Guerrero is the CEO. *Radio Ambulante* is a podcast by Radio Ambulante Estudios, produced and mixed on the Hindenburg PRO program. *Radio Ambulante* tells the stories of Latin America. I'm Daniel Alarcón. Thanks for listening.

Notes

Preface

1. Construction of a highway linking Managua to the Nicaraguan Caribbean coast began in 2017 and was completed in 2019. The project, according to some observers, was expected to encourage economic development in RACCS through the expansion of the tourist sector. See Moncada, "Así es el viaje," n.p.

2. Travel from Livingston, Guatemala to Punta Gorda, Belize—unlike travel from Guatemala City to Livingston—is straightforward, as boats leave on a daily basis from one dock to the other.

Introduction. Fictions of Blackness and Their Narrative Power

1. The passage is found in the book of Genesis 9:18–27.
2. Torquemada, *Monarquía Indiana*, 569.
3. See Katzew, *Casta Painting*.
4. See Miquel Valerio, *Sovereign Joy*.
5. Chance and Taylor, "Estate and Class in Colonial Oaxaca," 460.
6. Sigüenza y Góngora, "Alboroto y motín," 113.
7. Cope, *The Limits of Racial Domination*, 22
8. Cope, *The Limits of Racial Domination*, 22
9. Gonzalez, "A Categoria Político-Cultural de Amefricanidade," 72. Translation mine.
10. Vinson, "Introduction," 8.
11. Gonzalez, "A Categoria Político-Cultural de Amefricanidade, 79.
12. Martínez Duran and Contreras, "La abolición," 223–232.
13. For more on their participation, see Ben Vinson III's *Bearing Arms for His Majesty*, a meticulously researched account of Afrodescendant soldiers in New Spain.

14. Martínez Duran and Contreras, "La abolición," 227–228.

15. Martínez Duran and Contreras, "La abolición," 227–228.

16. Friehrer observes that unlike slaves in the Spanish Caribbean, Portuguese, and British colonies, it was not unthinkable for slaves in Central America to read and write, in "Slaves and Freedom in Colonial Central America," 39–57. This observation is substantiated by scholars working on other mainland contexts, including the Viceroyalties of New Spain, Peru, and Granada. See Herman L. Bennet's *Colonial Blackness* and Larissa Brewer-García's *Beyond Babel*.

17. For more on the extraordinary Afrodescendants who sought legal routes to end their enslavement, see Catherine Komisaruk's "Becoming Free, Becoming Ladino"; Rina Cáceres Gómez's extraordinary three-volume series, *Del olvido a la memoria*; and Ann Twinam's comparative volume, *Purchasing Whiteness*.

18. Meléndez Obando, "Slow Ascent of the Marginalized," 350–351.

19. In many instances in this book, I place the word "Black" in brackets to rhetorically highlight concepts that have historically been denied to Black populations in Central America. For example, the stories of Central American citizenry to which I signal here are *mestizo*, but even in the articulation that is taken for granted as being *mestizo*, there is an active refusal to see Black historical legacies in the concept of citizenry.

20. Haefkens, *Viaje*, 129.

21. Gómez Menjívar's article, "Passing into Fictions," covers the seventeenth and eighteenth centuries in the Captaincy of Guatemala. For a groundbreaking study of an earlier phase in the isthmus's colonial period, see Robinson A. Herrera's *Natives, Europeans, and Africans in Sixteenth-Century Santiago de Guatemala*.

22. *Mestizaje* has a long history of analysis, while the discussion of Blackness as it relates to *mestizaje* is an emerging area of study. Notable texts in this direction include Nancy Priscilla Naro's *Blacks, Coloureds and National Identity in Nineteenth-Century Latin America* and Juliet Hooker's *Theorizing Race in the Americas*.

23. Haefkens, *Viaje*, 289. Notably, Haefkens claims that enslaved peoples from Belize settled in Guatemala following the latter's independence. More research is needed in order to explore this resettlement further.

24. Haefkens, *Viaje*.

25. For more on the participation of Afrodescendants in military affairs during the colonial period, see Paul Lokken's "Undoing Racial Hierarchy" and "Useful Enemies."

26. Komisaruk, "Becoming Free, Becoming Ladino," 171.

27. Gudmundson, "What Difference Did Color Make?," 215.

28. Gudmundson, "What Difference Did Color Make?," 234.

29. Wade, "Rethinking Mestizaje," 243. See also Wade's *Degrees of Mixture, Degrees of Freedom*.

30. Hooker, "Race and the Space of Citizenship," 246–247.

31. For further reading on the transformation of Indigenous subject categories to that of the umbrella term *campesino* in El Salvador, please see Douglas Carranza Mena's "Los indígenas."

32. More research is needed to determine the extent to which this geopolitical spread from the Pacific coast to the Caribbean coast of the isthmus paralleled the "Manifest Destiny" ideology espoused in the United States, which likewise resulted in coast-to-coast land acquisition.

33. See Gómez Menjívar and Salmon's *Tropical Tongues*.

34. "Creole" is the term used in Belize for individuals whose ancestors were African slaves in British Honduras. A similar term, *criollo*, was used in Hispanophone colonies to refer to individuals born of Spanish parents who were born in the Spanish Crown's colonies. To complicate matters, *criollo* is now used in Hispanophone Central American contexts as a translation of Creole (as it is understood in Belize). *Criollo* in contemporary Central America also refers to the Kriol language spoken in Belize attributed to [Afrodescendant] Creoles. For more information as to the nuances of these terms, see Assad Shoman's *A History of Belize in 13 Chapters* and Gómez Menjívar and Salmon's *Tropical Tongues*.

35. There are two Afro-Indigenous groups in Central America, the Miskito and the Garifuna, resulting from the intermarriages of Indigenous peoples and African peoples forcibly taken to the Americas. Miskito communities were located along the coasts of Honduras and Nicaragua and during the colonial period, and the Treaty of Friendship and Alliance signed with the British in 1740 ensured their right to self-rule. For more on the history of Miskito peoples, see Charles Hale's *Resistance and Contradiction*. The second Afro-Indigenous group, the Garifuna, established communities in coastal Belize, Guatemala, and Honduras after they were deported to Roatán (Honduras) from St. Vincent by the British in 1797. Like the Miskito, they enjoyed autonomy and little interference from the Spanish colonial government and the Central American administrations until the early twentieth century, the period addressed directly in chapter 2 of this book. For further reading on the contemporary transnational Garifuna community, see Mark Anderson's *Black and Indigenous* and Serena Crosgrove et al.'s *Surviving the Americas*.

36. West Indians were recruited in the early twentieth century to work on railroads and banana plantations in Central American Caribbean coastal areas as well as for work on the Panama Canal. Historical records depict them as a proud, Anglophone, Protestant, educated community, who often appealed to the British Crown to denounce the ill treatment they suffered at the hands of *mestizo* Central Americans. Notably, Marcus Garvey's Universal Negro Improvement Association was inspired by his experience working as a timekeeper on banana plantations in Panama and observing the cruel treatment of West Indian workers. Due to the labor that they provided during a critical historical period in the history of

the region, this is the Afrodescendant population that has been best documented by scholars. A selection of notable texts would include E. David Cronon's *Black Moses*, Ronald N. Harpelle's *The West Indians of Costa Rica*, Glenn A. Chambers's *Race, Nation, and West Indian Immigration to Honduras*, and, Olive Senior's *Dying to Better Themselves*.

37. Hooker, "The Mosquito Coast," 246–277.

38. In Guatemala, they settled in the towns of Bananera, Livingston, and Puerto Barrios. In Honduras, the largest groups settled in Trujillo and La Ceiba. In Nicaragua, the largest number of West Indians settled in Bluefields and Pearl Lagoon. Costa Rica's largest West Indian community was founded in Port Limón. Lastly, Panama's largest West Indian communities are in Bocas del Toro and in the Canal Zone.

39. See Gómez Menjívar and Salmon, *Tropical Tongues*, 24–39.

40. Gates, *Black in Latin America*, 3.

41. See Rahier, *Black Social Movements*, and Hooker, *Theorizing Race in the Americas* and "The Mosquito Coast."

42. Wright, *Physics of Blackness*, 3.

43. See Ava DuVernay's documentary, *13th*, as well as Michelle Alexander's *The New Jim Crow*.

44. My gratitude to reviewer no. 1 during the first phase of the peer-review process at SUNY Press for offering these terms to understand the (re)inventions of Blackness in Central America over time.

45. Wright, *Physics of Blackness*, 35.

46. See María Elisa Velásquez's *Debates históricos contemporáneos*.

47. Stephen L. Carter writes about the wealthy Black families living in the original thirteen colonies, descendants of African ancestors who were never enslaved and who have historically exerted political influence in the Northeast. See, for example, his novels *The Emperor of Ocean Park* and *New England White*. See also https://www.huffingtonpost.com/entry/black-farmer-calls-out-liberal-racism-in-powerful-facebook-message_us_5925a027e4b0650cc020eb4d as well as Darius Rucker's excellent rendition of "Wagon Wheel" in https://www.youtube.com/watch?v=hvKyBcCDOB4.

48. When the United States acquired Louisiana in 1803, it also acquired a stretch of land in which Afrodescendants had for generations held prominent positions that sharply contrasted with the experiences of Afrodescendants elsewhere in the country. This led to New Orleans (a heavily Catholic, Romance language–influenced area) becoming a perpetual colonial space in the national imagination. The perception of New Orleans as exceptional and its exclusion from the normative common history imagined for the rest of the United States secured the sense of American exceptionalism. Counting New Orleans as an exotic space within its standardized fabric, Clark argues, diverted the United States' gaze of the nation away from its unattractive slaveholding past, allowing it to remain firmly fixed on less-troubling nation-building scenes played out on the Mayflower and

in Independence Hall. For more on the liminal US citizenry of New Orleans, see Emily Clark's *American Quadroon*.

49. As Ian Smart observed, Black Central American authors relayed an integrally Black perspective on race relations with which Afrodescendants could identify, regardless of their nationality. Smart finds that in contrast to *mestizo* writers' concern with interracial relationships, the West Indian writer is more politically grounded to the extent that spirituality and the luscious landscape foreground conflicts originating on the banana plantations and canal zones that permeate the interpersonal relationships of the community at large rather than romantic relationships.

50. These are translations of the contents of the texts, without any attempt to reconfigure the poetics of the pieces. Doing so lays bare the substance of the poems and prose studied in these chapters.

51. This is the case across Latin America, not just in Central America. Henry Louis Gates Jr. observes in his review of Blackness in Haiti, the Dominican Republic, Brazil, Cuba, Mexico, and Peru that what these societies share is "the unfortunate fact that persons of the seemingly 'purest' or 'unadulterated' African descent disproportionately occupy the very bottom of economic scale in these countries. In other words, the people with the darkest skin, the kinkiest hair, and the thickest lips tend to be overrepresented among the poorest members of society." Gates, *Black in Latin America*, 11. For excellent analyses of the impact of Afrodescendant phenotype on social class and economic opportunity in Latin America, see Edward Eric Telles's *Race in Another America* and *Pigmentocracies*, Ginetta E. B. Candelario's *Black Behind the Ears*, George Reid Andrews's *Blackness in the White Nation*, Alex Borucki's *From Shipmates to Soldiers*, and Mara Loveman's *National Colors*.

Chapter 1. Disappearing Acts

1. Gilroy, *The Black Atlantic*, 19.

2. See Stuart Hall's groundbreaking article, "Encoding and Decoding in the Television Discourse."

3. Francisco Gavidia, an emblematic Salvadoran poet, playwright, philologist, historian, essayist, and humanist, is credited with having taught Rubén Darío alexandrine verse. Gavidia's poetry places him steadfastly in the *modernista* tradition, though his prose celebrates national heroes and features quintessential Salvadoran themes. Gavidia believed that history, archaeology, and anthropology had failed the Salvadoran people by not shedding light on their origins, and thus exalted the exotic qualities of Indigenous cultures and rural landscapes in many of his works.

4. See James Mahoney's "Radical, Reformist and Aborted Liberalism" and *The Legacies of Liberalism*.

5. See Sergio Ramírez's *Balcanes y volcanes*.
6. Arroyo Calderón, *Cada uno en su sitio*, 25.
7. See Ruth María Tenorio Gochez's *Periódicos y cultura impresa en El Salvador* and François-Xavier Guerra's "Forms of Communication."
8. Guerra, "Forms of Communication," 12. See also Arroyo Calderón's *Cada uno en su sitio*.
9. Molina Jiménez, "Las bibliotecas nacionales de América Central," 77.
10. Molina Jiménez, "Las bibliotecas nacionales de América Central," 80.
11. Bolívar, "Carta de Jamaica," 28 (Spanish original). For the English translation used in this chapter, see Bolivar, *El liberatador*, 26.
12. Ramírez, *Balcanes y volcanes*, 288.
13. Ruiz, "El testamento poético de Darío," 17.
14. For an examination on the theme of Blackness focused exclusively on Rubén Darío's work, see Richard L. Jackson's "La presencia negra en la obra de Rubén Darío."
15. See David E. Whisnant's "Rubén Darío." According to Whisnant: "Darío's life and work have offered a tantalizing array of data for opposing exegetical agendas, sufficiently diverse and contradictory to admit a variety of interpretations" (42).
16. Patriotism reemerges in Darío's anti-Yankee poetry, which appears following the 1889 Spanish-American War and the United States' 1904 acquisition of the Panama Canal.
17. Shklovskij, "Art as Technique," 20.
18. Tinajero, *Orientalismo*, 16.
19. Shklovskij, "Art as Technique," 19.
20. Tinajero, *Orientalismo*, 22.
21. See Tzvetan Todorov's *The Conquest of America*. Todorov provides many examples of the phenomenon: Columbus spoke of the men he saw only because to him, they constituted a part of the landscape that so profoundly enchanted him, while Cortés's actions demonstrate that a superior understanding of the vanquished made destruction possible, defying the inclination to assume that comprehension goes hand in hand with sympathy.
22. The quotation is from the book of Genesis, chapter 9, verses 18–27. Religious interpretations of biblical verses were largely unchallenged until the Age of Enlightenment. See *The Authorized King James Version of the Bible*, 10.
23. See Whitford's *The Curse of Ham in the Early Modern Era*.
24. Darío, *Poesías completas*, 317.
25. Real de Azúa, "El modernismo literario," 41–75.
26. Real de Azúa, "El modernismo literario," 48.
27. Said, *Orientalism*, 40.
28. Grant, "Sequence and Theme," 895.
29. Darío dedicates the poem to Doctor Jerónimo Ramírez.

30. In "Alí," Zela goes from being her father's captive to her lover's luxurious object to another man's harem girl. Though the scope of this chapter does not allow us to delve deeper on the subject, Darío contributes to the discussion among French colonial intellectuals about the representation of Muslim women at the turn of the century. See Clancy-Smith, "The Colonial Gaze," where Clancy-Smith indicates that there were two schools of thought in relation to the Muslim woman in the nineteenth century. The first held that a Muslim woman was "nothing but an *objet de luxe*, a sensual, indolent, bored creature, caged like a bird in the harem" while the second held that she was "a servant or slave condemned by her husband to forced labor, and implicitly, forced sex" (214).

31. Darío, *Poesías completas*, 333.
32. Snowden, *Before Color Prejudice*, 77.
33. Snowden, *Before Color Prejudice*, 79.
34. Darío, *Poesías completas*, 336.
35. For a powerful study on the topic as it specifically relates to Black men, see Thomas A. Foster's *Rethinking Rufus*.
36. Gautier, *Enamels and Cameos*, n.p.
37. Gautier, *Enamels and Cameos*.
38. See Ángel Rama's *Las máscaras democráticas*. As Rama notes, "En el segundo momento de la Cultura modernizada internacionalista, la cualidad de 'literato' habrá de primar sobre la de 'intelectual.' Habrá más poetas líricos y prosistas de cuentos, estampas, esbozos, que expositores de ideas" (In the second phase of the modernized internationalist Culture, the quality of the literati had primacy over that of the 'intelectual.' There were many more lyricist poets and prose narrativists, ephemera, sketches, than expositors of ideas).
39. Rama, *Las máscaras democráticas*, 45.
40. Darío, *Poesías completas*, 336 (emphasis mine).
41. Darío, *Poesías completas*, 341.
42. See note 19 in this chapter.
43. Darío, *Poesías completes*, 344.
44. Darío, *Poesías completas*, 345.
45. Darío, *Poesías completas*, 346.
46. As critics have noted, the most significant departure from the original and later adaptations is the severity of Desdemona's murder. In Cinthio's version, the Moor's ensign counsels him to beat his wife to death with a stocking full of sand and later crush her head with a pillar in their bedroom—an act that he carried out without hesitation in order to preserve his reputation and prevent being labeled a cuckold. The translation of this text was prepared by the renowned critic William Hazlitt and the two quotes cited in this chapter read as follows in the original Italian: "Ma voi Mori siete de natura tanto caldi, ch'ogni poco di cosa vi muove ad ira, e a vendetta"/ "temo molto di non essere io quella, che dia

essempio alle giovani di non maritarsi il voler de'suoi; che la me la donne Italiane imparino di non si accompagnare con uomo, cui la natura, e il Cielo e il motto della vita disgiunge da noi." See Cinthio's "Un Capitano Moro."

47. Cinthio, "Un Capitano Moro," 300.

48. See Molina Tamacas's "*Júpiter*, de Gavidia." I study the play here as dramatic literature due to the initial mode of production, circulation, and consumption of the text and have an interest in exploring its performances in a future publication.

49. Sommer, *Foundational Fictions*, 5.

50. Sommer, *Foundational Fictions*, 7.

51. Sommer, *Foundational Fictions*, 40.

52. Arroyo Calderón, *Cada uno en su sitio*, 36.

53. Welter, "The Cult of True Womanhood," 152.

54. Gavidia, *Júpiter*, 17.

55. Zea, *Dos etapas*, 33.

56. Zea, *Dos etapas*, 33.

57. García Giráldez, "El debate sobre la nación," 22.

58. García Giráldez, "El debate sobre la nación."

59. See Sergio Ramírez's, *Tambor olvidado*.

60. Earle and Lowe, *Black Africans*, 77.

61. In the Spanish caste system, the term *bozal* was used to refer to Black slaves who were born in Africa and trafficked to the Americas.

62. See Baltasar Fra-Molinero's *La imagen de los negros en el teatro del Siglo de Oro*.

63. This idea earned Barrundia the label of dissident and traitor to the United Provinces of Central America, despite his having been elected vice president (which he declined) and serving as interim president.

64. Gavidia, *Júpiter*, 27.

65. Meléndez Valdés, *Poesías*, 304. The excerpt quoted in the conversation is from the last verse of the poem. The last seven verses read: "Hinche el corazón mío/ de un ardor celestial que a cuanto existe / como tú se derrame,/ y, oh Dios de amor, en tu universo te amé./ Todos tus hijos somos:/ el tártaro, el lapón, el indio rudo,/ el tostado africano,/ es un hombre, es tu imagen y es mi hermano" ([Lord] Fill this heart of mine/ with an endless celestial burning/ may it spill as you do/ and, oh God of love, in your universe I loved you/ All your children, we are:/ the Tarta, the Sami, the rude Indian,/ the toasted African,/ is a man, is your image and is my brother).

66. García Giráldez, "El debate sobre la nación," 22.

67. Gavidia, *Júpiter*, 45.

68. Gavidia, *Júpiter*.

69. Gavidia, *Júpiter*, 50–51.

70. Gavidia, *Júpiter*, 51.

71. See Mario Hernández Aguirre's *Gavidia*.
72. Gavidia, *Júpiter*, 58.
73. Gavidia, *Júpiter*, 163.
74. Lamming, *The Pleasures of Exile*, 109.
75. Lamming, *The Pleasures of Exile*, 109.
76. Gavidia, *Júpiter*, 170.
77. See Johannes Fabian's *Time and the Other*.
78. Zea, *Dos etapas*, 18.
79. See B. Christine Arce's *Mexico's Nobodies* for more about how this works in the Mexican context.
80. Pleitez, "Francisco Gavidia," n.p.
81. Darío, *Poesías completas*, 472.
82. Both of these images had circulated in the sixteenth and seventeenth centuries, when a more fruitful reference also had: the legend of Prester John, descendant of Balthasar and Black ruler of Ethiopia who was destined to spread Christianity throughout Africa. The legend had encouraged Spanish and Portuguese explorers, missionaries, and scholars to venture into Africa and filled imaginations with images of treasure troves presided over by a Black king. See Baltasar Fra Molinero's *La imagen de los negros*.
83. Hume, "Negroes . . . Naturally Inferior," 33.
84. See Georg Wilhelm Friedrich Hegel and Immanuel Kant in the edited anthology, *Race and the Enlightenment*.
85. See Juliet Hooker's "The Mosquito Coast and the Place of Blackness."
86. For more on race, color, and demographics at the turn of the nineteenth century, see Mara Loveman's *National Colors*.
87. Bloom, "Apophrades or the Return of the Dead," 141.

Chapter 2. Strategies of Containment

1. Holden and Zolov, "1903: The Hay–Bunau-Varilla Treaty," 86–88.
2. Darío, "1904: To Roosevelt," 91–92.
3. Lasso, *Erased*, 49.
4. In 1797, the British accused the phenotypically Black peoples of Yurumein (now called St. Vincent) of cooperating with rival French enemies and subsequently deported them to the island of Roatán, off the coast of Honduras. Garifuna deportees and descendants founded communities in present-day Belize, Guatemala, Honduras, and Nicaragua in Central America as well as in the United States. Today, the struggle to protect these ancestral homelands is manifest both in grassroots movements as well as in Garifuna cultural production, including film and social media. For more on the topic, see chapter 5 of this book; Gómez Menjívar's "Redes garifunas insurgents" (Insurgent Garifuna networks) and

"Tangible Afro-Indigenous Heritage"; and Pablo José López Oro's "Digitizing Ancestral Memory" and "Garifunanizando Latinidad."

5. See Aguilera Malta, *Canal Zone*, 13.
6. See Theodore Roosevelt, "1903: 'I Took Final Action in 1903,'" 94.
7. Aguilera Malta, *Canal Zone*, 42.
8. Lasso, *Erased*, 3.
9. Lasso, *Erased*, 10.
10. Stephenson Watson, *The Politics of Race in Panama*, 9.
11. See George W. Westerman's "Historical Notes of West Indians on the Isthmus of Panama."
12. Westerman, "Historical Notes."
13. See Trevor O'Reggio's *Between Alienation and Citizenship*.
14. Flores-Villalobos, *The Silver Women*, 15.
15. See John Biesanz, "Cultural and Economic Factors in Panamanian Race Relations."
16. Sepúlveda, *El tema del canal*, 41.
17. Biesanz, "Cultural and Economic Factors," 774.
18. Biesanz, "Cultural and Economic Factors," 775.
19. Marx and Engels are credited with coining the term "lumpenproletariat." It first appeared in *The German Ideology* (see Trotsky 7) and was used to describe a conceptually complex "knave" class that encompasses social scum, mobs, ragamuffins, and others commonly perceived as socially undesirable. See Nicholas Thoburn's *Deleuze, Marx and Politics*.
20. Aguilera Malta, *Canal Zone*, 55.
21. Aguilera Malta, *Canal Zone*, 59.
22. Aguilera Malta, *Canal Zone*, 60.
23. Aguilera Malta, *Canal Zone*, 61.
24. Aguilera Malta, *Canal Zone*, 13.
25. Aguilera Malta, *Canal Zone*, 51.
26. Panamanians rail against the economic downturn brought about by imperialism, but Coorsi's only passionate moment is in an erotic dance with a white woman. Thus, when Aguilera Malta could have framed him as a voice of anti-imperialist critique from within the Black Panamanian community, Coorsi is given the role of a sexually motivated Black man. This rhetorical strategy brings to bear the words of Frantz Fanon: "Black Magic, primitive mentality, animism, animal eroticism, it all floods over me. All of it is typical of peoples that have not kept pace with the human race. Or, if one prefers, this is humanity at its lowest" (126). See Frantz Fanon's *Black Skin, White Masks*.
27. Aguilera Malta, *Canal Zone*, 52.
28. Fanon, *Black Skin, White Masks*, 114. As Frantz Fanon reminds us, narratives of Black men as subjects of reason are not acceptable: partaking in reason

is futile, the Black man cannot simply say, "I think, therefore I am," because he is trapped by preconceptions about the inherent passion that fills his Black body.

29. Aguilera Malta, *Canal Zone*, 82 and 94.
30. Aguilera Malta, *Canal Zone*, 95.
31. Fanon, *Black Skin, White Masks*, 114.
32. Aguilera Malta, *Canal Zone*, 102.
33. Aguilera Malta, *Canal Zone*, 102.
34. Trotsky, *Fascism*, 7.
35. Watson, *The Politics of Race in Panama*, 69–93.
36. Navas de Miralda, *Barro*, 14.
37. Berman, *All That Is Solid Melts in the Air*, 15.
38. Navas de Miralda, *Barro*, 13–14.
39. Navas de Miralda, *Barro*, 13–14.
40. Their dignity demonstrated in their preference for Central American items, their controlled consumerism, and their intolerance for drinking, gambling, and prostitution—vices associated with the *costeños* throughout the novel.
41. For more about Froylán Turcios, see José A. Funes's *Froylán Turcios y el modernismo en Honduras*.
42. Euraque, "The Threat of Blackness to the Honduran Nation," 243.
43. Euraque, "The Threat of Blackness," 244.
44. Many Honduran presidents, including General Vicente Tosta and General Tiburcio Carías, openly opposed Black immigration and pledged to oppose Black immigrant labor after 1924. In the 1925 elections, Dr. Miguel Paz Barahona advocated for European immigration and the deportation of Black immigrants. Euraque, "The Threat of Blackness," 245.
45. Darío Euraque notes that these representations are deeply rooted in Nava de Miralda's connections to Olancho, the cradle of colonial Blackness in Honduras. He explains that Paca Nava de Miralda (as well as Froylán Turcios) was the child of Catalan immigrants who settled in Olancho, Honduras. Euraque explores the details of the mulatto presence in this area of Honduras and juxtaposes the situation with the racialization of the Garifuna who began to arrive in the eighteenth century in his *Conversaciones históricas*. See also Euraque's "Negritud garifuna y coyunturas políticas."
46. See Gómez Menjívar's "Tangible Afro-Indigenous Heritage" and "Xiomara Cacho Caballero: Writing from Central America's Narco Islands."
47. Kepner, *Social Aspects of the Banana Industry*, 53.
48. Euraque, "The Threat of Blackness," 241.
49. González, *Sojourners of the Caribbean*, 136.
50. See discussions in David Herman, Manfred Jahn, and Marie-Laure Ryan's *Routledge Encyclopedia of Narrative Theory*, and Bell and Ryan's *Possible Worlds Theory and Contemporary Narratology*.

51. Fabian, *Time and the Other*, 1. Though the history of anthropology indicates that this discipline contributed to the intellectual justification of the colonial enterprise, its utility has not been limited to intellectuals at the metropolises. The temporal concepts of this Eurocentric discourse—civilization, evolution, development, acculturation, modernization, industrialization, and urbanization—derive their conceptual content from evolutionary time and are equally at the behest of intellectuals in the periphery.

52. Navas de Miralda, *Barro*, 51.

53. Navas de Miralda, *Barro*, 51.

54. Gellner, *Thought and Change*, 18.

55. Navas de Miralda, *Barro*, 52.

56. Pocomania, also spelled Pukumina, is an African-based traditional religion that emerged in Jamaica in the 1860s. Religious syncretism is a feature of the religion, which holds that the Holy Ghost is the sole mediator between God the Father and humankind (eliminating the idea of Jesus Christ as intermediary). The idea of the experience of the Spirit has ritualistic implications, since a core belief of Pocomania is the coexistence of the spiritual world. One knows one's identity through relationship with these spirits, which all have the ability to possess and merit respect. Major rituals include street meetings and rituals for specific purposes, such as feast tables, altars, and baths. Prayer rituals involve Bible reading, hymn singing, and discussion. As a myth of return, Pocomania highlights the concept of a physical and/or metaphoric return to Africa. For more information, see Leslie R. James's entry "Pocomania" in *African American Religious Cultures*.

57. Navas de Miralda, *Barro*, 52–53.

58. Navas de Miralda, *Barro*, 53.

59. Navas de Miralda, *Barro*, 53. Note also that the national currency of Honduras today is the lempira, named after the Indigenous Lenca warrior who led a number of successful attacks against Spanish colonizers. The currency was changed from the peso to the lempira in 1931.

60. Bourdieu, *Outline of a Theory of Practice*, 96.

61. Bourdieu, *Outline of a Theory of Practice*, 96.

62. Navas de Miralda, *Barro*, 53.

63. Navas de Miralda, *Barro*, 83.

64. Jameson, "Third World Literature in the Era of Multinational Capitalism," 65–88.

65. Banana novels share a joint concern with respect to issues of national sovereignty, foreign occupation, and racial identity. See Mélida Ruth Sepúlveda's *El tema del canal en la novelística panamameña*.

66. Central America was not alone in the formation of leftist worker alliances. A notable example outside of the isthmus was the Alianza Popular Revolucionaria (1924), founded in Peru in response to the need for Latin American continental

alliances of like-minded political parties. See Kirk S. Bowman's *Militarization, Democracy and Development.*

67. Haya de la Torre, "1926: A Latin American Doctrine of Anti-Imperialism," 129.

68. See Díaz and Cox's "1912: Managing Nicaragua." Political leaders like Nicaraguan president Don Adolfo Diaz clamored for North American intervention, beseeching their business partners to take pity on the "unfortunate" Central American democracies: "We are weak and we need your strong help for the regeneration of our debilitated land. The hand which your Government generously and fraternally extends to us I accept without reserve or fear" (106).

69. Rodríguez, *Dividing the Isthmus*, 13.

70. The term "banana republic" was first used by O. Henry in reference to a fictional country called the "Republic of Anchuria." See O. Henry's *Cabbages and Kings*.

71. Fallas, *Mamita Yunai*, 21.

72. Fallas, *Mamita Yunai*, 21.

73. Fallas, *Mamita Yunai*, 23.

74. Miguel Ángel Asturias's earlier work, such as *Hombres de Maíz* (1949), focused on the Indigenous-*ladino* conflict that pervades the Guatemalan national imaginary and has led to centuries of exploitation of Mayan peoples in the country.

75. It is a scathing trilogy that decries the mass exodus of Mayan families, among others, who abandoned the highlands and migrated to the Caribbean Coast only to fall ill from malaria, inhumane living conditions, and unchecked exploitation at the hands of plantation owners. See David Caballero Mariscal's "Las minorías étnicas en la trilogía bananera de Miguel Ángel Asturias."

76. Asturias, *Viento fuerte*, 5-6.

77. This distinction between a familiar Central American country and the "other" side of it reappears in anti-imperialist text after anti-imperialist text. These novels are concerned with the transformation of *mestizos* into tools of the North American machine. Amaya Amador, *Prisión verde*, 40.

78. See Ian Smart, Richard L. Jackson, and Sonja Stephenson Watson for a deeper consideration of Beleño's Afrodescendance and the manner in which it influences the masterplot he develops in his Panamanian novels.

79. Suleiman, *Authoritarian Fictions*, 76.

80. See Valeria Grinberg Pla and Werner Mackenbach, "*Banana novel revis(it) ed*: etnia, género y espacio en la novela bananera centroamericana. El caso de *Mamita Yunai*," *Iberoamericana* 6.23 (2006): 161-176.

81. See Roland Barthes's "Death of the Author."

82. See Picado, "Our Blood Is Blackening!," 244.

83. Rubén Darío (see chapter 1 of this book) had in 1905 already used blackness as an adjective correlated to mediocrity. In his preface to *Cantos de*

vida y esperanza, he wrote: "Mi respecto por la aristocracia del pensamiento, por la nobleza del Arte, siempre es el mismo. Mi antiguo aborrecimiento a la mediocridad, a la mulatez intelectual, a la chatura estética, apenas si se aminora hoy con una razonada indiferencia." (My respect for the aristocracy of thought, for the nobility of Art, is as it has always been. My former abhorrence of mediocrity, of mullatoed intellectualism, junk aesthetic, is barely now lessening into a reasoned indifference.) Darío, *Poesías completas*, 529.

84. Picado, "Our Blood Is Blackening!," 244.
85. Stepan, *The Hour of Eugenics*, 10.
86. Stepan, *The Hour of Eugenics*, 184–189.
87. Palacios, *Nuestra América y el imperialismo*, 158, 163.
88. See Peter Szok's "Octavio Méndez Pereira and Foundational Fiction."
89. Griffin, "*Barro* Draws Picture of 1915 Banana Company," n.p.
90. Lasso, *Erased*, 2.
91. "More American than America," n.p.
92. During the historical period in question, West Indians in Central America developed a flourishing journalistic and literary movement as a result of their involvement in the UNIA (Universal Negro Improvement Association) movement headed by Marcus Garvey. This was the foundation of the Afro–Central American intellectual tradition, which encompasses creatives across a broad range of genres on- and offline.

Chapter 3. Mesoamerican Core, Kriol Periphery

1. Kirchhoff, "Mesoamérica," 92–107.
2. Winifred Creamer presents a thorough analysis of the archaeological models that have challenged Kirchhoff's concept of Mesoamerica. Her study includes such theories as: models of frontier and boundary, interaction sphere model, local evolutionary models, acculturation, core and periphery distinctions, and world systems models. For details, see her article, "Mesoamerica as Concept: An Archaeological View from Central America."
3. See Francisco Lizcano Fernández's "Las etnias centroamericanas en la segunda mitad del siglo XX."
4. See Gómez Menjívar and Salmon's *Tropical Tongues*.
5. Shoman, *A History of Belize*, 226.
6. Shoman, *A History of Belize*, 276.
7. Barbara S. Balboni and Joseph O. Palacio discuss the incorporation of Maya peoples in Belize in their volume, *Taking Stock: Belize at 25 Years of Independence*; Gómez Menjívar and Salmon consider their ethnolinguistic belonging in *Tropical Tongues*. For a discussion of the Belize-Guatemala land dispute,

see Gómez Menjívar and Salmon's "Mopan in Context: Mayan Identity, Belizean Citizenship, and the Future of a Language."

8. Francisco Lizcano Fernández identifies El Salvador, Honduras, and Nicaragua as *mestizo* countries; Guatemala as an *indomestizo* (with preeminence of both *mestizo* and Indigenous ethnicities) country; Costa Rica as a *criollo* country; Panama as an *afromestizo* (composed of *mestizo* and *mulato* peoples) country. While there exist *afrocriollo* (consisting of *criollo* and *mulato* peoples) elsewhere in Latin America—Cuba, Puerto Rico, the Dominican Republic, and Brazil—Lizcano Fernández does not find this ethnic identification in Central America. Belize, he states, is fundamentally Creole and *mestizo*, rendering it markedly distinct from the aforementioned nations. Lizcano Fernández's observations remained consistent into the twenty-first century, as substantiated during the research undertaken for Gómez Menjívar and Salmon's *Tropical Tongues*.

9. Cornejo Polar, "*Indigenismo* and Heterogeneous Literatures," 112.

10. Cornejo Polar, "*Indigenismo* and Heterogeneous Literatures," 114.

11. Miguel Ángel Asturias is widely recognized as an emblematic figure in Guatemala's cultural, nationalist, and modernizing debates from the end of the 1940s until his death in 1974. For specific treatment of his banana trilogy, see chapter 2 of this book, and for a broader understanding of his life's oeuvre, see Reni Prieto's *Miguel Ángel Asturias's Archaeology of Return*.

12. Arias, "El contexto guatemalteco," 806.

13. Caballero Mariscal, "Las minorías étnicas," 31–50.

14. Colonel Jacobo Árbenz Guzmán put forth the Agrarian Reform Act in 1952, a year after his election to the presidency. The act was aimed at large landowners holding over ninety hectares (224 acres) of land and put under scrutiny the United Fruit Company, which had benefited from land concessions offered by previous Guatemalan presidents.

15. Grandin, Levenson, and Oglesby's section, "Ten Years of Spring and Beyond," 197–280, in Grandin et al., *The Guatemala Reader*.

16. Grandin et al., "Ten Years of Spring and Beyond," 197–280.

17. Juan José Arévalo, "A New Guatemala," 208–210.

18. Asturias, *El papa verde*, 239.

19. Nonetheless, as literary critics Lucía Chen and Amina Figueroa Vergara argue, the two novels do not disconnect themselves from mythical references to Maya cosmogonies. The legacy of a firm Mayan epistemology contrasts sharply with floundering Black characters whose search for identity is never entirely fulfilled. See Lucía Chen's *La dictadura y la explotación* and Amina M. Figueroa Vergara's "A United Fruit Company."

20. "Ten years. Half a Katun, as they would say, following Mayan chronology, the archaeologists . . ." Although we've been taken far from the Mayan highlands, the narrator continues to measure time in Mayan terms and informs us that half

a *katun* has passed since the mulatto families were destroyed. See Asturias, *El papa verde*, 398.

21. For more on the nickname's racial baggage, see Joseph Boskin's *Sambo* and Shirley Ann Tate's *Decolonising Sambo*.

22. Asturias, *El papa verde*, 359.

23. Juambo is locked into his position by a sense of duty. He believes he owes the Green Pope for rescuing him from the clutches of a tiger after his parents abandoned him in the jungle, and for raising him. According to the story that Juambo has come to believe, his disease resulted from the trauma suffered in the jungle that night. Such is the degree of his gullibility that he remains in his boss's service even though he viciously punishes Juambo by pointing a cocked pistol to his head each time he experiences epileptic symptoms. The narrative unfolds and the reader understands—before Juambo himself does—the multiple inconsistencies of the Green Pope's tale. Juambo's gullibility and pitifulness prevents him from becoming a venerable character.

24. Willis, "Nobody's Mulata," 146–162.

25. See Miguel Ángel Asturias, *Los ojos de los enterrados*, 341.

26. See Asturias, *El papa verde*, 483.

27. Several linguists have proposed theories to account for the paucity of creole languages in former Spanish colonies, as compared to their prevalence in former British and French territories. For an introduction to the debate, see John Lipski's *A History of Afro-Hispanic Language*, and for a legal hypothesis of Spanish creole genesis, see Sandro Sessarego's "Casting Light on the Spanish Creole Debate."

28. Pérez-Brignoli, *A Brief History of Central America*, 130–131. Colonel Jacobo Árbenz Guzmán became president in 1951 during a tumultuous phase in Guatemalan politics. Internal affairs had become increasingly polarized as a result of a more organized reaction by landowners and the more visible presence of a workers' union and the newly organized Communist Party (1949). The declassified documents attesting to the scope and objective of CIA Operation PBSUCESS can be viewed online in the National Security Archive's Electronic Briefing Report. See http://www.gwu.edu/~nsarchiv/.

29. Grandin et al., "A Plan for Assassination," 243–245.

30. Grandin et al., "Denied in Full," 256–261, and, "Second Thoughts," 269–274.

31. See Prieto's *Asturias's Archaeology of Return*.

32. Morales, "La colorida nación infernal," 935.

33. Morales, "La colorida nación infernal," 936.

34. See note 28.

35. Asturias, *Mulata de tal*, 11.

36. Ribeiro, "Excerpts: *The Americas and Civilization*," 73, 74.

37. Ribeiro, "Excerpts: *The Americas and Civilization*," 73.

38. Following Judith Butler, "The term 'subjectivation' carries the paradox in itself: *assujetissement* denotes both the becoming of the subject and the process of

subjection—one inhabits the figure of autonomy only by becoming subjected to power, a subjection which implies a radical dependency." See Butler, *The Psychic Life of Power*, 83.

39. Asturias, *Mulata de tal*, 46.

40. The term can be used to express the different phases of the process of transitioning from one culture to another. Transculturation "does not consist merely in acquiring another culture, which is what the English word *acculturation* really implies, but the process also necessarily involves the loss or uprooting of a previous culture" and carries with it the idea of the creation of new cultural phenomena as a result of the fusion. Ortiz, "On the Social Phenomenon of 'Transculturation,'" 102–103.

41. Asturias, *Mulata de tal*, 47.

42. Acevedo Leal, "El engaño de la mujer," 894.

43. Examining the archetype further, Blanco Borelli explains: "Racialist discourses in Cuba constructed the *mulata* as a visceral, non-sentient, threatening object. As a visible representation of the miscegenation that Cuban elites were trying to contain, she needed placating. . . . The mulata, depending on her phenotype, operated in the space between blackness and whiteness. This indeterminate status created tragic encounters, as she was unable to dwell in either location. This liminal identity rendered her tragic, and this tragedy manifested itself in nineteenth-century plays, literature, and visual culture in the Americas, which also capitalized on the sentimentality and melodrama of the tragic *mulata* narrative." Blanco Borelli, *She Is Cuba*, 5–8.

44. Asturias, *Coloquio con Miguel Ángel Asturias*, 124.

45. See Morales, "La colorida nación infernal, 955.

46. Asturias, *Mulata de tal*, 331.

47. Yancy, *Black Bodies, White Gazes*, 5.

48. Acevedo Leal, "El engaño de la mujer," 900.

49. Asturias, *Mulata de tal*, 65.

50. Ramírez, *Tambor olvidado*, 141.

51. Ramírez, *Tambor olvidado*, 141.

52. Escudos, "David Ruiz Puga," n.p.

53. See Gómez Menjívar and Salmon's "Mopan in Context."

54. In order to secure its position as a future independent nation-state, Belize fortified the adjacency line (which is now the current geopolitical border between the countries) with UN Peacekeepers, maintained its alliance to England, and strengthened its economic and political relationship to the United States. See Shoman's *A History of Belize*.

55. Although the spelling Q'eqchi' is common in Guatemala, both Kekchi and Ketchi are used by Maya communities in Belize. I employ Kekchi in this book because it was the most prevalent in my fieldwork.

56. Gómez Menjívar and Salmon, "Mopan in Context," 71.

57. Translation by Gómez Menjívar and Salmon.

58. Escudos, "David Ruiz Puga," n.p.

59. This is in part due to the assumption that they fared better in the colonial period through their complicity with Spaniards to subjugate the Indigenous. Even critics who examine racial and ethnic issues in the isthmus have made statements such as: "By comparison to the brutalized Indigenous population, Black slaves were a privileged and expensive form of labor. They did not toil in the mines or the *latifundia*, but served as house slaves, craftsmen and teamsters. By reason of their history, modern Guatemalan blacks are seen as spirited and independent by nature." Willis, "Nobody's Mulata," 1074.

60. See the Belizean government's publication, *Belize: A New Nation in Central America*.

61. See Gómez Menjívar and Salmon's *Tropical Tongues*.

62. Bolland, *Colonialism and Resistance in Belize*, 56.

63. After their emancipation, the formerly enslaved Black workforce was replaced by indentured Indian and Chinese labor in virtually all Caribbean holdings as well as in Belize. See Moon-Ho Jung's *Coolies and Cane*.

64. Camille, "Population and Ethnicity of Belize, 1861," 55.

65. Ruiz Puga, *Got seif de Cuin!*, 9.

66. Camille, "Population and Ethnicity of Belize, 1861," 56.

67. Brett A. Houk and Brooke Bonorden, "The 'Borders' of British Honduras and the San Pedro Maya of Kaxil Uinic Village," *Ancient Mesoamerica* 31 (2020): 554–569.

68. Ruiz Puga, *Got seif de Cuin!*, 12.

69. As Gloria Anzaldúa describes the experience of the borderlands, "Internal strife results in insecurity and indecisiveness. The [borderlands subject's] dual or multiple personality is plagued by psychic restlessness. In a constant state of nepantilism, an Aztec word meaning torn between two ways, [the borderlands subject] is a product of the transfer of the cultural and spiritual values of one group to another. Being tricultural, monolingual, bilingual or multilingual, speaking a patois, and in a state of perpetual transition, the [borderlands subject] faces the dilemma of the mixed breed: which collectivity does [s/he] listen to?" Anzaldúa, *Borderlands/La Frontera*, 100.

70. Anzaldúa, *Borderlands/La Frontera*, 101.

71. Ruiz Puga, *Got seif de Cuin!*, 10.

72. Ruiz Puga, *Got seif de Cuin!*, 16.

73. Ruiz Puga, *Got seif de Cuin!*, 46.

74. Spivak, "Can the Subaltern Speak?," 271–331.

75. Browitt, "Exorcizando los fantasmas del pasado nacional," n.p.

76. Ruiz Puga, *Got seif de Cuin!*, 35.

77. Ruiz Puga, *Got seif de Cuin!*, 36.

78. Ruiz Puga, *Got seif de Cuin!*, 76.

79. Shoman, *A History of Belize*, 226.
80. Shoman, *A History of Belize*, 276.
81. Ruiz Puga, "Panorama literario del texto literario en Belice," n.p.
82. The atrocities that were committed during this time period against Maya peoples were reported in the four volumes that comprise *Guatemala: nunca más*, published by the Oficina de Derechos Humanos Arzobispado de Guatemala (ODHAG) in 1998.
83. See *La Prensa Libre*'s online newspaper article, "Belice afirma que 'hará todo lo possible por mantener su integridad territorial.'"

Chapter 4. Multicultural Plots

1. See Sonja Stephenson Watson's *The Politics of Race in Panama*.
2. Mosby, *Quince Duncan's "Weathered Men" and "The Four Mirrors*," 2. Mosby goes on to explain: "Beginning in the 1960s, Duncan asserted his claim to a Costa Rican national identity that also embraced Blackness and West Indian cultural identity with his celebrated works of fiction, collection of essays, and recompilations of Afro-Caribbean folktales" (2).
3. Mosby, *Quince Duncan's "Weathered Men" and "The Four Mirrors*," 7. The precursors to the post-Boom Afro–Latin American generation that Mosby describes are: Nelson Estúpiñan Bass and Luz Argentina Chiriboga from Ecuador, Nicomedes and Virginia Santa Cruz from Peru, Manuel and Juan Zapata Olivella from Colombia, Virginia Brindins de Salas from Uruguay, and Nicolás Guillén from Cuba. The generation of authors they influenced includes Quince Duncan from Costa Rica, as well as Gerardo Maloney, Carlos Guillermo Wilson, and Melva Lowe de Goodin from Panama, Nancy Morejón from Cuba, Norberto James and Blas Jiménez from the Dominican Republic, and Lucía Charún Illescas from Peru.
4. See Erik Ching's *Broadcasting the Civil War in El Salvador*.
5. Gioconda Belli and Rigoberta Menchú—to name just two of the many emblematic women writers of this period—reflected on gender and their commitments to social change in the context of raging civil wars. Writing from distinct coordinates in the isthmus, together they challenged mainstream paradigms in women's writing by centering "others" in literary discourses. As precarious and often perilous alliances were forged across generations, social classes, and Indigenous groups, women's literature positioned itself as literature of the oppressed, where the experiences of the "other"—understood as nonhegemonic or subaltern—had a rightful place. See Laura Barbas-Rhoden's *Writing Women in Central America*.
6. Barbas-Rhoden, *Writing Women in Central America*, 3.
7. For more on the "others" of Central American hegemonic ideologies across time and space, the reader might want to refer to Ileana Rodríguez's

House/Garden/Nation, Arturo Arias's *Recovering Lost Footprints*, Serena Cosgrove et al.'s *Surviving the Americas*, and Yajaira Padilla's *From Threatening Guerrillas to Forever Illegals*.

8. This cultural production runs the tropes of pain, pleasure, death, perversion, and abuse, among others. As Beatriz Cortez asserts, these narratives "emphasized the power of passion over reason through characters who sought to supersede the standards of decency, morality, and other principles fundamental to the symbolic order. Like the post-dictatorship narratives of Argentina and Chile, these post-civil war Central American narratives delved into the unattainability of happiness, the defense of the body that needed to engage in action, the predominance of life over death, and the immanence of power" (38). Cortez, *Estética del cinismo*, 27–38.

9. Cortez, *Estética del cinismo*, 38.
10. Meléndez and Duncan, *El negro en Costa Rica*, 9.
11. Palmer and Molina, *The Costa Rica Reader*, 229.
12. Palmer and Molina, *The Costa Rica Reader*, 230.
13. Rossi, *Limón Blues*, 418.
14. Brenes Molina, "Entrevista a Tatiana Lobo," 1–7.
15. Trigo, "Multiculturalismo, diversidad cultural y segmentación de mercados," 18.
16. Vargas Porras, "Celebran el día del negro," n.p.
17. Valdo, "Aprueban celebrar el Día de la Persona Negra," n.p.
18. United Nations, "UNESCO: United Nations Educational, Scientific, and Cultural Organization," n.p.
19. United Nations General Assembly, "Resolution adopted by the General Assembly on 18 December 2009. 64/169. International Year for People of African Descent," n.p.
20. For an in-depth study of the Universal Negro Improvement Association and Marcus Garvey himself, see Edmund David Cronon's *Black Moses*.
21. Kerns, "Postcoloniality in Anacristina Rossi's *Limón Blues*," 16–36.
22. Rossi, *Limón Blues*, 19–20.
23. Minor Keith was also known as "The Uncrowned King of Costa Rica" for his role in financing the sewers, markets, piping, railroad, phone, and electricity of San José.
24. Rossi, *Limón Blues*, 40.
25. Rossi, *Limón Blues*, 108.
26. Rossi, *Limón Blues*, 212; emphasis mine.
27. Rossi, *Limón Blues*, 275.
28. Rossi, *Limón Blues*, 275
29. Zalas Zamorra, "Encuentros y desencuentros culturales en la novela *Calypso*," n.p.
30. Zalas Zamorra, "Encuentros y desencuentros culturales en la novela *Calypso*," n.p.

31. Rossi, *Limón Blues*, 401.
32. Dow, *Mothering While Black*, 23–54.
33. Rossi, *Limón Blues*, 402.
34. Mackenbach, "Chocolate con crema en Parima Bay," 1–6.
35. As Dorothy Mosby explains, there are two traditions of oral transmission that lay the groundwork for storytellers of West Indian descent to put their stories into writing: the West African Ashanti tales of a trickster spider named Anansi and the calypsos, which are structured rhythmically to be remembered and repeated. Mosby, *Place, Language and Identity*, 32–33.
36. Halbwachs, *On Collective Memory*, 22.
37. Bloomfield, Barnes, and Huyse, *Reconciliation after Violent Conflict*, 12.
38. Lobo, *Calypso*, 25.
39. Lobo, *Calypso*, 137.
40. Lobo, *Calypso*, 104.
41. Lobo, *Calypso*, 101.
42. Lobo, *Calypso*, 144.
43. Lobo, *Calypso*, 216–217.
44. Lobo, *Calypso*, 232.
45. Palmer and Molina, *The Costa Rica Reader*, 55.
46. For a more in-depth discussion of this critical socioeconomic transition in Costa Rica's history, see Lowell Gudmundson's *Costa Rica before Coffee*.
47. Dunlop, "Viajes en Centroamérica," 84.
48. Mosby, *Place, Language and Identity*, 23.
49. Palmer and Molina, *The Costa Rica Reader*, 245–246.
50. Žižek, "Multiculturalism," 28–51.
51. Robinson, *Transnational Conflicts*, 20.
52. Izquierdo Miller, for instance, states that, due to her "Caribbean condition," she has identified with certain elements of the Afro-Caribbean religion as depicted in the novel. Her article prompts us to understand that the Black world of the text speaks to her experience as a Black woman with an intimate knowledge of that denied and neglected magically feminine Caribbean coast featured in the novel. See her essay, "Las orishas en *Calypso*."
53. Ana Cristina Rossi's *Limón Blues* has been listed twice on the mandatory reading list prescribed for the primary, secondary, and tertiary educational levels under the categories "Costa Rican Literature" and "Postmodern Costa Rican Literature."
54. Bloomfield, Barnes, and Huyse, *Reconciliation after Violent Conflict*, 11.
55. Bloomfield, Barnes, and Huyse, *Reconciliation after Violent Conflict*, 11.
56. Kamala Harris, vice president of the United States (2021–), was the second Black woman elected to serve in that capacity.
57. Many military and political leaders in the young Central American republics were Afrodescendants; they were neither listed as such nor did they advocate for the visibility of the formerly enslaved peoples in their nations. These

leaders have rarely been "seen" as Black men in power due to narratives that have presented them in the colorblind glory of the Independence movements. See Sergio Ramírez's *Tambor olvidado*.

58. See Campbell's "Un mensaje a la población costarricense."

59. See Waisbord and Amado's "Populist Communication by Digital Means," 1332.

60. See Campbell's "¡Gracias, Costa Rica!"

61. The last decades of the twentieth century saw a rise of grassroots organizations demanding full recognition of Afrodescendants as citizens, culminating especially in the 2001 UN World Conference against Racism, Racial Discrimination, Xenophobia, and Related Intolerance at which multiple Black leaders from the Americas participated. For more, see Jean Muteba Rahier's *Black Social Movements in Latin America*.

62. Rahier, *Black Social Movements in Latin America*, 4.

63. See the chapter on Honduras by Mark Anderson and on Guatemala by Carlos Agudelo in Rahier, *Black Social Movements in Latin America*.

64. Jan Hoffman French, *Legalizing Identities*, 185.

Chapter 5. From Caribbean Sea to Digital Shore

1. In Central America, national presses and university presses carry great weight, while the international press with the leading stamp of appeal is Alfaguara, which reaches Hispanophone readers across Latin America, Spain, and the United States. Alfaguara published Anacristina Rossi's multilingual *Limón Blues* (discussed in chapter 4) but as of the date of this writing has yet to publishe Black writers from Central America.

2. Mariske argues that the very first book fair in Latin America announced the "despertar editorial en México, los inicios de la labor editorial en gran escala; ya no sólo se imprimirían lujosos libros, de muy pocos títulos, y que eran los mismos que se editaban desde los inicios de la época colonial, sino que se empezó a hacer una labor editorial para la población mexicana en general a la par de la alfabetización de adultos y niños. También ayudaron los avances tecnológicos: gracias a las nuevas máquinas impresoras los libros se habían abaratado y los tirajes eran cada vez mayores; además, la instalación de luz eléctrica en el centro de la Ciudad de México permitía ahora leer en la noche." Mariske, "Ecos de la primera Feria del Libro," 188.

3. Salas, "Feria Internacional del Libro," n.p.

4. Jáuregui, "Writing Communities on the Internet," 294.

5. As suggested by a peer reviewer, I state from the outset that I do not emphasize any individual scholar or specific scholarly network as a barrier to publication but rather the factors engrained in the regional publishing industry.

6. Carrasco, "Literatura, intercambio, cultura," 168.

7. González, "Antología poética." n.p.

8. Flew, *New Media*, 2.

9. For a full discussion of Internet connections across the isthmus from the 1980s to the 2000s, as well as transnational flows of knowledge, data, and technologies in the region, see Ignacio Siles's *A Transnational History of the Internet in Central America*.

10. Cárdenas, *Constituting Central American–Americans*, 89.

11. See Juan G. Sánchez Martínez's "A Post-Ethnic/Racial Futurescape in Wingston González's *cafeina MC*."

12. Forbes, *Garífuna*, 78. Michelle Forbes further explains that there are three theories as to the African ancestry of Garifuna peoples, including the hypothesis that Africans in bondage were taken to St. Vincent from neighboring islands and the hypothesis that African voyagers had arrived on the island much prior to the arrival of Europeans in the lesser Antilles. However, the third hypothesis shapes Garifuna ethnogenesis and contributes to the formation of Garifuna identity: "Traditionally, the Garífunas hold fast to oral tradition that maintains that they were never slaves; their presence on St. Vincent was due to at least one or two shipwrecked slaving barges. . . . The source of this account derives loosely from historical papers (Scott 1667; Young 1795), from which contemporary chroniclers from St. Vincent (Anderson 1938; Duncan 1970) extracted specific sections to offer a most celebratory relation of Garífuna ancestry" (78).

13. Taylor, *The Black Carib Wars*, 23.

14. Most research on creole languages is concerned with relations between the creole/vernacular and the standard. See McWhorter's *The Missing Spanish Creoles* as well as the sources in Gómez Menjívar and Salmon's *Tropical Tongues*.

15. Wade, *Race and Ethnicity*, 26.

16. Taylor, *The Black Carib Wars*, 23.

17. Taylor, *The Black Carib Wars*, 5.

18. The permanent link to the film on Amazon Prime is https://www.amazon.com/Garifuna-Peril-Ruben-Reyes/dp/B01EYY53EK.

19. Taylor, *The Black Carib Wars*, 149.

20. Arrivillaga Cortés, "La diaspora garífuna entre memorias y fronteras," 85.

21. Mariano Galvez, chief of state of Guatemala while it was part of the Federal Republic of Guatemala, stated in a decree dated November 26, 1831: "And in order that the district and its principal town be a monument to legislation and freedom, as well as to honour the memory of the patriotic American legislator, whose penal system the State intends to adopt, and as a symbol of safety and protection, they shall bear the name Livingston." Gullick, *Exiled from St. Vincent*, 32.

22. DJ Labuga, "Garifuna Music & Talk with DJ Labuga," 00:00:00–02:20:30.

23. Payeras, "Prefacio," 7.

24. González, "Antología poética," n.p.

25. Douglas Taylor, *The Black Caribs of British Honduras*, 105.

26. Intrasentential code-switching occurs within a sentence. For example, when the poetic voice in this poem says, "Belice city." This type of code-switching poses interesting challenges to arrive at a translation since "Belize City" is an equivalent, but not a true measure of what is achieved with the intrasentential code-switching. Intersentential code-switching occurs at sentence boundaries and presents a different set of challenges for the translator. One example in this poem would be: "Ajá. The star spangled banner. Do you have a girlfriend wingston? Tus primas son brujas. Tus tíos son brujos."

27. See Gómez Menjívar's article in *Istmo* and López Oro's chapter in *Indigenous Interfaces*.

28. Wilson and Stewart, *Global Indigenous Media*, 18.

29. Flew, *New Media*, 13–14.

30. Gómez Menjívar and Chacón, *Indigenous Interfaces*, 12.

31. As late as 2012 during the course of fieldwork, Livingston's Internet cafes operated with tourists first in mind, and formal typing classes for locals were still held on typewriters. Before moving to Guatemala City, winning well-deserved prizes, and receiving the scholarly attention that led to his work being translated into English and German, González faced a clear structural challenge for producing and distributing his poetry.

32. González, "Antología poética," n.p.

33. González, "Antología poética." n.p. A different version of the poem, without the first three verses I highlight here, has been published and translated by Simmons in *Palabras*.

34. Anderson, *Black and Indigenous*, 8.

35. López Oro, "Digitizing Ancestral Memory," 206.

36. Kahn, *Seeing and Being Seen*, 169.

37. Gifitti, also spelled gifiti and guiffity, is an alcoholic drink made with rum and various roots and herbs that sometimes include chamomile, marigold stems, anise, peppercorns, cloves, bitterwood, garlic, and ginger, among others.

38. Wingston, "Antología poética," n.p.

39. González, "Antología poética," n.p.

40. Cabrera, "Wingston González," n.p.

41. Ochoa, "Wingston González, n.p.

42. Álvarez and Spiegeler, "Antojología de Carl Rigby," n.p.

43. Álvarez and Spiegeler, "Antojología de Carl Rigby," n.p.

44. García Espinosa, "For an Imperfect Cinema," 220.

45. Edison, "Carlos Rigby," n.p.

46. Roof, "The Nicaribbeans," 4.

47. Mosby, "Nuevos nómadas," n.p.

48. "Antojología de Carl Rigby," n.p.

49. Castro Jo, "Raza, consciencia de color y militancia negra," 30–31.

50. Ryan, *Popularizing Media*, 14.

51. Rincón and Marroquín, "Latin American *Lo popular* as a Theory of Communication," 43.

52. Rincón and Marroquín, "Latin American *Lo popular*," 43.

53. See the website "Antojología de Carl Rigby" as well as the full documentary, *Antojología* on YouTube (0:00:00–1:02:56).

54. The verses in figure 5.3 have been extracted from the poem "Odo clasial" (Classical Ode), and it is shown in print form in Rigby's hands a few frames later. The ode begins with the verse "Cuesta mucho ser blanco" (It costs a lot to be white) and incorporates images of Rigby as a child learning about the primacy of class over race in human experience. The full text of the poem is reproduced in Norbert-Bertrand's digital publication, *Gojón No. 28 Especial: Carlos Rigby y poetas caribeños*, n.p.

55. For more about the shift in themes in Black writing from the twentieth to the twenty-first century as specifically related to Quince Duncan, Melanie Taylor Herrera, Wingston González, and Xiomara Cacho Caballero, see the chapters by Gloria Chacón, Ángela Castro, Juan Guillermo Sánchez Martínez, and Jennifer Carolina Gómez Menjívar in *Améfrica in Letters*.

56. Luciano Barraco's "Race and Revolution in Bluefields."

57. Lipski, "Linguistic Consequences of the Sandinista Revolution."

58. For more on the concentration of literary presses in the capital cities of Latin America, see Bowker Editores's *La impresa del libro en América Latina*.

59. See Ella Chmielewska's "Framing [Con]text" and Tracey Bowen's "Reading Gestures and Reading Codes."

60. See Langston Hughes's "Harlem." The full text of the poem is:

What happens to a dream deferred?
Does it dry up
like a raisin in the sun?
Or fester like a sore—
And then run?
Does it stink like rotten meat?
Or crust and sugar over—
like a syrupy sweet?
Maybe it just sags
like a heavy load.
Or does it explode?

61. Martín-Barbero, "A Nocturnal Map," 313.

62. John Lipski's "Linguistic Consequences of the Sandinista Revolution and Its Aftermath in Nicaragua."

63. See Gómez Menjívar's "Redes garífunas insurgentes."

Conclusion. The Battlegrounds of Central American Identity

1. See Gómez Menjívar and Salmon, *Tropical Tongues*.
2. See Alarcón and Vargas's "Cocorí." The full English-language translation of the episode transcript in included as the appendix to this book with permission from Radio Ambulante Estudios.
3. Carlos Luis Fallas's *Mamita Yunai* is a canonical text in the banana novel genre; it is described briefly in chapter 2 of this book and more fully in Ana Patricia Rodríguez's *Dividing the Isthmus*. Joaquín Gutiérrez is described in the episode as an influential man who "published six novels, three collections of poems, four travel books, and one memoir. He translated four works of Shakespeare into Spanish. His books, in turn, have been translated into twelve languages. One of those books is *Cocorí*, which was so successful that it has been published in French, German, Russian, Polish, and Portuguese, among other languages. He was a member of the Costa Rican Academy of the Spanish Language and winner of the National Culture Award; he received an honorary doctorate from the University of Costa Rica; and one of the most relevant newspapers in the country declared him a Person of the Century in national literature. Joaquín Gutiérrez is also remembered as a man committed to leftist struggles. He was a member of the Costa Rican Communist Party. He traveled to Vietnam during the war to write chronicles and worked in China as a translator of the works of the revolutionary Mao Zedong. He was a candidate for the vice presidency of the country twice in the 1980s, with the Pueblo Unido coalition. He did not win either time." See Daniel Alarcón and Luis Fernando Vargas's "Cocorí."
4. Luis Fernando Vargas summarizes *Cocorí* thus: "It's the story of a boy named Cocorí, who lives on a beach that borders the jungle, in what is supposed to be like the Costa Rican Caribbean. It's a very, very rustic town. And one day, a ship arrives in the morning, a large ship, with passengers. Cocorí goes along with his neighbors bringing fruit as a gift in a little boat. They board the ship and Cocorí meets a girl. To him, she is the prettiest girl he has ever seen. And the girl gives him a rose that the boy considers as beautiful as she is. But the next day, the rose dies and the girl leaves. And Cocorí, very sad, wonders why beautiful things last so little and why ugly and bad things, like the dangerous animals in the jungle and the carnivorous plants where he lives, last what seems like an eternity. He then goes on an adventure into the heart of the jungle to ask old and supposedly wise animals to try and figure this out, right? Why is the weather so inclement? . . . The complexity is that Cocorí is of African descent and the girl is White, and that begins to give everything meaning. In other words, the girl is the most beautiful thing Cocorí has ever seen; she looks like a rose. And Cocorí, on the other hand, on the first page of the book, is compared to a *caimito*, which is a tropical fruit with a dark skin that is not very popular, that is, it is not an apple, and this is the beginning of the idea that what is external,

what is not from Cocorí's home, is better, more beautiful." See Daniel Alarcón and Luis Fernando Vargas's "Cocorí."

5. See Alarcón and Vargas's "Cocorí."
6. Loveman, *National Colors*, 301.
7. Loveman, *National Colors*, 303.

Works Cited

Acevedo Leal, Anabella. "'El engaño de la mujer es siempre un misterio': construcciones y desconstrucciones de la sexualidad en *Mulata de tal*." In Miguel Ángel Asturias, *Mulata de tal: edición crítica*, 891–905. Mexico City: Fondo de Cultura Económica, 2000.
Agudelo, Carlos. "The Afro-Guatemalan Political Mobilization." In *Black Social Movements in Latin America: From Monocultural Mestizaje to Multiculturalism*, edited by Jean Muteba Rahier, 75–94. New York: Palgrave, 2012.
Aguilera Malta, Demetrio. *Canal Zone*. Mexico City: Ediciones de Andrea, 1966.
Aguirre, Mario Hernández. *Gavidia: Poesía, Literatura, Humanismo*. San Salvador: Ministerio de Educación, Dirección General de Cultura, 1965.
Alarcón, Daniel, and Luis Fernando Vargas. "Cocorí." *Radio Ambulante*, Season 11, Episode 19, NPR, February 8, 2022. https://radioambulante.org/en/translation/cocori-translation.
Alexander, Michelle. *The New Jim Crow: Mass Incarceration in the Age of Colorblindness*. New York: New Press, 2020.
Álvarez, María José, and Eduardo Spiegeler. *Antojología de Carl Rigby* (2019). YouTube. https://www.youtube.com/watch?v=xZkP8Vz2pmM.
Amaya Amador, Ramón. *Prisión verde*. Yoro, Honduras: Editorial Universitaria, 1990.
Anderson, Mark. *Black and Indigenous: Garifuna Activism and Consumer Culture in Honduras*. Minneapolis: University of Minnesota Press, 2009.
———. "Garifuna Activism." In *Black Social Movements in Latin America: From Monocultural Mestizaje to Multiculturalism*, edited by Jean Muteba Rahier, 53–74. New York: Palgrave, 2012.
Andrews, George Reid. *Blackness in the White Nation: A History of Afro-Uruguay*. Chapel Hill: University of North Carolina Press, 2010.
Anzaldúa, Gloria. *Borderlands/La Frontera: The New Mestiza*. New York: Aunt Lute Books, 1987.

Arce, B. Christine. *México's Nobodies: The Cultural Legacy of the Soldadera and Afro-Mexican Women*. Albany: State University of New York Press, 2016.

Arévalo, Juan José. "A New Guatemala." In *The Guatemala Reader: History, Culture, Politics*, edited by Greg Grandin, Deborah T. Levenson, and Elizabeth Oglesby, 206–210. Durham, NC: Duke University Press, 2011.

Arias, Arturo. "El contexto guatemalteco y el exilio de Asturias después de la caída de Árbenz." In *Mulata de tal: edición crítica*, edited by Arturo Arias, 803–818. Nanterre, France: Signatarios del Acuerdo Archivos, 2000.

———. *Recovering Lost Footprints, Volume 2: Contemporary Maya Narratives*. Albany: State University of New York Press, 2017.

Arrivillaga Cortés, Alfonso. "La diáspora garífuna entre memorias y fronteras" *Boletín de Antropología* Universidad de Antioquia 24.41 (2010): 84–95.

Arroyo Calderón, Patricia. "Cada uno en su sitio y cada cosa en su lugar. Imaginarios de desigualdad en América Central (1870–1900)." Electronic thesis or dissertation, Ohio State University, 2015.

Asturias, Miguel Ángel. *Viento fuerte*. Buenos Aires: Aguilar, S.A. de Ediciones, 1969.

———. *El papa verde*. Buenos Aires: Aguilar, S.A. de Ediciones Juan Bravo, 1969.

———. *Mulata de tal: edición crítica*. Mexico City: Fondo de Cultura Económica de México, 2000.

———. *Coloquio con Miguel Ángel Asturias*. Guatemala City: Editorial Universitaria, 1968.

———. *Los ojos de los enterrados*. Buenos Aires: Editorial Losada, 1960.

Balboni, Barbara S., and Joseph O. Palacio. *Taking Stock: Belize at 25 Years of Independence*. Benque Viejo del Carmen, Belize: Cubola Productions, 2007.

Baltasar Fra Molinero. *La imagen de los negros en el teatro del Siglo de Oro*. Madrid: Siglo Veintiuno de España Editores, 1995.

Baracco, Luciano. "Race and Revolution in Bluefields: A History of Nicaragua's Black Sandinista Movement." *Wadabagei* 10.1 (2007): 4–23.

Barbas-Rhoden, Laura. *Writing Women in Central America: Gender and the Fictionalization of History*. Athens: Center for International Studies at the Ohio University, 2003.

Barthes, Roland. "Death of the Author." In *Image, Music, Text*, 142–147. New York: Hill and Wang, 1977.

"Belice afirma que "hará todo lo posible por mantener su integridad territorial' al presentar ante La Haya memoria de respuesta a Guatemala." *La Prensa Libre*, June 6, 2022. https://www.prensalibre.com/guatemala/politica/belice-presenta-ante-la-haya-memoria-de-respuesta-a-la-demanda-de-guatemala-breaking/.

Belize, the Government of Belize, Belmopan. *Belize: A New Nation in Central America*. Benque Viejo del Carmen, Belize: Cubola Productions, 1976.

Bell, Alice, and Marie-Laure Ryan. *Possible Worlds Theory and Contemporary Narratology*. Lincoln: University of Nebraska Press, 2019.

Bennet, Herman L. *Colonial Blackness: A History of Afro-Mexico*. Bloomington: Indiana University Press, 2009.

Benson, Devon Spence. *Anti-Racism in Cuba: The Unfinished Revolution*. Chapel Hill: University of North Carolina Press, 2016.
Berman, Marshall. *All That Is Solid Melts in the Air: The Experience of Modernity*. London: Verso, 1983.
Biesanz, John. "Cultural and Economic Factors in Panamanian Race Relations." *American Sociological Review* 14.6 (1949): 772–779.
Blanco Borelli, Melissa. *She Is Cuba: A Genealogy of the Mulata Body*. New York: Oxford University Press, 2016.
Bloom, Harold. "Apophrades or the Return of the Dead." In *The Anxiety of Influence: A Theory of Poetry*, 139–156. New York: Oxford University Press, 1973.
Bloomfield, David, Teresa Barnes, and Luc Huyse. *Reconciliation after Violent Conflict: A Handbook*. Stockholm: International Institute for Democracy and Electoral Assistance, 2003.
Bolland, Nigel. *Colonialism and Resistance in Belize: Essays in Historical Sociology*. Benque Viejo del Carmen, Belize: Cubola Productions, 2003.
Bolívar, Simón. "Carta de Jamaica." In *Fuentes de la cultura latinoamericana I*. Mexico City: Fondo de Cultura Económica, 1995.
———. *El liberatador: Writings of Simon Bolivar*. New York: Oxford University Press, 2003.
Borucki, Alex. *From Shipmates to Soldiers: Emerging Black Identities in Rio de la Plata*. Albuquerque: University of New Mexico Press, 2015.
Borucki, Alex, David Eltis, and David Wheat. "Atlantic History and the Slave Trade to Spanish America." *American Historical Review* 120.2 (2015): 433–461.
Boskin, Joseph. *Sambo: The Rise and Demise of an American Jester*. New York: Oxford University Press, 1986.
Bourdieu, Pierre. *Outline of a Theory of Practice*. London: Cambridge University Press, 1977.
Bowen, Tracey. "Reading Gestures and Reading Codes: The Visual Literacy of Graffiti as Both Physical/Performative Act and Digital Information Text." In *Mapping Minds*, edited by Monika Raesch, 85–94. Oxford, UK: Interdisciplinary Press, 2010.
Bowker Editores. *La impresa del libro en América Latina*. Buenos Aires: Bowker Editores Argentina, 1968.
Bowman, Kirk S. *Militarization, Democracy and Development: The Perils of Praetorianism in Latin America*. Philadelphia: University of Pennsylvania Press, 2002.
Brenes Molina, José Jacinto. "Entrevista a Tatiana Lobo: literatura y sociedad." *Revista Comunicación* 12 (2002): 1–7.
Brewer-García, Larissa. *Beyond Babel: Translations of Blackness in Colonial Peru and New Granada*. London: Cambridge University Press, 2020.
Browitt, Jeff. "Exorcizando los fantasmas del pasado nacional: *Got seif de Cuin!* de David Ruiz y *Margarita, está linda la mar* de Sergio Ramírez." *Istmo*:

revista de estudios culturales centroamericanos, January 26, 2002. http://collaborations.denison.edu/istmo/n03/articulos/fantasmas.html.

Browne, Randy M. *Surviving Slavery in the British Caribbean*. Philadelphia: University of Pennsylvania Press, 2017.

Butler, Judith. *The Psychic Life of Power: Theories in Subjection*. Stanford, CA: Stanford University Press, 1997.

Caballero Mariscal, David. "Las minorías étnicas en la trilogía bananera de Miguel Ángel Asturias: el personaje de Juambo, el 'Sambito.'" *Revista destiempos* 32 (2011): 31–50.

Cabrera, Claudia. "Wingston González." Goethe Institut, December 1, 2016. http://www.goethe.de/ins/mx/lp/prj/lit/aut/gua/es13534358.htm.

Cáceres Gómez, Rina. *Rutas de la esclavitud en África y América Latina*. San Pedro: Editorial Universidad de Costa Rica, 2001.

———. *Del olvido a la memoria: Africanos y afromestizos en la historia colonial de Centroamérica*. Paris: UNESCO, 2008.

Candelario, Ginetta E. B. *Black Behind the Ears: Dominican Racial Identity from Museums to Beauty Shops*. Durham, NC: Duke University Press, 2007.

Cañizares-Esguerra, Jorge, Matt D. Childs, and James Sidbury. *The Black Urban Atlantic in the Age of the Slave Trade*. Philadelphia: University of Pennsylvania Press, 2013.

Camille, Michael A. "Population and Ethnicity of Belize, 1861." In *Belize: Selected Proceedings from the Second Interdisciplinary Conference*. Lanham, MD: University Press of America, 1996.

Campbell, Epsy. "Un mensaje a la población costarricense. #EsPorCostaRica." Facebook, April 1, 2018. https://www.facebook.com/EpsyCampbellBarr/videos/10156340149899452/.

———. "¡Gracias, Costa Rica! Mi último mensaje como Vicepresidenta de la República." Facebook, May 8, 2022. https://www.facebook.com/EpsyCampbellBarr/videos/388508236521995.

Cárdenas, Maritza E. *Constituting Central American-Americans: Transnational Identities and the Politics of Dislocation*. New Brunswick, NJ: Rutgers University Press, 2018.

Carr, Robert. *Black Nationalism in the New World: Reading the African-American and West Indian Experience*. Durham, NC: Duke University Press, 2002.

Carranza Mena, Douglas. "Los indígenas y las identidades poscampesinas en El Salvador." *Istmo: revista virtual de estudios culturales centroamericanos*, January 26, 2002. http://istmo.denison.edu/n03/articulos/identidades.html

Carrasco, Iván. "Literatura, intercambio, cultura." *Revista Austral de Ciencias Sociales* 7 (2017): 165–170.

Castro, Ángela. "The Palimpsestic Afro-Panamanian Woman in Melanie Taylor Herrera's *Camino a Mariato*." In *Améfrica in Letters: Literary Interventions from Mexico to the Southern Cone*, edited by Jennifer Carolina Gómez Menjívar, 97–108. Nashville, TN: Vanderbilt University Press, 2022.

Castro Jo, Carlos. "Raza, conciencia de color y militancia negra en la literatura nicaragüense." *Revista Wani* 33 (2003): 21–32.
Chacón, Gloria Elizabeth. "Transatlantic Routing and Rooting in Quince Duncan's *Kimbo*." In *Améfrica in Letters: Literary Interventions from Mexico to the Southern Cone*, edited by Jennifer Carolina Gómez Menjívar, 83–96. Nashville, TN: Vanderbilt University Press, 2022.
Chambers, Glenn A. *Race, Nation, and West Indian Immigration to Honduras, 1890–1940*. Baton Rouge: Louisiana State University Press, 2010.
Chance, John K., and William B. Taylor. "Estate and Class in Colonial Oaxaca: Oaxaca in 1792." *Comparative Studies in Society and History* 19.3 (1977): 454–487.
Chen, Lucía. *La dictadura y la explotación: un estudio de la trilogya bananera de Miguel Ángel Asturias*. Mexico City: Cuadernos Americanos UNAM, 2000.
Ching, Erik. *Broadcasting the Civil War in El Salvador*. Austin: University of Texas Press, 2021.
Chmielewska, Ella. "Framing [Con]text: Graffiti and Place." *Space and Culture* 10.2 (2007): 145–169.
Chomsky, Aviva. *Central America's Forgotten History: Revolution, Violence, and the Roots of Migration*. Boston, MA: Beacon Press, 2021.
Cinthio. "Un Capitano Moro." 1565. In *Shakespeare's Library: A Collection of the Plays, Romances, Novels, Poems and Histories Employed by Shakespeare in the Composition of His Works*, 285–308. London: Reeves and Turner, 1875.
Clammer, Paul, Ray Bartlett, and Celeste Brash. *Lonely Planet: Belize*. Fort Mill, SC: Lonely Planet, 2019.
Clancy-Smith, Julia. "The Colonial Gaze: Sex and Gender in the Discourses of French North Africa." In *Franco-Arab Encounters*, edited by David C. Gordon, Carl L. Brown, and Matthew Gordon, 201–228. Beirut: American University of Beirut Press, 1996.
Clark, Emily. *American Quadroon: Free Women of Color in the Revolutionary Atlantic World*. Chapel Hill: University of North Carolina Press, 2013.
Clealand, Danielle Pilar. *The Power of Race in Cuba: Racial Ideology and Black Consciousness during the Revolution*. New York: Oxford University Press, 2017.
Cope, Douglas. *The Limits of Racial Domination: Plebeian Society in Colonial Mexico City, 1660–1720*. Madison: University of Wisconsin Press, 1994.
Cornejo Polar, Antonio. "*Indigenismo* and Heterogeneous Literatures: Their Double Sociocultural State." In *The Latin American Cultural Studies Reader*, edited by Ana del Sarto, Alicia Ríos, and Abril Trigo, 100–152. Durham, NC: Duke University Press, 2004.
Cortez, Beatriz. *Estética del cinismo: pasión y desencanto en la literatura centroamericana de posguerra*. Guatemala City: F & G Editores, 2009.
Cosgrove, Serena, José Idiáquez, Andrew Gorvetizian, and Leonard Joseph Bent. *Surviving the Americas: Garifuna Persistence from Nicaragua to New York City*. Cincinnati, OH: University of Cincinnati Press, 2021.

Creamer, Winfred. "Mesoamerica as Concept: An Archaeological View from Central America." *Latin American Research Review* 22.1 (1987): 35–62.
Cronon, E. David. *Black Moses: The Story of Marcus Garvey and the Universal Negro Improvement Association*. Madison: University of Wisconsin Press, 1955.
Darío, Rubén. "1904: To Roosevelt." In *Latin America and the United States: A Documentary History*, edited by Robert H. Holden and Eric Zolov, 91–92. New York: Oxford University Press, 2011.
———. "La raza de Cham." In *Parisiana*, 211–217. Managua, Nicaragua: Editorial Mundo Latino, 1917.
———. *Poesías completas. Ordenadas por Luis Alberto Ruiz*. Bogota, Colombia: Ediciones Zamora, 1967.
de la Fuente, Alejandro, and George Reid Andrews. *Afro-Latin American Studies: An Introduction*. New York: Oxford University Press, 2018.
de Torquemada, Juan. *Monarquía Indiana*, 1615. Mexico City: Porrúa, 1975.
Díaz, Adolfo, and Philander Cox. "1912. Managing Nicaragua." In *Latin America and the United States*, edited by Robert H. Holden and Eric Zolov, 98–100. New York: Oxford University Press, 2000.
DJ Labuga. "Garifuna Music & Talk with DJ Labuga: Presenta Wingston González." YouTube, July 30, 2015. https://www.youtube.com/watch?v=3xFG1bfDZjY.
Dow, Dawn Marie. *Mothering While Black*. Berkeley: University of California Press, 2019.
Dunlop, Glasgow. "Viajes en Centroamérica." In *Costa Rica en el siglo XIX: antología de viajeros*, edited by Ricardo Fernández Guardia, 81–82. San José, Costa Rica: Editorial Universitaria Centroamericana, 1982.
DuVernay, Ava. *13th*. Performances by Melina Abdullah, Michelle Alexander, Cory Booker, Dolores Canales, and Gina Clayton. Netflix, 2016.
Earle, T. F., and K. J. P. Lowe. *Black Africans in Renaissance Europe*. Cambridge, UK: Cambridge University Press, 2005.
Edison, Thomas Wayne. "Carlos Rigby." Oxford African American Studies Center, May 31, 2017. https://doi.org/10.1093/acref/9780195301731.013.74921.
Escudos, Jacinta. "David Ruiz Puga: más allá del exotismo." *Istmo: revista de estudios culturales centroamericanos*, January 17, 2005. http://collaborations.denison.edu/istmo/n10/foro/ruiz.html.
Euraque, Darío. "The Threat of Blackness to the Honduran Nation: Race and Ethnicity in the Honduran Banana Economy, 1920s and 1930s." In *Banana Wars: Power, Production, and History in the Americas*, edited by Steve Striffler and Mark Moberg, 229–252. Durham, NC: Duke University Press, 2003.
———. *Conversaciones históricas con el mestizaje en Honduras y su identidad nacional*. San Pedro Sula, Honduras: Centro Editorial, 2004.
———. "Negritud garifuna y coyunturas políticas en la Costa Norte de Honduras, 1940–1970." In *Memorias del mestizaje: política y cultura en Centroamérica, 1920–1990*, 295–323. Guatemala: CIRMA, 2004.

Fabian, Johannes. *Time and the Other: How Anthropology Makes Its Object.* New York: Columbia University Press, 1983.
Fallas, Carlos Luis. *Mamita Yunai.* San José, Costa Rica: Editorial de Arte y Literatura, 1987.
Fanon, Frantz. *Black Skin, White Masks.* New York: Grove Press, 1967.
Fernández Durán, Reyes. *La corona española y el tráfico de negros: del monopolio al libre comercio.* Madrid: Ecobook, 2011.
Figueroa Vergara, Amina M. "A United Fruit Company na Guatemala de Miguel Ángel Asturias." *Anais Eletrônicos do VIII Encontro Internacional da ANPHLAC* (2008): 27–39.
Flew, Terry. *New Media.* South Melbourne, Victoria: Oxford University Press, 2014.
Forbes, Michelle Ann. "Garífuna: The Birth and Rise of an Identity through Contact Language and Contact Culture." PhD dissertation, University of Missouri–Columbia, 2011.
Foster, Thomas A. *Rethinking Rufus: Sexual Violations of Enslaved Men.* Athens: University of Georgia Press, 2019.
Fra-Molinero, Baltasar. *La imagen de los negros en el teatro del Siglo de Oro.* Mexico City: Siglo XXI, 1995.
Friehrer, Thomas. "Slaves and Freedom in Colonial Central America: Rediscovering a Forgotten Black Past." *Journal of Negro History* 64.1 (1979): 39–57.
Funes, José A. *Froylán Turcios y el modernismo en Honduras.* Tegucigalpa: Banco Central de Honduras, 2006.
García Espinosa, Julio. "For an Imperfect Cinema." In *Film Manifestos and Global Cinema Cultures: A Critical Anthology*, edited by Scott MacKenzie, 220–230. Berkeley: University of California Press, 2014.
García Giráldez, Teresa. "El debate sobre la nación y sus formas en el pensamiento político centroamericano del siglo XIX." In *Las redes intelectuales centroamericanas: un siglo de imaginarios nacionales 1820–1920*, edited by Marta Casaús Arzú and Teresa García Giráldez, 71–121. Guatemala City: F & G Editores, 2005.
García Peña, Lorgia. *The Borders of Dominicanidad.* Durham, NC: Duke University Press, 2016.
Gates, Henry Louis, Jr. *Black in Latin America.* New York: New York University Press, 2011.
Gautier, Théophile. *Enamels and Cameos.* Project Gutenberg, March 6, 2011. https://www.gutenberg.org/files/29521/29521-h/29521-h.htm.
Gavidia, Francisco. *Júpiter.* San Salvador: Dirección de Publicaciones e Impresos, 2002.
Gellner, Ernest. *Thought and Change.* Chicago: University of Chicago Press, 1964.
Gilroy, Paul. *The Black Atlantic: Modernity and Double Consciousness.* Cambridge, MA: Harvard University Press, 1993.

Godreau, Isar P. *Scripts of Blackness: Race, Cultural Nationalism, and U.S. Colonialism in Puerto Rico.* Urbana: University of Illinois Press, 2015.

Gómez Menjívar, Jennifer Carolina. "Liminal Citizenry: Black Experience in the Central American Intellectual Imagination." PhD dissertation, Ohio State University, 2011.

———. "Passing into Fictions: Blackness, Writing, and Power in the Captaincy General of Guatemala." *Chasqui* 45.1 (2016): 103–115.

———. "Redes garifunas insurgents: derechos culturales y derechos a la comunicación desde los espacios virtuales." *Istmo: revista virtual de estudios culturales centroamericanos* 37 (2018): 172–189.

———. "Tangible Afro-Indigenous Heritage: Land and Sea in *Garifuna in Peril*." In *The Rise of Central American Film*, edited by Mauricio Espinoza and Jared List. Gainesville: University Press of Florida, forthcoming in 2023.

———. "Xiomara Cacho Caballero: Writing from Central America's Narco Islands." In *Améfrica in Letters: Literary Interventions from Mexico to the Southern Cone*, edited by Jennifer Carolina Gómez Menjívar, 170–193. Nashville, TN: Vanderbilt University Press, 2022.

Gómez Menjívar, Jennifer Carolina, and Gloria Elizabeth Chacón. *Indigenous Interfaces: Spaces, Technology, and Social Networks in Mexico and Central America.* Tucson: University of Arizona Press, 2019.

Gómez Menjívar, Jennifer Carolina, and William Noel Salmon. "Mopan in Context: Mayan Identity, Belizean Citizenship, and the Future of a Language." *Native American and Indigenous Studies* 5.2 (2018): 70–90.

———. *Tropical Tongues: Language Ideologies, Endangerment, and Minority Languages in Belize.* Chapel Hill: University of North Carolina Press, 2018. Project MUSE, March 27, 2019. https://muse.jhu.edu/book/65713.

Gonzalez, Lélia. "A Categoria Político-Cultural de Amefricanidade." *Tempo Brasileiro* 92.93 (1988): 72.

González, Nancie L. *Dollar, Dove, and Eagle: One Hundred Years of Palestinian Migration to Honduras.* Ann Arbor: University of Michigan Press, 1992.

———. *Sojourners of the Caribbean: Ethnogenesis and Ethnohistory of the Garifuna.* Champaign: University of Illinois Press, 1988.

González, Wingston. "Antología poética." Wingston González, May 30, 2007. https://www.artepoetica.net/Wingston_Gonzalez.htm.

Grandin, Greg, Deborah T. Levenson, and Elizabeth Oglesby, eds. *The Guatemala Reader: History, Culture, Politics.* Durham, NC: Duke University Press, 2011.

Grant, Richard B. "Sequence and Theme in Victor Hugo's *Les Orientales*." *Publication of the Modern Language Association* 94.5 (1979): 894–908.

Griffin, Wendy. "*Barro* Draws Picture of 1915 Banana Company." *Honduras This Week Online: Your Central American Weekly Review*, December 2001. http://www.marrder.com/htw/2001dec/cultural.htm.

Gudmundson, Lowell. *Costa Rica before Coffee: Society and Economy on the Eve of the Export Boom.* Baton Rouge: Louisiana State University Press, 1986.

———. "What Difference Did Color Make? Blacks in the White Towns of Nicaragua in the 1880s." In *Blacks and Blackness in Central America*, edited by Lowell Gudmundson and Justin Wolfe, 209–245. Durham, NC: Duke University Press, 2010.

Gudmundson, Lowell, and Justin Wolfe. *Blacks and Blackness in Central America: Between Race and Place*. Durham, NC: Duke University Press, 2010.

Guerra, François-Xavier. "Forms of Communication, Political Spaces, and Cultural Identities in the Creation of Spanish American Nations." In *Beyond Imagined Communities: Reading and Writing in Nineteenth-Century Latin America*, edited by Sara Castro-Klarén and John Charles Chasteen, 3–23. Washington, DC: Woodrow Wilson International Center for Scholars, 2003.

Gullick, C. J. M. R. *Exiled from St. Vincent: The Development of Black Carib Culture in Central America up to 1945*. B'Kara, Malta: Progress Press, 1976.

Haefkens, Jacob. *Viaje a Guatemala y Centroamérica*. 1832. San Carlos: Editorial Universitaria Universidad de San Carlos de Guatemala, 1969.

Halbwachs, Maurice. *On Collective Memory*. Chicago: University of Chicago Press, 1992.

Hale, Charles. *Resistance and Contradiction: Miskitu Indians and the Nicaraguan State*. Stanford: Stanford University Press, 1994.

Hall, Stuart. "Encoding and Decoding in the Television Discourse." In Stuart Hall, *Writings on Media: History of the Present*, 247–266. Durham, NC: Duke University Press, 2021.

Harpelle, Ronald N. *The West Indians of Costa Rica: Race, Class, and the Integration of an Ethnic Minority*. Montreal: McGill-Queen's University Press, 2001.

Haya de la Torre, Victor. "1926: A Latin American Doctrine of Anti-Imperialism." In *Latin America and the United States: A Documentary History*, edited by Robert H. Holden and Eric Zolov, 122–124. New York: Oxford University Press, 2000.

Hegel, Georg Wilhelm Friedrich. "Race, History and Imperialism (1822)." In *Race and the Enlightenment: A Reader*, edited by Emmanuel Chukwudi Eze, 109–153. Cambridge, MA: Blackwell, 1997.

Herman, David, Manfred Jahn, and Marie-Laure Ryan. *Routledge Encyclopedia of Narrative Theory*. London: Routledge, 2010.

Herrera, Robinson A. *Natives, Europeans, and Africans in Sixteenth-Century Santiago de Guatemala*. Austin: University of Texas Press, 2003.

Henry, O. *Cabbages and Kings*. New York: McClure, Phillips, 1905.

Hoffman French, Jan. *Legalizing Identities: Becoming Black or Indian in Brazil's Northeast*. Durham: University of North Carolina Press, 2009.

Holden, Robert H., and Eric Zolov. "1903: The Hay–Bunau-Varilla Treaty." In *Latin America and the United States: A Documentary History*, edited by Robert H. Holden and Eric Zolov, 86–88. New York: Oxford University Press, 2011.

Hooker, Juliet. "Race and the Space of Citizenship: The Mosquito Coast and the Place of Blackness and Indigeneity in Nicaragua." In *Blacks and Blackness* in Central America: Between Race and Place, edited by Lowell Gudmundson and Justin Wolfe, 246–277. Durham, NC: Duke University Press, 2010.

———. Theorizing Race in the Americas: Douglass, Sarmiento, Du Bois, and Vasconcelos. New York: Oxford University Press, 2017.

Hughes, Langston. "Harlem." In Langston Hughes: Poems, 238. New York: Random House, 1999.

Hume, David. "Negroes . . . Naturally Inferior (1748)." In Race and the Enlightenment: A Reader, edited by Emmanuel Chukwudi Eze, 29–34. Cambridge, MA: Blackwell, 1997.

Izquierdo Millar, Inés. "Las orishas en Calypso." Espéculo: Revista de estudios literarios 31 (2007): 1–3.

Jackson, Richard L. "La presencia negra en la obra de Rubén Darío." Revista iberoamericana 33.64 (1967): 395–417.

James, Leslie R. "Pocomania." In African American Religious Cultures, edited by Anthony B. Pinn et al., 322–330. Santa Barbara, CA: ABC-Clio, 2009.

Jameson, Frederic. "Third World Literature in the Era of Multinational Capitalism." Social Text 15 (1986): 65–88.

Jáuregui, Carlos A. "Writing Communities on the Internet: Textual Authority." In Latin American Literature and Mass Media, edited by Edmundo Paz Soldán and Debra A. Castillo, 288–300. New York: Garland, 2001.

Jung, Moon-Ho. Coolies and Cane: Race, Labor, and Sugar in the Age of Emancipation. Baltimore: Johns Hopkins University Press, 2006.

Kahn, Hilary. Seeing and Being Seen: The Q'eqchi' Maya of Livingston, Guatemala and Beyond. Austin: University of Texas Press, 2006.

Kant, Immanuel. "This Fellow Was Quite Black . . . (1764)." In Race and the Enlightenment: A Reader, edited by Emmanuel Chukwudi Eze, 38–64. Cambridge, MA: Blackwell, 1997.

Katzew, Ilona. Casta Painting: Images of Race in Eighteenth-Century Mexico. New Haven: Yale University Press, 2004.

Kepner, Charles David. Social Aspects of the Banana Industry. New York: Columbia University Press, 1936.

Kerns, Sofia. "Postcoloniality in Anacristina Rossi's Limón Blues." South Carolina Modern Language Review 5.1 (2006): 16–36.

Kirchhoff, Paul. "Mesoamérica, sus limites geográficos, composición étnica y carácteres culturales." Acta Americana 1 (1943): 92–107.

Komisaruk, Catherine. "Becoming Free, Becoming Ladino: Slave Emancipation and Mestizaje in Colonial Guatemala." In Blacks and Blackness in Central America, edited by Lowell Gudmundson and Justin Wolfe, 150–174. Durham, NC: Duke University Press, 2010.

Lamming, George. The Pleasures of Exile. University of Michigan Press, 1992.

Lasso, Marixa. Erased: The Untold Story of the Panama Canal. Cambridge, MA: Harvard University Press, 2019.

Lipski, John. *A History of Afro-Hispanic Language: Five Centuries, Five Continents.* Cambridge, UK: Cambridge University Press, 2005.

———. "Linguistic Consequences of the Sandinista Revolution and Its Aftermath in Nicaragua." In *Undoing and Redoing Corpus Planning*, edited by Michael G. Clyne, 61–94. Berlin: Mouton de Gruyter, 1997.

Lizcano Fernández, Francisco. "Las etnias centroamericanas en la segunda mitad del siglo XX." *Revista Mexicana del Caribe* 9.17 (2004): 7–42.

Lobo, Tatiana. *Calypso*. San José: Grupo Editorial Norma, 2000.

Lokken, Paul. "Undoing Racial Hierarchy: Mulatos and Militia Service in Colonial Guatemala." *SECOLAS Annals: Journal of the Southeastern Council on Latin American Studies* 11.1 (1999): 25–36.

———. "Useful Enemies: Seventeenth-Century Piracy and the Rise of Pardo Militias in Spanish Central America." *Journal of Colonialism and Colonial History* 5.2 (2004). https://muse.jhu.edu/article/173268

López Oro, Pablo José. "Digitizing Ancestral Memory." In *Indigenous Interfaces: Spaces, Technology, and Social Networks in Mexico and Central America*, edited by Jennifer Carolina Gómez Menjívar and Gloria Elizabeth Chacón, 165–179. Tucson: University of Arizona Press, 2019.

———. "Garifunanizando AfroLatinidad: Blackness, Indigeneity, and Latinidad." In *Hemispheric Blackness and the Exigencies of Accountability*, edited by Jennifer Carolina Gómez Menjívar and Héctor Nicolás Ramos Flores, 211–225. Pittsburgh, PA: University of Pittsburgh Press, 2022.

Loveman, Mara. *National Colors: Racial Classification and the State in Latin America.* New York: Oxford University Press, 2014.

Mackenbach, Werner. "Chocolate con crema en Parima Bay: Una novela costarricense cuenta del encanto perdido del Caribe." *Revista Comunicación* 12 (2002): 1–6.

Mahoney, James. *The Legacies of Liberalism: Path Dependence and Political Regimes in Central America.* Baltimore: Johns Hopkins University Press, 2002.

———. "Radical, Reformist, and Aborted Liberalism: Origins of National Regimes in Central America." *Journal of Latin American Studies* 33.2 (2001): 221–256.

Marsiske, Renate. "Ecos de la primera Feria del Libro del Palacio de Minería y el proyecto editorial vasconcelista." *Perfiles educativos* 35.142 (2013): 188–201.

Martín, Barbero. "A Nocturnal Map." In *The Latin American Cultural Studies Reader*, edited by Ana del Sarto, Alicia, Ríos, and Abril Trigo, 310–328. Durham, NC: Duke University Press, 2004.

Martínez Duran, Carlos, and Daniel Contreras. "La abolición de la esclavitud en Centroamérica." *Journal of Inter-American Studies* 4.2 (1962): 223–232.

McWhorter, John. *The Missing Spanish Creoles: Recovering the Birth of Plantation Contact Languages.* Berkeley: University of California Press, 2000.

Meléndez, Carlos, and Quince Duncan. *El negro en Costa Rica.* San José, Costa Rica: Editorial Costa Rica, 1972.

Meléndez Obando, Mauricio. "Slow Ascent of the Marginalized: Afrodescendants in Costa Rica and Nicaragua." In Blacks and Blackness in Central America: Between Race and *Place*, edited by Lowell Gudmundson and Justin Wolfe, 334–352. Durham, NC: Duke University Press, 2010.

Meléndez Valdés, Juan. *Poesías de don Juan Meléndez Valdés*. Librería de Don Francisco Oliva. Barcelona: A. Bergnes, 1838.

Molina Jiménez, Iván. "Las bibliotecas nacionales de América Central durante los siglos XIX y XX." In *Bibliotecas y cultura letrada en América Latina: siglos XIX y XX*, edited by Carlos Aguirre and Ricardo Donato Salvatore, 73–104. Lima, Peru: Pontificia Universidad Católica, Fondo Editorial, 2018.

Molina Tamacas, Carmen. "'*Júpiter*, de Gavidia, en las ondas" de radio." *El Diario de Hoy*, September 13, 2006. http://archivo.elsalvador.com/noticias/2006/09/13/escenarios/esc6.asp.

Moncada, Roy. "Así es el viaje para llegar a Bluefields en la primera Carretera que conecta al Pacífico con el Atlántico de Nicaragua." *La Prensa: El diario de los nicaragüenses*, May 13, 2019. https://www.laprensani.com/2019/05/13/nacionales/2548954-asi-es-el-viaje-para-llegar-bluefields-en-la-primera-carretera-que-conecta-al-pacifico-con-el-atlantico-de-nicaragua.

Morales, Mario Roberto. "La colorida nación infernal del sujeto popular interétnico: a propósito de *Mulata de tal*." In Miguel Ángel Asturias, *Mulata de tal: edición crítica*, 934–955. Mexico City: Fondo de Cultura Económica de México, 2000.

"More American than America." *Time*, January 24, 1964. https://content.time.com/time/subscriber/article/0,33009,875649,00.html.

Mosby, Dorothy. "'Nuevos nómadas': Negritud y ciudadanía en la literatura centroamericana." *Istmo: revista virtual de estudios culturales centroamericanos*, May 17, 2008. http://istmo.denison.edu/n16/proyectos/mosby.html.

———. *Place, Language and Identity: Afro-Costa Rican Literature*. Columbia: University of Missouri Press, 2003.

———. Quince Duncan's "Weathered Men" and "The Four Mirrors": Two Novels of Afro-Costa Rican Identity. Cham, Switzerland: Palgrave, 2018.

Naro, Nancy Priscilla. *Blacks, Coloureds and National Identity in Nineteenth-Century Latin America*. London: Institute of Latin American Studies, 2003.

Navas de Miralda, Paca. *Barro*. Guatemala City: Editorial del Ministerio de Educación Pública, 1951.

Nöel, Samantha A. *Tropical Aesthetics of Black Modernism*. Durham, NC: Duke University Press, 2021.

Norbert-Bertrand, Barbe. *Gojón No. 28 Especial: Carlos Rigby y poetas caribeños*, November 28, 2018. https://en.calameo.com/read/005259387a290f87fb2bb.

Ochoa, Salazar. "Wingston González: literatura desde la retaguardia." *La Hora*, July 24, 2015. http://lahora.gt/wingston-gonzalez-literatura-desde-la-retaguardia/.

ODHAG-REMHI. *Guatemala: nunca más*. San Sebastián: Oficina de Derechos Humanos Arzobispado de Guatemala, 1998.

O'Reggio, Trevor. *Between Alienation and Citizenship: The Evolution of Black West Indian Society in Panama 1914–1964*. Lanham, MD: University Press of America, 2006.
Ortiz, Fernando. "On the Social Phenomenon of 'Transculturation' and Its Importance in Cuba." In *Cuban Counterpoint: Tobacco and Sugar*, 102–103. Durham, NC: Duke University Press, 1995.
Padilla, Yajaira. *From Threatening Guerrillas to Forever Illegals: US Central Americans and the Cultural Politics of Non-belonging*. Austin: University of Texas Press, 2022.
Palacios, Alfredo. *Nuestra América y el imperialismo*. Buenos Aires: Palestra, 1961.
Palmer, Steven, and Iván Molina, eds. *The Costa Rica Reader: History, Culture, Politics*. Durham, NC: Duke University Press, 2004.
Payeras, Javier. "Prefacio: Wingston González y el jazz singer." In Wingston González, *Los magos del crepúsculo (y blues otra vez)*. Guatemala City: Editorial Cultura, 2005.
Perez-Brignoli, Hector. *A Brief History of Central America*. Berkeley: University of California Press, 1989.
Picado, Clodomiro. "Our Blood Is Blackening!" In *The Costa Rica Reader: History, Culture, Politics*, edited by Steven Palmer and Iván Molina, 243–244. Durham, NC: Duke University Press, 2004.
Pleitez, Mario. "Francisco Gavidia, iniciador de la literatura en El Salvador y máximo humanista salvadoreño." *Istmo revista de estudios culturales y literarios centroamericanos*, February 22, 2005. http://collaborations.denison.edu/istmo/n10/articulos/francisco.html.
Prieto, Reni. *Miguel Ángel Asturias's Archaeology of Return*. Cambridge, UK: Cambridge University Press, 1993.
Rahier, Jean Muteba, ed. *Black Social Movements in Latin America: From Monocultural Mestizaje to Multiculturalism*. New York: Palgrave, 2012.
Rama, Ángel. *Las máscaras democráticas del modernismo*. Montevideo: Arca Editorial, 1985.
Ramírez, Dixa. *Colonial Phantoms: Belonging and Refusal in the Dominican Americas*. New York: New York University Press, 2018.
Ramírez, Sergio. *Balcanes y volcanes: la pluma debajo del sombrero*. Alicante, Spain: Biblioteca Miguel Cervantes, 2015.
———. *Tambor olvidado*. San José, Costa Rica: Santillana, 2008.
Real de Azúa, Carlos. "El modernismo literario y las ideologías." *Escritura: Teoría y crítica literarias* 3 (1977): 41–75.
Ribeiro, Darcy. "Excerpts from *The Americas and Civilization*." In *The Latin American Cultural Studies Reader*, edited by Ana del Sarto, Alicia Ríos, and Abril Trigo, 58–82. Durham: Duke University Press, 2004.
Rigby, Carl. "Home: Antojología de Carl Rigby." https://www.antojologiadecarlrigby.com/en/home/.

Rincón, Omar, and Amparo Marroquín. "The Latin American *Lo popular* as a Theory of Communication." In *Citizen Media and Practice: Currents, Connections, and Challenges*, edited by Hilde C. Stephensen and Emiliano Treré, 42–56. Abingdon, UK: Routledge, 2020.

Rivero, Yeidy M. *Tuning Out Blackness: Race and Nation in the History of Puerto Rican Television*. Durham, NC: Duke University Press, 2005.

Robinson, William I. *Transnational Conflicts: Central America, Social Change and Globalization*. London: Verso, 2003.

Rodríguez, Ana Patricia. *Dividing the Isthmus: Central American Transnational Histories, Literatures, and Cultures*. Austin: University of Texas Press, 2009.

Rodríguez-Silva, Ileana M. *Silencing Race: Disentangling Blackness, Colonialism, and National Identities in Puerto Rico*. New York: Palgrave, 2012.

Rodríguez, Ileana. *Transatlantic Topographies: Islands, Highlands, and Jungles*. Minneapolis: University of Minnesota Press, 2004.

———. *Women, Guerrillas, and Love: Understanding the War in Central America*. Minneapolis: University of Minnesota Press, 1996.

Rossi, Anacristina. *Limón Blues*. San José: Alfaguara, 2002.

Roof, María. "The Nicaribbeans: African-Descended Writers in Nicaragua." *Cincinnati Romance Review* 40 (2016): 45–86.

Roosevelt, Theodore. "1903: 'I Took Final Action in 1903.'" In *Latin America and the United States: A Documentary History*, edited by Robert H. Holden and Eric Zolov, 92–94. New York: Oxford University Press, 2000.

Ruiz, Luis Alberto. "El testamento poético de Darío." *Poesías completas: Ordenadas por Luis Alberto Ruiz*. Bogota, Colombia: Ediciones Zamora, 1967.

Ruiz Puga, David. *Got seif de Cuin!* Guatemala City: Editorial Nueva Narrativa, 1995.

———. "Panorama literario del texto literario en Belice, de tiempos coloniales a tiempos post-coloniales." *Istmo: revista de estudios culturales centroamericanos*, January 27, 2001. http://collaborations.denison.edu/istmo/n01/articulos/panorama.html.

Ryan, Susan. *Popularizing Media: The Politics of Video in the Nicaraguan Revolution*. New York: New York University Press, 1996.

Said, Edward W. *Orientalism*. New York: Vintage Books, 1979.

Salas, Laura. "Feria Internacional del Libro será dedicada a la cultura afrodescendiente." CRHoy.com, August 16, 2012. https://archivo.crhoy.com/feria-internacional-del-libro-sera-dedicada-a-la-cultura-afrodescendiente/entretenimiento/.

Sánchez Martínez, Juan G. "A Post-Ethnic/Racial Futurescape in Wingston González's *cafeina MC*." In *Américas in Letters: Literary Interventions from Mexico to the Southern Cone*, edited by Jennifer Carolina Gómez Menjívar, 42–67. Nashville, TN: Vanderbilt University Press, 2022.

Saunders, Tanya L. *Cuban Underground Hip Hop: Black Thoughts, Black Revolution, Black Modernity*. Austin: University of Texas Press, 2015.

Senior, Olive. *Dying to Better Themselves: West Indians and the Building of the Panama Canal*. Kingston, Jamaica: University of the West Indies Press, 2014.
Sepúlveda, Mélida Ruth. *El tema del canal en la novelística panamameña*. Caracas: Universidad Católica Andrés Bello, 1975.
Sessarego, Sandro. "Casting Light on the Spanish Creole Debate: A Legal Perspective." In *Hispanic Linguistics: Current Issues and New Directions*, edited by Alfonso Morales-Front et al., 328–341. Amsterdam: John Benjamins, 2020.
Shklovskij, Viktor. "Art as Technique." In *Literary Theory: An Anthology*, edited by Julie Rivkin and Michael Ryan, 8–14. Malden, MA: Blackwell, 1998.
Shoman, Assad. *A History of Belize in 13 Chapters*. Belize City: Angelus Press, 2011.
Sigüenza y Góngora, Carlos de. "Alboroto y motín" [1692]. In *Seis obras*, edited by I. A. Leonard and W. G. Bryant. Caracas: Biblioteca Ayacucho, 1984.
Siles, Ignacio. *A Transnational History of the Internet in Central America, 1985–2000: Networks, Integration, and Development*. Cham, Switzerland: Springer, 2020.
Simmons, Rose. "Three Poems: Wingston González." In *Palabras: Dispatches from the Festival de la Palabra*, edited by Yamile Silva and Hank Willenbrink, 87–94. South Gate, CA: No Passport Press, 2013.
Siu, Lok. *Memories of a Future Home: Diasporic Citizenship of Chinese in Panama*. Stanford, CA: Stanford University Press, 2007.
Snowden, Frank M. *Before Color Prejudice: The Ancient View of Blacks*. Cambridge, MA: Harvard University Press, 1983.
Sommer, Doris. *Foundational Fictions: The National Romances of Latin America*. Berkeley: University of California Press, 1993.
Spivak, Gayatri. "Can the Subaltern Speak?" In *Marxism and the Interpretation of Culture*, edited by Cary Nelson and Lawrence Grossberg, 271–331. Urbana: University of Illinois Press, 1988.
Stepan, Nancy Leys. *The Hour of Eugenics: Race, Gender and Nation in Latin America*. Ithaca, NY: Cornell University Press, 1991.
Stephens, Michelle Ann. *Black Empire: The Masculine Global Imaginary of Caribbean Intellectuals in the United States*. Durham, NC: Duke University Press, 2005.
Stephenson Watson, Sonja. *The Politics of Race in Panama: Afro-Hispanic Literary Discourses of Contention*. Gainesville: University Press of Florida, 2014.
Suleiman, Susan Rubin. Authoritarian Fictions: The Ideological Novel as a Literary Genre. New York: Columbia University Press, 1983.
Szok, Peter. "Octavio Méndez Pereira and Foundational Fiction." *Revista Mexicana del Caribe* 7.14 (2002): 145–165.
Tate, Shirley Ann. *Decolonising Sambo: Transculturation, Fungibility and Black Futurity*. Bingley, UK: Emerald, 2020.
Taylor, Christopher. *The Black Carib Wars: Freedom, Survival, and the Making of the Garifuna*. Jackson: University Press of Mississippi, 2012.
Taylor, Douglas. *The Black Carib of British Honduras*. New York: Wenner-Gren Foundation, 1951.

Telles, Edward Eric. *Race in Another America: The Significance of Skin Color in Brazil*. Princeton, NJ: Princeton University Press, 2004.

Telles, Edward Eric, and the Project on Ethnicity and Race in Latin America (PERLA). *Pigmentocracies: Ethnicity, Race, and Color in Latin America*. Chapel Hill: University of North Carolina Press, 2014.

Tenorio Gochez, Ruth María. "Periódicos y cultura impresa en El Salvador: 'cuán rápidos pasos da este pueblo hacia la civilización europea.'" PhD dissertation, Ohio State University, 2006.

Thoburn, Nicholas. *Deleuze, Marx and Politics*. London: Routledge, 2003.

Tinajero, Araceli. *Orientalismo en el modernismo hispanoamericano*. London: Purdue University Press, 2004.

Todorov, Tzvetan. *The Conquest of America: The Question of the Other*. New York: Harper and Row, 1983.

Torquemada, Juan de. *Monarquía Indiana* [1615]. Mexico City: Porrúa, 1975.

Trigo, Abril. "Multiculturalismo, diversidad cultural y segmentación de mercados." In *Identidad y multiculturalismo: retos de la sociedad global*. Barranquilla: Cátedra Fulbright/Universidad del Norte, 2006.

Trotsky, Leon. *Fascism: What It Is and How to Fight It*. New South Wales, Australia: Resistance Books, 2002.

Twinam, Ann. *Purchasing Whiteness: Pardos, Mulattos, and the Quest for Social Mobility in the Spanish Indies*. Stanford, CA: Stanford University Press, 2015.

UNESCO. "Introducing UNESCO: Who We Are." United Nations Educational, Scientific and Cultural Organization, January 1, 2009. https://www.un.org/youthenvoy/2013/08/unesco-united-nations-educational-scientific-and-cultural-organization/

United Nations General Assembly. "A/RES/64/169: International Year for People of African Descent," December 18, 2009. https://undocs.org/Home/mobile?FinalSymbol=A%2FRES%2F64%2F169&Language=E&DeviceType=Desktop&LangRequested=False

Valdo, Melissa. "Aprueban celebrar el Día de la Persona Negra y la Cultura Afrocostarricense por Ley." *La Nación: Edición Electrónica*, March 28, 2011. http://161.58.191.209/2011-03-28/ElPais/UltimaHora/ElPais2730589.aspx?Page=1#comentarios.

Valerio, Miguel. *Sovereign Joy: Afro-Mexican Kings and Queens, 1539–1640*. Cambridge, UK: Cambridge University Press, 2022.

Vargas Porras, Edwin. "Celebran el día del negro." *Al Día*, August 22, 2010. http://www.aldia.cr/ad_ee/2010/agosto/22/nacionales2492721.html.

Velásquez, María Elisa. *Debates históricos contemporáneos: africanos y afrodescendientes en México y Centroamérica*. Mexico City: Centro de Estudios Mexicanos y Centroamericanos, 2013.

Vinson, Ben, III. *Bearing Arms for His Majesty: The Free Colored Militia in Colonial Mexico*. Stanford, CA: Stanford University Press, 2002.

———. "Introduction: African (Black) Diaspora History, Latin American History." *The Americas* 63.1 (2006): 1–18.
Wade, Peter. *Degrees of Mixture, Degrees of Freedom: Genomics, Multiculturalism, and Race in Latin America*. Durham, NC: Duke University Press, 2017.
———. *Race and Ethnicity in Latin America*. Pluto Press, 2010. JSTOR, www.jstor.org/stable/j.ctt183p73f.
———. "Rethinking Mestizaje: Ideology and Lived Experience." *Journal of Latin American Studies* 37.2 (2005): 239–257.
Waisbord, Silvio, and Adriana Amado. "Populist Communication by Digital Means: Presidential Twitter in Latin America." *Information, Communication and Society* 20.9 (2017): 1330–1346.
Weaver, Frederick Stirton. *Inside the Volcano: The History and Political Economy of Central America*. Boulder, CO: Westview Press, 1994.
Welter, Barbara. "The Cult of True Womanhood: 1820–1860." *American Quarterly* 18.2 (1966): 151–174.
Westerman, George W. "Historical Notes of West Indians on the Isthmus of Panama." *Phylon* 22.4 (1961): 340–350.
Whisnant, David E. "Rubén Darío as a Focal Figure in Nicaragua: The Ideological Uses of Cultural Capital." *Latin American Research Review* 27.3 (1992): 7–49.
Whitford, David M. *The Curse of Ham in the Early Modern Era: The Bible and the Justifications for Slavery*. London: Routledge, 2017.
Williams, Eric. *From Columbus to Castro: The History of the Caribbean*. New York: Vintage Books, 1984.
Willis, Susan. "Nobody's Mulata." In *Mulata de tal: edición crítica*, edited by Arturo Arias, 1060–1075. Nanterre, France: Signatarios del Acuerdo Archivos, 2000.
Wilson, Pamela, and Michelle Stewart. *Global Indigenous Media: Cultures, Poetics, and Politics*. Durham, NC: Duke University Press, 2008.
Wright, Michelle M. *Physics of Blackness: Beyond the Middle Passage Epistemology*. Minneapolis: University of Minnesota Press, 2015.
Yancy, George. *Black Bodies, White Gazes: The Continuing Significance of Race*. Lanham, MD: Rowman & Littlefield, 2008.
Yúdice, George. *Nuevas tecnologías, música y experiencia*. Barcelona: Gedisa, 2007.
Zalas Zamorra, Edwin. "Encuentros y desencuentros culturales en la novela *Calypso*." VIII Congreso de Filología, Lingüística y Literatura Carmen Naranjo, November 26, 1999. http://www.tec.cr/sitios/Docencia/ciencias_lenguaje/revista_comunicacion/VIII%20Congreso%20-%20Carmen%20Naranjo/ponencias/literatura/otrosautores/pdf%27s/esalas.pdf.
Zea, Leopoldo. *Dos etapas del pensamiento en hispanoamérica: del romanticismo al positivism*. Mexico City: Fondo de Cultura Económica, 1949.
Žižek, Slavoj. "Multiculturalism, or, the Cultural Logic of Multinational Capitalism." *New Left Review* 1.225 (1997): 28–25.

Index

Note: Page numbers in *italics* indicate figures; page numbers following "n" refer to endnotes.

#EsPorCostaRica (It's for Costa Rica), 146

acculturation, 233n40
Afro–Costa Rican culture, 21, 129–30, 138, 142, 179
afrocriollo community, 231n8
Afrodescendance in Central America, 6–7, 9, 20, 25–26, 93, 116, 131, 147, 186, 220n36, 237–38n57; constitutive citizenry, recognized as, 189; existence of plurality, 16–17; *gente decente*, 3–4; geographical and linguistic diversity of, 13–16; liminal citizenry, recognized as, 185; in Mesoamerican identity issues, 96; movement and dispersal of, 8–9; *negro-moreno*-turned-*mestizo* hegemonic ideology, 8; racial diversity of, 9–10; regional diversity of, 11–13; rightful belonging of, 185–86
Afro-Indigenous Garifuna communities, 17–18, 24, 65, 76
afromestizos, 7–8, 231n8
The Afro-Spanish American Author, (Jackson), 21

Agrarian Reform Act (1952), 100, 231n14
Aguilera Malta, Demetrio, 65, 87, 97, 187, 226n26; anti-imperialist masterplots, 82–83; *Canal Zone*, 65–74
Alfaguara, 238n1
"Alí" (poem by Darío), 32, 33–34, 38–44, 53, 223n30
Alianza Popular Revolucionaria, 228–29n66
Amaya Amador, Ramón, 85–86
"Améfrica" theory, 5
Amefricans, 5
American Quadroon (Clark), 21
The Americas and Civilization (Ribeiro), 101
Anderson, Mark, 160
anti-imperialist literature, 82–83; *Bananos: La vida de los peones en la Yunai*, 86; *Bananos y hombres*, 86; *Barro*. See *Barro* (Nava de Miralda); *Canal Zone*. See *Canal Zone* (Aguilera Malta); *Curundurú*, 86; *Dividing the Isthmus*, 83, 242n3; *El papa verde*, 84, 97–99; *Flor de banana*, 86; *Gamboa*

263

anti-imperialist literature *(continued)*
Road Gang, 86; *Los ojos de los enterrados*, 84–85, 98–100; *Luna verde*, 86; *Mamita Yunai*, 83–84, 242n3; *Prisión verde*, 85–86; *Sangre en el trópico*, 86; simplicity of characterization of, 87; *Viento fuerte*, 84
Antojología (documentary-anthology), 165–77, 169; effect of mediations, 169; on YouTube, 150, 241n53
Antonio Cuadra, Pedro, 166
Anzaldúa, Gloria, 234n69
apophrades, 58
Árbenz, Jacobo, 96, 100–101
Arce, B. Christine, 19
Arce, Manuel José, 45
Arévalo, Juan José, 96–97
Arias, Arturo, 96
Arrivillaga Cortés, Alfonso, 222n21
Arroyo Calderón, Patricia, 46
assujetissement, 232–33n38
Asturias, Miguel Ángel, 23, 24, 84–86, 94, 187, 229, 231n11; *El papa verde*, 97–100; *indigeneista* approach, 95–96; *indomestizo* approach, 101; *Los ojos de los enterrados*, 98–100; *Mulata de tal*, 94, 96, 100–106; spiritual socialism in writings of, 97; *Weekend in Guatemala*, 100
Azul (Darío), 32

Balboni, Barbara S., 230n7
banana novels, 84–85, 187, 228n65; *Barro* by Nava de Miralda, 74–81; *El papa verde*, 97–98; *Flor de banana*, 86; of Honduras, 23–24; *Los ojos de los enterrados*, 98; *Mamita Yunai*, 83–84; *Mulata de tal*, 94, 96
Bananos: La vida de los peones en la Yunai (Quintana), 86

Bananos y hombres (Lyra), 86
barbarism, 10, 57, 78
Barbas-Rhoden, Laura, 126
Barro (Nava de Miralda), 65, 66, 74, 89, 90; about Garifuna peoples in Honduras, 76–81; about industrialization and modernization of Honduras, 74; about nationalism in Honduras, 76, 81; about North American imperialism impact in Hondurans, 74–76; about racism in Honduras, 76–77. See also *Canal Zone* (Aguilera Malta); *El papa verde* (Asturias)
Barrundia, José Francisco, 50, 224n63
Before Color Prejudice (Snowden), 42
Beleño, Joaquín, 86
Belize-Guatemala border dispute, 94, 107–8, 110, *109–11*, 111. See also *Got seif de Cuin!* (Ruiz Puga)
Belize, 16, *17*, 18, 93–94, 233n54, 234n60; Creole identity in, 107; Garifuna communities in, 225n4; Hispanophone discourses in, 107–8; Maya people in, 94
Belize City, 16, *17*, 113, 240n26
Belli, Gioconda, 125, 235n5
Belize-Guatemala border dispute, 109–110
belonging(ness), 8, 10, 21–22, 23, 188; legitimate (*mestizo*), 91; linguistic, 91; narratives about associative, 20, 121; narratives about national, 125, 184–85; narratives about rightful, 20, 121, 185
Berman, Marshall, 74
best practices, 131, 145
biotypology, 84, 87–90
Black heritage, 3, 7, 10, 180, 186, 218n19
"Black Caribs," 152, 153. See also Garifuna

The Black Image in Latin American Literature (Jackson), 21
Black/Indigenous divide, 24, 94, 120
Black in Latin America (Gates), 18
Black Literature and Humanism in Latin America (Jackson), 21
Black masses, 45, 68, 69–70, 73, 74
Blackness in Central America, 4, 180, 183, 188, 191; analysis based on print media, 22–23; axes and coordinates of, 18–22; biotypology, discourse of, 87–90
Black Panamanian community, 226n26
Blacks in Central America (Valencia Chalá), 21
Black slaves, 3, 7, 43, 45, 48, 52, 224n61
Black Star Line, 134
Black Writers and Latin America: Cross Cultural Affinities (Jackson), 21
Black Writers and the Hispanic Canon (Jackson), 21
Black Writers in Latin America (Jackson), 21
"blood-mending," 2
Bloom, Harold, 58
Blumenbach, Johann Friedrich, 9
Bolívar, Simón, 32, 64
Bolland, Nigel, 113
The Borders of Dominicanidad (García Peña), 21
Borelli, Blanco, 233n43
Bourdieu, Pierre, 80
British Honduras, 113–14, 116, 117, 219n34
Browitt, Jeff, 117

Cabrera, Claudia, 163
Cabrera, Miguel, 2
caimito, 195, 206, 242n4

Calderón de la Barca, Pedro de, 49
Caliban language, 54–55
Calypso (Lobo), 131, 138–42
Campbell Barr, Epsy, 145–47, 183; on Facebook, 146
canal literature/novels, 187; Beleño's trilogy, 86; *Canal Zone* by Aguilera Malta, 65–74; of Panama, 23–24
Canal Zone (Aguilera Malta), 65–66, 89, 90, 97; about nationalism in Panama, 67, 68; about racism in Panama, 68, 69, 72–73; rhetoric of progress in Panama, 66–67; West Indian immigrants, 67, 68–74. See also *Barro* (Nava de Miralda); *El papa verde* (Asturias)
Cantos de vida y esperanza (Darío), 229–30n83
Captaincy of Guatemala, 1–2, 9
Cardenal, Ernesto, 166
Cárdenas, Maritza E., 151
Carías, Tiburcio, 227n44
"Carta de Jamaica" (Bolívar), 32, 64
Carter, Stephen L., 20, 220n47
cartography, 22, 65, 87, 90–91
Casta paintings, 2
Castro Jo, Carlos, 167
Celis, Santiago, 45, 46, 49, 51–53
census categories (Blackness) *negro-no declarado* (Black-Undeclared), 180; *negro-otro* (Black-Other), 180; *negro/afro-costarricense* (Black/Afro-Costa Rican), 179; *negro antillano* (Caribbean Black), 180; *negro colonial* (Colonial Black), 180; *negro inglés* (English/British Black), 179; *negro*/Maya divide, 98–99, 104; *negros-morenos-citizens* transformation, 7–8; *negros bozales*, 10; *negros criollos*, 10. See also Afrodescendance in Central America

Central American Blackness. *See* Blackness in Central America
Central American Caribbean coast, 12–14, 20, 25, 89; Caribbean Coastal Towns, *12*; industrialization impact, 63; literary production, 126–28, 149–178; multilingual, 107
Central American Pacific coast, 20, 23, 25; literary production, 29–62; monolingual, 112, 149
Central American identity: battle for recognition of Blackness, 184–85; impertinence and accountability, 185–89; literary discourses, 185; print media, role of, 179–80, 187
Central American Writers of West Indian Origin (Smart), 21, 91
Central Valley of Costa Rica, 128–29
CERD. *See* Commission for Eradication of Racial Discrimination
Céspedes, Benjamín de, 104
Chacón, Gloria, 157
"Charaibes Noirs," 152
Chatoyer, Joseph, 153
Chen, Lucía, 231n19
Chinese groups, 3, 85, 113, 118, 143
Chiquimala, 154
chombo, 69, 70, 71
Chow, Juan, 166
chumecos, 136
cine imperfecto (imperfect cinema), 165
Cinthio, 223n46
civilization/barbarism dichotomy of, 58, 78–79
The Civilizers (documentary), 25
Clancy-Smith, Julia, 223n30
Clark, Emily, 21, 220n48
Cocorí (Gutiérrez), 181, 183, 242n3, 242n4; impact, 183–184

Cocorí (podcast episode for *Radio Ambulante*), 180–84, 242n2; full text of, 193–215
code-switching: intrasentential, 240n26; between Spanish-English-Garifuna, 156–57, 159–60
"Colección Teatro," 45
Commission for Eradication of Racial Discrimination (CERD), 183
Consejo Regional Autónomo del Atlántico Norte (CRAAN), 130
"Constancia" (For the Record) (poem by Rigby), 173, *174*
Constitution of Federal Republic of Central America, 7
The Control of the Tropics (Kidd), 64
Cornejo Polar, Antonio, 95
Cortez, Beatriz, 126, 236n8
cosmopolitanism of Central America, 30, 64; Darío's and Gavidia's contributions to, 31, 33, 56–58; rise of print culture, 30–31
Costa Rica, 16, 63, 127, 179, 231n8; Afro–Costa Rican culture, 21, 129–30, 138, 142, 179; Black Heritage Festival, 129–30; *Calypso* about Black women enslavement in, 138–42; culture, 129; demographic and political imbalance, 128–29; economic development in, 142–43; *Limón Blues* about racism in, 129, 132–38; NGOization, 130; politics of multiculturalism, 126–28, 144; racism in, 127, 128, 144, 181, 182–83; reconstruction of national imaginary, 145; representation of Campbell Barr, 145–47; strategic plan between UNESCO and CRAAN, 130–31; West Indian settlement, 131–32, 220n38; whiteness in, 143–44

CRAAN. *See* Consejo Regional Autónomo del Atlántico Norte
Creamer, Winfred, 230n2
Creole: communities, 179, 219n34, 231n8; heritage, 93; identity, 93; language in Central American Caribbean coast, 16; Spanish languages in Central America, 99–100
criollo, 3, 45, 219n34
Cruz, Ramón E., 76
Cuadra, Manolo, 166
The Curse of Ham, 1–2, 35, 36, 43
Curundurú (Beleño), 86

Darío, Rubén, 10, 22–23, 29, 31, 53, 56–58, 104, 187, 221n3, 222n15, 223n30; "Alí" poem by, 32, 33–34, 38–44; *Cantos de vida y esperanza*, 229–30n83; "El porvenir" poem by, 32, 33–38; *Epístolas y poemas* about Blackness, 32–33; "To Roosevelt" poem, 64
defamiliarization, 34
Deguis, Juliana, 20
Delgado, José Matías, 6, 45, 47, 49, 50–53
"de pequeño..." (poem by González), 154–56; code-switching between Spanish-English-Garifuna, 156–57, 159–60; demands for "ethnic authenticity," 154, 162–63; launched into cyberspace, 162, 163; "(o leleru Bungiu)," 160–62; variations of cyberpoet/digital poetic voices in, 156, 157–58
Día del Negro (Day of the Black Person), 148
digital media. *See* new media
digital print, 22, 149, 189, 193
Divan occidental (Goethe), 41

Dividing the Isthmus (Rodríguez), 83, 242n3
Dollar, Dove, and Eagle (González), 25
Dos etapas del pensamiento en hispanoamérica (Zea), 56
Douglass, Frederick, 134
Dow, Dawn Marie, 136
Duncan, Quince, 22, 125–26, 127, 181, 235nn2–3

Edgell, Zee, 125
Edison, Thomas Wayne, 166
El papa verde (Asturias), 84–85, 97; about ethnolinguistic divides in Guatemala, 99–100; narration of Black and *mestizo* masses, 97–98; about *negro*/Maya divide, 97–99. See also *Barro* (Nava de Miralda); *Canal Zone* (Aguilera Malta)
"El porvenir" (poem by Darío), 32, 33–34, 39; *América*-Europe connection in, 34–35; hegemonic belief in Blackness, 36–37; Old World narrative to frame Africa, 35–36; Orientalism in, 37–38
El Salvador, 7, 93, 192, 231n8; *campesino* in, 219n31; Peace Accords in, 144
Émaux et Camées (Gautier), 41
Engels, Friedrich, 226n19
Enrique, Don, 115, 116
Escudos, Jacinta, 107
ethical ethnotourism, 145
Ethiopian (Black) people, 9
etnias autóctonas (autochthonous ethnicities), 148
eugenics, 23, 87–90
Euraque, Darío, 227n45
Eurocentric discourse, 228n51

Fabian, Johannes, 55

Facundo (Sarmiento), 58
Fallas, Carlos Luis, 83, 84, 181, 197, 242n3
Fanon, Frantz, 226n26, 226n28
Federación Obrera Hondureña (FOH), 76
Federal Republic of Central America, 7, 32, 33, 41, 48, 153, 185–86
Ferdinand VII (King of Spain), 48
Figueroa Vergara, Amina, 231n19
Flew, Terry, 151
Flor de banana (Beleño), 86
FOH. *See* Federación Obrera Hondureña
Forbes, Michelle, 239n12
The Four Mirrors (Mosby), 125
French, Jan Hoffman, 148
Friehrer, Thomas, 218n16

Galvez, Mariano, 153, 239n21
Gamboa Road Gang (Beleño), 86
García Espinoza, Julio, 165
García Peña, Lorgia, 21
Garifuna communities, 160, 179, 186, 219n35; Afro-Indigenous community in Livingston, 151; deproture of ancestors, 15; Garifuna language in Central American Caribbean coast, 16; in Labuga/Livingston, 153–54; in United States, 157, 160; in Yurumein, 151–53; on Facebook and YouTube, 157
Garifuna in Peril (film), 153
Garvey, Marcus, 132–34, 136, 219n36
Gates, Henry Louis, Jr., 18, 221n51
Gautier, Théophile, 41
Gavidia, Francisco, 23, 29, 31, 44–45, 56–58, 187, 221n3
Gellner, Ernest, 78
gente decente (respectable people), 3–4

The German Ideology (Marx and Engels), 226n19
Gifitti, 240n37
Gilroy, Paul, 29
Giraldi, Giovanni (Cinthio) Battista, 44, 55
Goethe, Johann Wolfgang von, 41
Gómez Menjívar, 230n7
Gonzalez, Lélia, 5
González, Nancie L. Solien, 25, 77
González, Wingston, 22, 24, 150, 151, 154, 177–78, 188, 240n31; award for *Translaciones*, 164; online comments of followers, 164–65; poem about experience of belonging to community, 154–63. *See also* Rigby, Carl Earlington
Got seif de Cuin! (Ruiz Puga), 94, 112–19, 121
Gramática de la lengua castellana (Nebrija), 49
"Great White Fleet" of steamships, 63
Grinberg Pla, Valeria, 87
Guadalupe Hidalgo, Treaty of, 82
Guatemala: nunca más, 235n82
Guatemala, 4, 16, 93, 231n8; Afrodescendance and Mayanness of, 100–106; Asturias's banana trilogy about, 84–85; Belize-Guatemala border dispute, 94, 107–11; *etnias autóctonas*, 148; Garifuna communities, 225n4; geography and language, 13; Guatemalan Caribbean Coastal Towns, 14; *indigenismo*, 93, 95–96; Indigenous borders and Black limits in, 106, 112–19; Maya people in, 94; Mesoamerican departures in, 119–21; Mesoamerican distinction in Central America, 95; Miskitu community settlement in, 17;

national discourses in, 24; Peace Accords in, 144; spiritual socialism, 97; UFCO, 63; West Indian settlement in, 220n38
Gudmundson, Lowell, 10
Gutiérrez, Joaquín, 181, 242n3
Guzmán, Jacobo Árbenz, 231n14, 232n28

Haefkens, Jacob, 8–9, 218n23
Hafez (Persian poet), 41
Hale, Charles, 219n35
Hall, Stuart, 29
Hartman, Saidiya, 20
Haya de la Torre, Victor, 82
Hay–Bunau-Varilla Treaty, 63–64, 82
Hazlitt, William, 223n46
Hegel, Georg Wilhelm Friedrich, 57
Herodotus, 38
Hombres de Maíz (Asturias), 229
Honduran Workers Federation. *See* Federación Obrera Hondureña (FOH)
Honduras, 16, 63, 231n8; *etnias autóctonas*, 148; Garifuna peoples in Honduras, 76–80, 225n4; geography and language, 13; Honduran Caribbean Coastal Towns, 15; industrialization and modernization of, 74; Miskitu community settlement in, 17; nationalism in, 76, 81; North American imperialism impact in, 74–76; *Prisión verde* about, 85–86; racism in, 76–77; West Indian settlement, 220n38
Hooker, Juliet, 11–12, 18
The Hour of Eugenics (Stepan), 88
Hughes, Langston, 175
Hugo, Victor, 33
human cartography in print, 90–91

Hume, David, 57

ignorado (Unknown), 179
Indians, 3, 179, 186
indígena (Indigenous), 179
indigenismo, 93, 95–96, 120
indigenista authors and novels, 95–96
Indigenous (*campesino*) labor force, 14
Indigenous Interfaces (Gómez Menjívar and Chacón), 157
Indigenous Lenca warrior, 228n59
indomestizo identity, 105
Instituto Nicaragüense de Cultura, 174–75
International Year for People of African Descent (2011), 131
Internet, 145, 151, 239n9, 240n31
Introduction to American Expansion Policy (Kidd), 64
Isabella I of Castille, 49
Iximché. *See* Santiago de los Caballeros in Guatemala

Jackson, Richard L., 21, 166
John, Prester, 225n82
Juambo (*Sambito*), 98, 99, 232n23
Juárez, Juan Rodríguez, 2
Júpiter (drama by Gavidia), 29, 44–45; about events of 1811 uprising, 45–46; literary references in, 49–51; narratives of gender models, 46–48; independence movement in, 48–49; on Radio YSUCA 91.7, 45
Justo, Don, 118

Kalípona community in Yurumein, 151–53
Kant, Immanuel, 57
"Karaib Negroes," 152
Keith, Minor C., 133, 236n23

Kekchi communities, 107, 233n55
Kerns, Sofia, 132
Kidd, Benjamin, 64
Kirchhoff, Paul, 93, 230n2
"knave" class, 226n19
Kriol language, 16, 18, 93, 110, 113, 119

"La beca del guerrillero" (The Scholarship of the Guerrilla), 167, 168
ladinos, 9, 10, 93, 95, 179
La India, 166
Lamming, George, 54
La Prensa Libre newspaper, 108
La sibila de Oriente y la gran reina de Sabá (Calderón de la Barca), 49
Lasso, Marixa, 64, 67
latifundia, 234n59
Leal, Anabella Acevedo, 106
Limón Blues (Rossi), 129, 131, 132, 139, 237n53; government's abuse of power and complicity, 133–34; intertextuality of, 134–36, 137–38; about structural racism in Costa Rica, 132–33, 136–37
literary mapping of Central American people, 90
Lizcano Fernández, Francisco, 231n8
Lobos, 3
Lobo, Tatiana, 23, 24, 127, 138–42, 188
lo indio, 11
lo negro, 11
López Oro, Paul Joseph, 160
"Lo rojoinegro de lo azuliblanco" (Rigby), 171
Lose Your Mother (Hartman), 20
Los hijos de la fortuna (Calderón de la Barca), 49
Los ojos de los enterrados (Asturias), 84–85; about ethnolinguistic divides in Guatemala, 99–100; about negro/Maya divide, 98–99. See also El papa verde (Asturias)
lumpenproletariat, 69–70, 73–74, 226n19
Luna verde (Beleño), 86
Lyra, Carmen, 86

Mackenbach, Werner, 87, 138
maifrenes, 135–36
Malay people, 9
Mamita Yunai (Fallas), 83, 181, 242n3
manumission in Central America, 5–7, 25, 45
Mao Zedong, 242n3
Mariscal, David Caballero, 84
Marroquín, Amparo, 169
Martín-Barbero, Jesús, 169
Martínez, Palacios, 164
Marx, Karl, 226n19
Matory, J. Lorand, 18
Maya people, 179, 231–32n20, 231n19; in Belize, 94; ethnolinguistic heritage of, 114–15; at Guatemalan/British Honduras border, 116; Maya languages in Guatemala, 106–7; in Mulata de tal, 101–6
McField, David, 166
Meléndez, Carlos, 127
Meléndez Valdes, Juan, 51
Memories of a Future Home (Siu), 25
Menchú, Rigoberta, 126, 235n5
Menjívar, Gómez, 218n21
Mennonite, 179
meseteño, 136
Mesoamerica, 23, 93, 230n2; Afrodescendance and Mayanness of Guatemala, 100–106; Belize-Guatemala border dispute, 94, 107–19, 109–11; Black/Indigenous divide in, 94, 97–98; Hispanicization, 93–94, 119, 120

mestizaje, 4, 9–11, 18, 20, 93, 187, 218n22
mestizos, 3, 9–11, 14, 20, 25, 63, 77, 81, 93, 95, 218n19, 231n8
México's Nobodies (Arce), 19
Miller, Izquierdo, 237n52
minimal departure, principle of, 77
miskito (Miskito), 179
Miskitu communities, 17, 179, 219n35
modernismo, 31
Molina Jiménez, Iván, 31
Molina Tamaca, Carmen, 45
Monarquía Indiana (Torquemada), 2
Mopan communities, 107
Morales, Roberto, 104–5
moreno, 6, 10
Moriscos, 3
Mosby, Dorothy, 21, 125, 126, 143, 166, 235n2–3, 237n35
mulata, 233n43
mulata archetype, 101, 101, 105–6
Mulata de tal (Asturias), 94, 100–106
Mulattos, 3, 7, 10, 97, 186
multiculturalism in Costa Rica, 126–28, 144

nationalism: in Honduras, 76, 81; in Panama, 67, 68
Nava de Miralda, Paca, 65, 87, 154, 187, 227n45; anti-imperialist masterplots, 82–83; *Barro*, 65, 66, 74–81
Nebrija, Elio Antonio de, 49
"negative *mestizaje*," 2, 21
nepantilism, 234n69
new media, 23, 146–147, 150–51, 157
New Orleans, 220n48
New Spain, social hierarchy in, 3–4
newspapers, 30, 45, 48, 68, 108, 132, 170, 199, 235n83, 242n3
Nicaragua, 16, 63, 179, 231n8; Garifuna communities, 225n4;

mestizo competence, 11; Peace Accords in, 144
Nicaraguan Cultural Institute. *See* Instituto Nicaragüense de Cultura
no-indígena (Non-Indigenous), 179
no-te-entiendo, 10
Novelas amorosas y ejemplares (Sotomayor), 50
Nueva Armenia, 77–78

Obando, Mauricio Meléndez, 7
ODHAG. *See* Oficina de Derechos Humanos Arzobispado de Guatemala
"Odo clasial" (Classical Ode) (poem by Rigby), 241n54
Oficina de Derechos Humanos Arzobispado de Guatemala (ODHAG), 235n82
On the Natural Varieties of Humankind (Blumenbach), 9
Operation PBSUCCESS, 100, 232n28
Orientalist/Orientalism, 33, 34; in Darío's poems, 33–34, 37–38; formalism over divisive political rhetoric, 41
ostranenie technique, 33, 34, 35, 39
Othello (Shakespeare), 44, 53
"others," 191; of Central American hegemonic ideologies, 188, 235–36n7; Costa Rica, 86; Guatemala, 84; Honduras, 85; Panama, 86
Outline of a Theory of Practice (Bourdieu), 80

Palacio, Joseph O., 230n7
Palacios, Alfredo, 88
Panama, 16; Black identities in, 179–80; Palacios's views on, 88; West Indian settlement, 220n38
Panama Canal, 63–64, 69, 72, 83; Aguilera Malta's *Canal Zone*

Panama Canal *(continued)*
    about, 65–74; in Central American politics, 63–64
Pan American Conferences of Eugenics and Homoculture, 88
Pan American Sanitary Conferences, 88
"Para los terremotólogos" (For the Seismologists), 170, *170*
Pasos, Joaquin, 166
Paz Barahona, Miguel, 227n44
The Physics of Blackness (Wright), 18–19
Picado, Clodomiro, 87
Place, Language, and Identity in Afro-Costa Rican Literature (Mosby), 21
plebe (plebeians), 3–4
Pocomania, 79, 228n56
Port Limón, 32, 135, 136, 138
"positive *mestizaje*," 2, 21
Powell Benard, Lorein, 180–81
Prieto, René, 100–101
print media of Central America, 126, 149, 187, 190–91; anti-imperialism in, 64–65; in technical writing of censuses, 179–80; used by Black communities, 180–84
Prisión verde (Amaya Amador), 85–86
proyectos de rescate cultural, 129
Puerto Rico, 82
Pukumina. *See* Pocomania

Q'eqchi', 233n55
Quesada, Carlos Alvarado, 145
Quintana, Emilio, 86

racism: in Costa Rica, 127, 128, 144, 181, 182–83; by denial, 5; in Honduras, 76–77; institutional, 128; in Panama, 68, 69, 72–73
Radio Ambulante podcast, 20
Rahier, Jean Muteba, 18, 147–48
Rama, Ángel, 41, 223n38
Ramírez, Sergio, 106
Reconciliation after Violent Conflict, 145
The Reddish Black of the Blue and White. *See* "Lo rojoinegro de lo azuliblanco" (Rigby)
"Red/Yellow" Caribs, 152, 153
religious syncretism, 228n56
Repertorio salvadoreño magazine, 45
Resistance and Contradiction (Hale), 219n35
Ribeiro, Darcy, 101
Rigby, Carl Earlington, 22, 24, 150, 151, 165, *171*, 177–78, 188, 241n54; commitment to ideals of Sandinista revolution, 166–67; documentary-anthology about, 167, *168*, 170, 171–77, *176*; poems for *Antojología* project, 170, *170*, 173, *174*; recognizing value of video production, 167, 168–69
Rincón, Omar, 169
Robinson, William I., 144
Robleto, Hernán, 86
Ródrigo E. J. Campbell Foundation, 165
Rodríguez, Ana Patricia, 83, 242n3
Roosevelt, Theodore, 66, 67
Rossi, Anacristina, 23, 24, 126–27, 129, 132, 188, 237n53
Ruiz, Juan Patricio Morlete, 2
Ruiz Puga, David, 23, 24, 94, 112, 121, 187
Ryan, Marie-Laure, 77
Ryan, Susan, 168

Salmon, William Noel, 107, 110, 230n7
Salvadoran Dirección de Publicaciones e Impresos, 45
Sandino, Augusto, 76
Sangre en el trópico (Robleto), 86
Santiago de los Caballeros in Guatemala, 4

self, discovery of, 34
Shakespeare, William, 44, 53
Shklovskij, Viktor, 33
Sibaja, José Francisco, 83, 84
Sigüenza y Góngora, Carlos de, 3–4
Siu, Lok, 25
Smart, Ian, 21, 91, 166, 221n49
Snowden, Frank M., 42
Sommer, Doris, 45, 46
Sotomayor, María de Zayas y, 49–50
Spaniards, 3, 4, 10, 234n19
spiritual socialism of Guatemala, 97, 100
Spivak, Gayatri, 116
Stelzner, Uli, 25
Stepan, Nancy Leys, 88
Stephenson Watson, Sonja, 67, 73
Stewart, Michelle, 157
structural racism in Costa Rica, 132–33, 136–37
St. Vincent, 151, 160, 225n4
subjectivation, 232–33n38
Swaby Campbell, Tanisha, 183

Taft, William Howard, 67
Taylor, Christopher, 153
Teacher's Union of Costa Rica, 129
Teágenes y Caricela (Calderón de la Barca), 49
Telegraph Company, 63
The Tempest (Lamming), 54
tente-en-el-aire, 10
Time and the Other (Fabian), 55
Todorov, Tzvetan, 222n21
tornatrás, 10
Torquemada, Juan de, 2
Tosta, Vicente, 227n44
transculturation, 233n40
Translaciones (González), 164
Trigo, Abril, 129
Tropical Radio, 63
Trotsky, Leon, 73
Turcios, Froylón, 76, 227n45

UFCO. *See* United Fruit Company
UNESCO. *See* United Nations Educational, Scientific and Cultural Organization
UNIA. *See* Universal Negro Improvement Association
United Fruit Company (UFCO), 63, 77, 100, 144, 231n14
United Nations Educational, Scientific and Cultural Organization (UNESCO), 130
United Provinces of Central America, 13, 17
United States (US): acquisition of Louisiana, 220n48; CIA invasion of Guatemala, 100; Hay–Bunau-Varilla Treaty, 63–64; investment in Guatemala, 118; role in Belize/Guatemala border dispute, 94
Universal Declaration of Human Rights, 131
Universal Negro Improvement Association (UNIA), 131, 134–35, 219n36, 230n92
US Panama Canal Company, 69

Valencia Chalá, Santiago, 21, 131–32
Valle, José Cecilio del, 48, 52
Vargas, Luis Fernando, 180, 182, 242n4
Venegas, Elibeth, 129
Viceroyalty of New Spain, 1, 4
Victoria (Queen of Great Britain), 114, 115
Viento fuerte (Asturias), 84–85
Vinson III, Ben, 5

Wade, Peter, 10, 152
Walcott, Derek, 149
Walthe, Thomas, 25
Weathered Men (Mosby), 125
Web 2.0 principles in new media, 157

Weekend in Guatemala (Asturias), 100
West Indians, 17–18; in Central America, 230n92; in Costa Rica, 131–32; immigrants, 65, 67, 68–74, 186; industrialization impact, 63; recruitment in Central American Caribbean coastal areas, 219n36; tradition, 91. *See also* "Black" community
whiteness in Costa Rica, 143–44
white North American labor force, 67–68
Wilson, Carlos "Cubena" Guillermo, 73–74, 125
Wilson, Pamela, 157

Wright, Michelle M., 18–20

xenophobia, 23
xinka, 179

Yancy, George, 105
Yucatec communities, 108
Yurumein. *See* St. Vincent

Zalas Zamorra, Edwin, 136
zambiagos, 3, 10
zambos, 86, 97
zaramullos, 3
Zea, Leopoldo, 47, 56
Zelaya, José Santos, 14
Žižek, Slavoj, 144

www.ingramcontent.com/pod-product-compliance
Lightning Source LLC
Chambersburg PA
CBHW030527230426
43665CB00010B/794